10·17·77

The Complete Outdoorsman's Guide to

BIRDS

OF EASTERN NORTH AMERICA

The Complete Outdoorsman's Guide to

BIRDS

OF EASTERN NORTH AMERICA

by

John P. S. Mackenzie

Illustrated by

Terence Shortt

PAGURIAN PRESS LIMITED

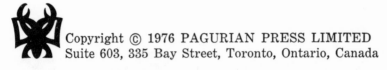

Distributed in the United States of America
and internationally by:

PUBLISHERS MARKETING GROUP
A BAKER & TAYLOR COMPANY

Executive Offices
1515 Broadway
New York, N.Y. 10036

Distribution Center
Gladiola Avenue
Momence, Illinois 60954

ISBN 0-88932-027-6

Printed and bound in the United States.

Preface

This attractive book has been designed to supplement the standard identification guides such as my own *Field Guide to the Birds* and *Birds of North America* by Robbins et al. These two guides, well known to practically everyone who watches birds, are strictly recognition manuals, relying heavily on color illustration to do the job, and assisted by rather telegraphic texts. Basically, they are visual presentations.

There has always been the need for a somewhat expanded presentation, giving more on behavior, feeding preferences, nesting habits, seasonal status, migratory movements, etc. and this is precisely why this outdoorsman's guide has been prepared. To a certain extent the *Audubon Bird Guide* (in two volumes) by Pough, published some years ago and still very useful, filled this need. However, the very completeness of the above guides, with the inclusion of even the rarities, may confuse the beginner and the less than "hard-core" birder. This book by John Mackenzie, on the other hand, is a selective treatment of the 270 species most likely to be encountered in the northeastern part of our continent.

The illustrations by Terry Shortt, the dean of Canadian bird portraitists, are a delight to the eye and support the text admirably. I have been an admirer of Mr. Shortt ever since I first saw his work more than 40 years ago. In 1965 it was my pleasure to be in the field with him in the Galapagos Islands for six glorious weeks while he was preparing a diorama for the Royal Ontario Museum and I was filming for the Canadian Broadcasting Corporation. It was while on this expedition that I came to know him not only as a skilled field naturalist, but also as a friend.

Bird-watching has come of age, along with an environmental awareness that has made itself felt across the land. Recently when a rare Ross' gull made its appearance at Newburyport harbor in Massachusetts, nearly 2000 birders flocked in to see it on a single weekend. You will not find the Ross' gull in the pages of this book, but in studying them you will be better informed about the birds that you have a reasonable chance of seeing. And that is really what bird-watching is all about.

Roger Tory Peterson
Old Lyme, Connecticut

To the late Colonel H. F. (Mike) Seymour, who, in teaching me the difference between a snipe and a dowitcher, and many more things, started a process of many years which led me to write this book.

Contents

Introduction

Our decision to write about the birds of northeastern North America was made in full consciousness of the vast amount of splendid material which is already available. Almost everyone is aware of birds to some extent, for even in crowded urban areas there are birds — Robins, sparrows, pigeons and starlings throughout the year and others, such as the nighthawk, in summer. Many people include in their libraries at least one book on field identification, most often Roger Tory Peterson's durable and beautifully presented "A Field Guide to the Birds" which was first published in 1934. It covers the birds of eastern North America and is accompanied by his guide to the birds of the west. A more recent book by Robbins, Bruun and Zim "A Guide to Field Identification — Birds of North America", published in 1966, includes range maps and sonograms which illustrate bird songs in graphic form. Another excellent series is the Audubon Bird Guide in two volumes, one for the small land birds and the other for water, game and large land birds, both written by Richard H. Pough and first published in 1946. Our copy of some 700 pages has both volumes bound in one cover, and contains more detailed life stories than either Peterson or Robbins, whose texts do not attempt to go beyond identification.

The literature in the areas beyond identification is vast and, to a large extent, more scientific than most people care to attempt. In any emerging science the results of constant research must be made available, and thus such areas of study as territorial behavior, nesting habits, food requirements, geographic distribution, migration impulses, navigation and range, become the subject of separate works. Broad studies of behavioral patterns are often made on a world-wide basis. Another treatment, the area into which this book falls, is the description of birds in a geographic area. The "Birds of Massachusetts", for example, is a classic.

The purpose of this book is to describe the birds of the northeastern United States and eastern Canada. In the 270 specie studies which follow, we have attempted to take the reader further than identification guides are designed to do, to describe the typical habitat of each, to discuss something of its relationship with man and its environment and to present a fairly complete physical description of both sexes and, in many cases of juveniles, in both nuptual (spring) and post-nuptual (autumn) plumage. In doing so, we have drawn heavily on the work of others, in addition to our own notes and recollections. In all the years in which we have been watching and studying birds as weekend and holiday amateurs, we have felt the need for a work which falls somewhere between the identification guides and the scientific literature, and isolates those species likely to be seen in our area. The general identification guides, of necessity include hundreds of species not seen in the northeast, and the process of elimination can be a tedious part of the learning process. We hope that this book will be as useful to others as it has been to us in its preparation.

Notes on Bird Watching

Birds are the most readily observable form of wild life. They are present in almost every habitat — deep forests, small woodlots, fields, hedges, town and city in North America and it is possible to join with others in the Arctic and sub-Arctic, are seen only briefly as migrants in the spring and fall. Others arrive in the spring from their wintering areas to nest, and are seen through the summer. And then there are still others, such as some sparrows and owls, which migrate into our area from the north, and are seen only in winter. A few species are with us for all seasons of the year.

The extent to which each individual becomes involved in his awareness of birds is a matter of wide choice. Nature groups exist in almost every town and city in North America and it is possible to join with others in organized walks, particularly during the migration period, to observe and list the numbers and varieties seen. Bird listing is a popular end for most observers and, while entirely harmless, should not represent the final objective. Even as you reach for the magic number of one hundred species in a day, you can be broadening your scope by studying behavior, song and habitat. This leads, almost naturally, into an interest in the environment — trees, plants, grasses and marshes, and into involvement in the conservation of the environment essential to the maintenance of these various life forms.

While birds are elusive and easily disturbed by abrupt movement or a sharp noise, their natural curiosity can be exploited. It is important for the observer to remain perfectly still if possible when birds are seen, but if one must move closer it should be directly toward the object, slowly and deliberately. When perching birds hide in a bush or in the grass, they can usually be persuaded to show themselves by "squeaking". This consists of sucking on the knuckles or on the back of the hand with moist lips, making a loud kissing sound. Alternatively, and more simply, one makes a *pssh* sound with the mouth, placing the tongue against the lower jaw below the teeth and exhaling slowly through the mouth, alternately opening and closing the lips. This technique is particularly effective with chickadees and warblers.

In late summer and early autumn when singing has ceased most small birds tend to skulk in the underbrush. One should then sit comfortably in the woods and make the squeaking noise. If birds are present they will suddenly appear, invariably led by the chickadees, until several species are flitting about in the trees overhead.

Binoculars and Telescopes

Some form of magnification is essential to the enjoyment of birds seen at a distance of more than a few feet. Good binoculars were once an expensive luxury and the best of the European makes still are. It is now possible to purchase practical and quite acceptable binoculars at moderate cost, although good tinted glass which has a minimum of distortion is essential. There is no "best" combination of magnification and size, but it is important to use a glass which is wide enough to allow a fairly wide field of vision and sufficient light, usually a minimum of 30 millimeters. A glass of over 50 millimeters tends to become heavy and bulky. The usual magnifications for hand-held binoculars range from seven times to ten times, which means reducing the apparent distance to one-seventh to one-tenth. Thus a glass marked 7 x 35 reduces the distance to the object observed to one-seventh the distance through an aperture of 35 millimeters, a reasonable combination. To observe water birds and other marsh birds effectively, a telescope mounted on a tripod or clamped to the car window is essential. This requires a more substantial investment — one in which it is pointless to compromise with requirements. A zoom lens makes it possible to focus on the bird with as wide a field of vision as possible, and then to zoom to maximum magnification. Small scopes, with a small field of vision, are frustrating and are not recommended.

Feeding Stations

In winter it is possible to attract and hold for most of the season a resident population by providing seeds and suet. Mixed seeds and sunflower seeds are available commercially in small packages and, more economically, in bulk. Feeders can be purchased in many designs and are easily made. They should be hung out of reach of squirrels and cats or placed on poles with a shield below to stop climbing animals. Suet can be melted and mixed with seed or, better still, hung in large chunks or in net bags. Feeders should not be filled until migration is finished, usually late November, for birds which would otherwise move south may be attracted to remain in an area where they can not survive the winter, even if fed regularly.

Bird Houses

Many birds require holes for nesting and these can be encouraged to nest in gardens which provide suitable boxes. Designs vary, depending on the species, as do the sizes of entrances. Purple Martin houses are described later.

Organization of This Book

The 270 species described in this book comprise substantially all of those known to nest in, or pass through, northeastern North America with some regularity. Many are seen only in coastal areas, others, like the Peregrine Falcon, are now so rare that they are unlikely to be seen at all, and we have omitted a few, like the ptarmigans, which are seen only in the far north. We have followed the sequence of the checklist of the American Ornithological Union which starts with the least specialized birds (loons) and ends with the most complex (finches). This process conforms with the usual practice of organization, although some identification guides depart modestly from this sequence. We have generally disregarded sub-species, a hideously complicated subject, and the reader should recognize that sub-specific differences do exist which are largely geographic and involve some differences in appearance.

With each family and species, we have shown the scientific name which consists of two Greek or Latin words, the first to distinguish its genera or group, the second the specific name of the bird. During the forty years since Dr. Peterson wrote his field guide many English language names have been changed, species have been combined or separated. We have used the most current English usage and have indicated former names as well. The reader using an old field guide and this book should check the scientific name as an accurate key to reading both.

Length of Birds

Most books which show the measurements of birds take the length from the tip of the bill to the tip of the tail from specimens measured on their backs on a flat surface. These measurements are invariably longer than the bird is when seen in life. In this book, we use lengths of the birds when seen in natural positions and have relied on figures used in the Robbins, Bruun and Zim field guide.

Check lists showing the names of birds in one's own area are available from local bird clubs in most of the United States and Canada. They usually indicate which species breed locally, those seen only on migration and those which are rare and therefore unlikely to be seen often.

For those interested in bird songs, a number of excellent recordings are available which, again, can usually be obtained from local ornothological groups or from commercial outlets.

John P. S. Mackenzie
Lois K. Parkhill

Adjala, Ontario — 1975.

Glossary of Terms

Abdomen	The underpart of the body between the breast and the tail.
Belly	Used interchangeably with abdomen.
Coniferous	Evergreen trees bearing cones.
Crest	Long feathers protruding from the head.
Crown	The top of the head.
Deciduous	Trees, usually broad-leafed, which shed their leaves each year.
De-curved	Downcurving, usually applied to the bill.
Diurnal	Day-time.
Flanks	The sides of the body toward the rear.
Gregarious	Flocking.
Nocturnal	Night-time.
Primaries	The principal flight feathers, attached to the outer bone, or hand, of the wing.
Rump	The part of the upperside between the back and the tail.
Secondaries	Flight feathers attached to the forearm, or second bone from the end of the wing.
Species	Members of the same group of birds which can interbreed freely with other members of the same group and which cannot normally breed with members of another group.
Speculum	A patch of color on the wing, usually close to the body, common in ducks.

Northern Fulmar

Leach's Storm Petrel

Pied-billed Grebe

Common Loon

Representative members of the fulmar, grebe, storm petrel, and loon families.

Loons
Family Gaviidae

Loons are large, picturesque and somewhat primitive diving birds which feed on fish in open water. Indigenous to the north, they are larger and heavier than ducks, but in fact, do not belong to the duck family (ANSERI-FORMES) at all. Web-footed like ducks, loons have long, sharp, pointed bills without the serrated edge of the broad, flat duckbill.

Less adaptable than ducks, loons depend on their diving ability to secure food. Their legs are set far at the back of the large body, making it almost impossible for them to walk normally on land. They usually push themselves along on their breasts, but avoid unnecessary contact with land by placing the nest on shore at the edge of the water.

The loon's wings are narrow and pointed with relatively low lifting power. Thus this bird rises with difficulty from the water. Once airborne they fly strongly and directly, the head low and neck straight, the recessed legs extending beyond the short tail, giving the impression in flight of a hinged handkerchief carrying a stick. Loons, although not valued as game birds, are entirely protected under International Migratory Treaty.

There are only four species of loon, all of which breed in Arctic Canada and Eurasia, the Common, Arctic, Yellow-billed and Red-throated. Only two are likely to be seen in the northeastern United States or Canada, the Common and the Red-throated. The Red-throated migrates, in part, southward across the continent, some birds wintering in the Great Lakes, and in part, across the eastern Arctic, wintering in waters off Labrador. The Red-throated also breeds in Quebec, on the north shore of the St. Lawrence River and on Anticosti Island. Only the Common Loon nests in settled areas and can be seen in most of the more remote lakes in the Canadian shield.

COMMON LOON
Gavia immer
LENGTH 24 INCHES, WINGSPAN 54 INCHES

The Common Loon, silent in winter, has three separate summer calls, the long wail, most often heard at night and before a storm, a yodel of haunting beauty and a tremulous laugh. It is probably the latter which has led to the popular expression "crazy as a loon" or "loony", but exciting as they are to hear, all three calls have been somewhat over-dramatized in wilderness literature. They are easily imitated, and two experienced people have been known to call one another for a long period, each thinking a loon was replying.

Loons are found singly or in pairs in open water on deep lakes. Normally there is only one pair per lake, but if the lake is large and the outboard motor count reasonable, it will support more.

The loon is a large bird which seldom comes ashore except to breed. Ideally suited to catching fish under water, it travels long distances and can remain submerged for two or three minutes, but usually stays down for less. It propels itself mostly with its webbed feet and occasionally with its wings. By compressing its feathers and exhaling, the loon can ride low in the water and even sink at will. It also feeds on frogs, shellfish and vegetation.

This species moults in late winter when it is flightless for a time. It emerges from its drab gray and white winter colors to a hard, glossy plumage which looks all black from a distance. The head is dark with a green sheen, there's a striped white bar across the throat, and another bar, somewhat larger and lower, across the back of the neck. The back and flanks are a mass of orderly black and white checks, bars and spots. The undersides are white.

The loon cannot rise from the land and, off water, requires a take-off run varying from a few yards to a quarter of a mile, depending on the wind. It taxis along, feet galloping and wings churning the water. The flight is then direct and fast, with the head carried low, giving a rather hump-backed appearance.

The nest is built at the edge of the water, often on top of a muskrat house. The two eggs are incubated for a month and the young then require a further ten weeks before they can fly. Loons are impatient of close neighbors and will attempt to drive nesting ducks from their shore by harrassing them from underwater.

The breeding range, on suitable fresh water, extends from Alaska to Baffin Island and south to the northern United States. Loons move to coastal waters for the winter, from Newfoundland to Texas in the east and from Alaska to California in the west. Young birds remain in coastal waters for a year or two until they reach maturity.

Grebes
Family Podicipedidae

The grebes are a small, or select, worldwide family of diving birds, numbering only seventeen in all. (By comparison, there are 110 species of cardinals and 301 thrushes.) Six species are resident in, or off, the shores of North America, of which only three are likely to be seen in the east: the Red-necked and the Horned, which breed sparingly in the northeastern States and eastern Canada and are principally seen on migration, and the more common Pied-billed, which nests from coast to coast. Two others are only in the west: the large Western Grebe and the Eared Grebe.

Grebes in spring are elegant, brightly colored, ornamental waterbirds, all having tufts, or a crest of some kind on the head, and all performing elaborate courtship ceremonies. They are similar to the primitive loon with their sharp pointed bills (either straight or slightly upturned) and short tails, which in the grebe can scarcely be seen. They are remarkably quick divers, and their legs, placed at the back of the body, are enclosed by the skin of the trunk, leaving only the feet free to move, and making the grebe almost incapable of walking on land. The toes have skin flaps or lobes, which make excellent paddles and offer a minimum resistance on the return stroke. The nests are usually placed on masses of floating vegetation so that the adult bird may slide directly into the water.

Grebes have white-tipped secondaries (not present in the loon) and a silvery sheen to the underparts, which were formerly prized as millinery trim and rugs in Greenland.

RED-NECKED GREBE (formerly HOLBOELL'S GREBE)
Podiceps grisegena
LENGTH 13 INCHES

Relatively uncommon everywhere, this western breeding grebe is seen only in a few localities in the east. The range extends from Alaska to North Dakota. On migration it is seen on the St. Lawrence River and in the Great Lakes. The winter is spent in salt water on both coasts, in the east from Newfoundland south as far as Florida.

The Red-necked Grebe nests in fresh water marshes and on the edge of shallow lakes. The nest is made of rotten vegetation built up in a mound above the water, usually among old reeds. Like the loon, the grebe can compress its feathers and sink, which it does when disturbed, often with the young clinging to its back.

The Red-necked, which is much larger than the more common Pied-billed Grebe, has a long heavy neck like a rusty red pipe, and a short body. In breeding plumage, from March to June, the head is dark on top with a suggestion of a crest, the face and chin are white and the long pointed bill is yellow. (It should not be confused with the Horned Grebe whose neck is also red, but short, and whose cheeks are dark.) The back is dark, the sides mottled rusty and white, and the underparts white. In early winter it loses the red on the neck, and the bird becomes grayish underneath and darker on top.

The voice on the breeding ground is an unfortunate medley of wails, brays, squeaks and whinnies. Red-necks rely on what Mr. Webster (of the dictionary) calls "fantastic ceremonies of dancing in the water with weeds dripping from their bills".

HORNED GREBE
Podiceps auritus
LENGTH 10 INCHES

This handsome but stubby-necked grebe has much the same range (Alaska south to North Dakota) and habitat as the Red-necked, but even fewer birds nest in the east than the Red-necked. Breeding populations can be found on Anticosti Island and the Magdelan Islands in Quebec, and in a thin strip across the north of Lake Superior, east to Algonquin Park, in Ontario. A few birds actually winter in open water on the Great Lakes, but the majority go to salt water on both coasts, and we see them on migration.

The ornate breeding plumage — which lasts only until the end of June when it fades, is black on top, red underneath. The headdress consists of two pale yellow horns, or ear tufts, mixed in with an ochre ruff, the whole resembling the furred brim of a small fur hat pushed down over the eyes. The neck, front, breast and flanks are red, the underparts white. The upper parts, head, neck and back are black and the rudimentary tail is nothing but a small lump of feathers. The bill is short, straight and dark. In late summer and early winter, the face, throat and flanks, like the underparts, are white. The top of the tufted head remains black as do the nape of the neck and back. The Eared Grebe, with its golden ear plumes, should not be confused with the Horned in spring plumage — its neck is entirely black.

Like the Red-necked, the Horned Grebe nests in fresh water marshes and shallow lakes, and often in ponds with bare shores and little or no cover. The nest is of rotting marsh vegetation, either floating or tethered, on a marshy islet near the shore.

PIED-BILLED GREBE

Podilymbus podiceps
LENGTH 9 INCHES

This is the only grebe in North America with a thick blunt bill. The bill in breeding plumage is pied-white with a dark band near the tip. Other than a black throat patch and a white patch on the tail this bird is a dingy dark brown. In the winter the throat patches and bill stripe disappear.

This least exotic grebe, the Pied-billed is the only grebe which is seen in the east in summer in any numbers; it is then present all over the east, indeed the range extends from the southern Northwest Territories to Argentina. It arrives in the north early in spring, first in large marshes and bays and later in ponds when they are clear of ice. It is a shy and retiring bird, although in early spring one can usually see it in open water in marshes. It prefers to remain hidden in deep cover in the marsh, and, when surprised in open water, will sink until only its bill remains above the surface and swim to cover. The nest is usually built in fairly deep water on the top of a mass of floating vegetation and anchored to reeds. Those birds building in shallow water on a pile from the bottom risk flooding if the water rises. This grebe can be found in fresh water ponds, lakes, rivers and, in the west in sloughs, but in each it requires good cover of growing and rotting vegetation.

The Pied-bill Grebe may often go unseen but, if present, can be heard. Its far carrying *kow, kow, kow,* repeated about a dozen times is accompanied by grunts and wails. In the autumn, one can be surrounded by them all day and perhaps see only one or two.

Grebes are not valued as game, and are protected by law.

Fulmars and Shearwaters
Family Procellariidae

A number of species of birds, including fulmars and shearwaters, roam the open ocean for most of the year, coming ashore in various parts of the world only to breed. Their lives have been well documented on film in recent years and widely shown on television in a number of nature series. Most of us will never see them for, even if they can be seen from the shore, they will only be unrecognizable specks in the distance. For those making an ocean crossing or a trip off-shore, the birds will become more real.

The Northern Fulmar (*Fulmarus glacialis*) is a gull-like bird with a wingspan of forty-two inches, but weighs under two pounds. It breeds in colonies in the Arctic, North Atlantic and North Pacific Oceans and wanders widely over the sea in winter. This is the bird which follows ships in mid-ocean after the gulls have returned to shore, hanging in the air in the updraft at the stern, waiting for garbage. It flies on stiff straight wings with a few flaps and long glides. Darwin thought it to be the most abundant bird in the world, and it is certainly so in the Atlantic.

The shearwaters have longer and narrower wings than the fulmar, a long narrow tail and are darker in color. They too flap and glide, but usually close to the water. It is always a thrilling sight to watch them skimming up and down the long rollers in the Atlantic, especially during storms which never seem to bother them. They land on the water to feed on squid and small fish and are always present in some numbers when fish are being cleaned at sea. Of the ten species recorded off the coast of the northern United States and Canada only three, the Cory's, Greater, and Sooty occur regularly and in any significant numbers in the Atlantic.

Storm Petrels
Family Hydrobatidae

Storm Petrels are known to sailors as "Mother Carey's Chickens" or "Sea Pigeons". They are dainty little birds from seven to nine inches in length with a wingspan of about eighteen inches, which flutter about the waves of the open ocean, almost running on the water with webbed feet. They feed on plankton, tiny fish and shrimps. Two species can be seen in the North Atlantic, Leach's and Wilson's. Both are dark brown birds with large white patches on the wings and on the upper and lower sides of the rump. They differ in appearance in that Leach's has a forked tail and Wilson's a rounded one. The bill is sturdy and the upper mandible hooks downward.

Wilson's, which is the more common, is present only in summer for it breeds on islands around Cape Horn during South America's summer. At sea it can be seen more readily than Leach's for it follows ships in small flocks.

Leach's Storm Petrel breeds on islands in both the Pacific and Atlantic. These include, in eastern North America, several points in Labrador, Newfoundland, Gaspé, Cape Breton, Nova Scotia, Maine and Massachusetts. It nests in burrows, and is now mostly excluded from mainland breeding because of predation from domestic animals and rats. The incubation period is about six weeks, and the sitting bird may be on the nest without food for up to a week. It is then relieved at night and takes its turn at sea to feed. During the day a petrel colony appears to be deserted, for the burrow entrances are well hidden and all activity is at night.

Pelicans
Family Pelecanidae

WHITE PELICAN
Pelecanus Erythrorhynchos
LENGTH 4 FEET, WINGSPAN 9 FEET

One tends to think of pelicans as tropical birds closely associated with salt water, but the White Pelican breeds only on fresh water lakes from California to South Dakota in the south and from extreme northern Alberta, across the prairies to Lake of the Woods in western Ontario. The winter is spent on salt water from the southern United States to Guatemala where it joins the non-migratory Brown Pelican.

White Pelicans move north in the spring in flocks, traveling in V-formation, with a slow measured wing-beat. They also soar in groups, often very high, and on descending, do so almost vertically, pulling out of their dive with a great roar of air through feathers. They feed in formation on the surface, swimming side by side, beating their wings on the water and driving schools of small fish to shallow water. The fish are then scooped up in the enormous bills and the water drained off. Pelicans have a remarkably fast digestive system and are reputed to eat their own weight (fifteen pounds) in fish every day. They nest in colonies, building the nest on islands in lakes, either in forested or treeless country.

Pelicans need little description. They are large birds with a long neck and equally long bill. This one has the typical bill with the soft sack below, yellowish in color, and is entirely white except for a few black flight feathers and secondary feathers on the wings, which give it a lacy look in flight. It flies with the neck tucked in against the body.

Boobies
Family Sulidae

GANNET
Morus bassanus
LENGTH 31 INCHES, WINGSPAN 70 INCHES

Although the Gannet breeds in colonies in Newfoundland and in Quebec on Anticosti Island and the Magdalens, the colony at Bonaventure Island near

Gannet

Double-crested Cormorant

White Pelican

The Double-crested Cormorant, the Gannet, and the White Pelican are shown here in their typical habitat and as they appear in flight.

Percé at the tip of the Gaspé Peninsula is the most famous. The Bonaventure colony can be approached by boat to the foot of the cliff-face, or on foot from the opposite side of the island. Immediate access by foot is now restricted, relieving the nesting birds of much disturbance. A 1965 count showed that the Bonaventure population was increasing and then exceeded 13,000 pairs. Other breeding colonies can be found in the British Isles, Iceland and the Faroe Islands, north of Scotland.

The Gannet is a large white seabird belonging to the same family as the booby and closely related to the pelican, but without the pelican's large bill. The head and neck are washed with yellow and there are black tips on the final third of the wings. The bill is long and pointed, as is the tail. Young birds are sooty gray with a black trailing edge on the wings.

The colonies in spring are full of confusion and noise. The nests, which are made of seaweed, are placed close together wherever there is level ground, although sometimes an egg rolls out of the nest and down the cliff. There is much quarreling and threatening as birds attempt to leave and return, those on nests sticking their bills in the air or waving them around making an obstacle course of the take-off run. But the social structure and respect for territory, however minute, is such that little damage is done to eggs or young.

Incubation is about six weeks and young birds are left on their own on the cliffs at about twelve weeks. After a week without food, the young birds finally launch themselves into the sea.

Gannets live entirely on small fish which they take in spectacular, almost vertical, dives from about one hundred feet. They land with a great splash and swim underwater to make their catch. When they locate a school of fish they dive again and again as a flock.

In winter they stay in small groups, in coastal waters from Virginia to Florida, never very far from land, and often associating with gulls.

Cormorants
Family Phalacrocoracidae

DOUBLE-CRESTED CORMORANT
Phalacrocorax auritus
LENGTH 27 INCHES, WINGSPAN 50 INCHES

My earliest recollections of interesting large birds (crows were not "interesting") are of Great Blue Herons (which we incorrectly called cranes) and of cormorants which, ironically, turned out to be called "crow ducks." We used to watch these great black birds sitting on the pilings of wharves and channel markers in the tidal estuaries of New Brunswick with their wings stretched out, shroud-like, to dry. What we didn't know then is that cormorants, like their tropical relative the Anhinga, lack the plumage oils typical of waterbirds and, although they can remain in the water up to half an hour at a time, must dry out for long periods.

The Double-crested Cormorant is the only one of its family to have moved inland. It now breeds on a broad range of continental fresh waters and is present in summer in lakes and rivers of the prairie regions of the United States and Canada, in a narrow banding surrounding the Great Lakes and St. Lawrence River and around the shores of eastern North America. On the Atlantic coast it may be confused with the Great Cormorant (*Phalacrocorax carbo*) which is somewhat larger and has a white face patch during the breeding season. Cormorants are rather ugly birds with a long black body, snake-like neck, bare face and a long bill hooked downward at the tip. When perched, they sit upright with their bills held high. The Double-crested has a red face naked of feathers and, during breeding season, two plumes, one over each eye.

The Double-crested is a colonial nester, often in a community with pelicans, and builds a bulky nest on a cliff ledge, low on small islands and sometimes in trees, in areas inaccessible to predators. The Cormorant sits on the nest for one month and feeds its fledglings for another two. Occasionally it lays its eggs in an abandoned Blue Heron's nest. It lives entirely on fish, almost invariably those of little value, fish which are often predators of valuable species. It also contributes significantly, by its droppings, to the nitrates and phosphates of the waters.

In the water the cormorant rides low like a loon with its tail submerged. It dives for its food, but never from the air. It first alights, then disappears with a serpentine motion, remaining submerged for about thirty seconds. On leaving the water it must use feet and wings to become airborne, but once up, flies strongly and directly. It migrates in flocks, either in line or in a V-formation, and winters on the coast south from Long Island, and inland, from Tennessee south to the West Indies and Central America.

Herons, Bitterns, and Egrets
Family Ardeidae

The herons, bitterns and egrets all belong to the same family — a worldwide family numbering sixty-three species. Fifteen of these are present in North America and seven are known to breed in the northeast. Others have been sighted on rare occasions, but are unusual and are not described here.

ARDEIDAE are wading birds which take most of their food, primarily fish, in marshes and at the marshy edges of streams and lakes. Typically they have long legs, long neck and bill and a short tail. However, four of the species seen here have shorter necks: the Green Heron, the Black-crowned Night Heron, the Cattle Egret and the American Bittern. Plumage is loose and most develop plumes, or aigrettes, at the head, neck or back during the breeding season. The crown is generally dark. One noticeable distinction between cranes and herons is that herons fly with neck S'ed back against their bodies whereas cranes fly neck outstretched. The heron wing beat is generally slow.

Nesting is varied, some in the marsh and others in trees. The tree nesters tend to breed in colonies, often in very large numbers.

American Bittern

Green Heron

Least Bittern

Black-crowned Night Heron

Great Blue Heron

The herons and bitterns are wading birds, taking most of their food
(primarily fish) in marshes and marshy lakes and streams.

24

GREAT BLUE HERON
Ardea herodias
LENGTH 38 INCHES, WINGSPAN 70 INCHES

This is the largest, most elegant and most numerous of our herons, standing about four feet high with a six foot wingspan. It is also the most evident, for it prefers to feed in open shallow water at the edge of a marsh, pond, lake or stream, while other species tend to withdraw into the cover of reeds. It feeds on small fish, water snakes, mice, frogs, insects and salamanders which are caught with lightning jabs of its long pointed bill. In its hunting it often remains motionless for long periods watching the water, but it also stalks with deliberate steps. When at rest, the long neck may either be held straight or arched back against the body. In flight its neck and head are curled back with the legs trailing. It often flies to the very top of a tree where it lands gracefully, or to dead branches where it tends to camouflage itself with its head and neck erect.

The Great Blue Heron has a commanding stance, half the bird being tawny gray neck and half bluish gray body. The neck is brownish gray, mottled black and white on the front, the mottling ending in plumes over the chest. The head is narrow with a long fairly stout bill which tapers to a point and the narrow face is white. A rich black plume runs along the top of the head and extends well beyond. The yellowish legs are nearly two feet long, almost two thirds of its length.

This heron is a colonial nester, the colonies remaining intact for many years unless molested. The nests are usually at the tops of high trees on islands or in remote woods, often some distance from water. Nests, sometimes in bushes or even on the ground, are massive affairs about three feet across which are repaired and used for many years. Heronries used to be severely molested for the eggs, but legal protection and a better informed public has made it possible for these birds to continue to breed and live in close proximity with man.

The breeding range extends across most of southern Canada through the United States to Mexico. Large concentrations build up in autumn, particularly in tidal marshes in New England and in the Maritimes where hundreds of birds may be seen feeding on the mud flats. In winter a few birds remain in British Columbia, the Great Lakes and the Maritimes and New England, but most move to the southern United States and South America.

GREEN HERON
Butorides virescens
LENGTH 14 INCHES, WINGSPAN 25 INCHES

This little heron is about the size of a crow and is very attractive when seen in a good light which is not often, for it hides in the shade of overgrown bogs, and the green is scarcely evident. The face, throat and neck are chestnut brown, there is a black crest on the top of the head which is raised when the bird is alarmed, the bill is sturdy, fairly long and tapered.

The back is dark green, but looks black in poor light, the wings are dark and noticeably broad when the bird flies. The legs are dark red. Immature birds have a reddish tinge on the face and are striped below like a bittern. This heron flies with its short neck outstretched and with rapid wing beats. The voice is a harsh *kyow*, with a mixture of grunts and squawks. The Green Heron can only be confused with the Little Blue Heron which has a much longer neck and dark legs. The confusion is unlikely to occur, for the Little Blue does not breed in the northeast although on occasion young birds, which are white, wander north to New England and south-eastern Canada in late summer and autumn.

The Green Heron is common in the extreme western United States and through the eastern and southern parts of the country. In Canada it breeds in southern Ontario and Quebec and, rarely, in southern New Brunswick. Pairs usually nest alone, but in some areas they are found in small colonies and with other herons. The nest is built of sticks in thick foliage, usually in an evergreen from ten to twenty feet up, and may be placed a long way from water.

This heron feeds on small fish and insects in ponds, marshes and streams, stalking with a slow walk at the edge of the water.

CATTLE EGRET
Bubulcus Ibis
LENGTH 17 INCHES, WINGSPAN 37 INCHES

One of the remarkable explosions of bird populations in the Americas is that of the Cattle Egret. It was first seen in Brazil in 1877, probably having crossed the Atlantic from its native Africa, in Guyana in 1911 and in Florida about 1940. By 1957 it was known to be breeding in Florida, Louisiana and North Carolina and the first nest was discovered in Canada in 1962, one bird having been seen ten years earlier. The interested observer now has a reasonable chance of seeing this bird either in pastures with cattle or in marshes. In the southern United States it is now quite abundant.

This crow-sized white heron has a short neck, an orangy yellow bill and reddish legs. Immature birds have dark legs. It may be confused with the Snowy Egret (*Leucophoyx thula*) which has a long neck, black legs with yellow feet and a black bill, or with the immature Little Blue Heron which has gray legs and a pale bill dark tipped. Both of these birds are rarely seen in the northeast. The Cattle Egret in breeding plumage has longish buffy feathers on the head and breast.

It is one of the few insect-eating herons, taking the large insects (and small amphibians) kicked up by rhinoceros and hippopotamus and other grazing animals on the plains of Africa. It moved into grasslands created by extensive forest clearance in South America, feeding near domestic cattle to replace the wild animals of Africa. Since it lacks competition for its diet, and roosts comfortably in both urban and country surroundings, it is reasonable to assume that it will prosper in its new range. It nests communally with other herons, building untidy platform nests of stout sticks.

GREAT EGRET (name changed from Common Egret in 1973)

Casmerodius albus
LENGTH 32 INCHES, WINGSPAN 55 INCHES

Fifty years ago the Great, or Common Egret, as it was formerly called, came close to being exterminated. Great numbers of the birds were slaughtered during the nineteenth and early twentieth centuries for the long tail plumes which were widely used in the millinery trade as decoration. Legislation was passed early in the century in the United States, both protecting the bird and banning the use of plumes in that country. A warden of the Audubon Society was shot by plume hunters in Florida, causing an outcry and more rigid enforcement. Once a rarity, it has now recovered and is again common through the southern States, breeding on the west coast and east from Texas, north to the Great Lakes and on the coast north to New Jersey. In Canada the Great Egret has nested in southern Ontario at the western end of Lake Erie. It has been seen as a late summer wanderer in New England, the Maritimes, Quebec and various parts of southern Ontario.

It is almost as large as the Great Blue Heron, but is all white with black legs and feet. It has a long neck and orange bill. In flight, the head is held back against the body, and the legs trail behind.

BLACK-CROWNED NIGHT HERON

Nycticorax nycticorax
LENGTH 20 INCHES, WINGSPAN 44 INCHES

This is a stout, short-necked heron which roosts in large groups in trees for most of the day and feeds at night. The crown is black, as are the back and sturdy bill. The legs are yellow and the rest of the bird is white, including a patch across the eyes and several long white feathers running down the back. The tail is short, extending only to the end of the large wide wings. Immature birds are brown with white stripes, the wings brown with white spots and they may easily be confused with the mature American Bittern.

It nests in colonies, usually in trees and sometimes in bushes, as near to extensive marshes as it can, but sometimes at a distance from its feeding ground. It often nests in association with other herons.

Although essentially nocturnal, some birds move about during the day, particularly on migration, but generally fly to the marshes at dusk, when their *quonk* call can be heard. When a large number of birds come to the marsh in the evening they do so from some height, then fall almost vertically with a series of side-slips to land. They feed on fish, frogs, insects and mice.

This heron breeds in the western and central United States and along the Gulf and east coasts. In Canada the central population extends north to the Prairie Provinces, and in the east along the shores of Lake Erie, Lake Ontario and the St. Lawrence River and in New Brunswick.

LEAST BITTERN

Ixobrychus exilis
LENGTH 11 INCHES, WINGSPAN 17 INCHES

This tiny heron is perhaps not as rare as might appear from the few times we see it, for it is secretive and shy. In many years of tramping about marshes I have recorded only six sightings, but have heard its low cooing voice and its harsh cackle much more frequently. The Least Bittern lives in the cattail marshes and prefers to remain hidden when disturbed. When it flies it moves only a short distance, dropping again into the reed cover. In areas where the water is too deep for wading it manages to move about the marsh by clinging to the reeds, and behaves more like a rail than a heron. On migration it often feeds at the edge of drainage canals close to marshes and along open water leads. The nest is built in the marsh supported by a clump of vegetation.

It is difficult to suggest where best to find the Least Bittern, other than in extensive marshes, but it is worth finding for its rich brown colors and markings. The crown is black, the face, neck and wings chestnut colored. When the bird flies the beige inner front part of the wing can be seen. The back and short tail are black with two whitish lines down the back. The throat and abdomen are almost white, and the yellow bill is long, tapering to a point.

In the United States it breeds in fresh water marshes throughout Maine and Minnesota and on the west coast. The Canadian breeding range extends through southern Ontario from the north side of Lake Huron to southern Quebec, about as far east as Lake St. Peter. It nests again in extreme southern New Brunswick and in southern Manitoba. The winter is spent from the southern United States southward.

AMERICAN BITTERN

Botaurus lentiginosus
LENGTH 23 INCHES, WINGSPAN 45 INCHES

In marshes, reedy streams and lake sides all over North America, from Great Slave Lake south, the spring and early summer song of this heron can be heard, a deep, hollow *oong-ka-tchoonk*, repeated several times. The pumping rhythm of this song has given rise to such colloquial names as "Thunder pumper" and "Stake driver", the first because it sounds not unlike a suction pump, and the second because it sounds like a stake being hammered into the bog.

We seldom see this "Marsh Hen", as we knew it in my youth, before it flushes, which it does only when closely approached. It then flies off with a few croaks, not usually very far. It prefers to "freeze", compressing its feathers to the body and pointing its long bill straight in the air. Since the bird is brown-on-light-brown, striped and spotted, it tends to resemble the wheat colored marsh reeds and becomes remarkably invisible. I looked into a small grass and reed filled enclosure at a zoo for some moments once, thinking the enclosure empty. It wasn't until there was a slight movement that I realized there was an American Bittern in "freeze position" looking back at me, with eyes positioned to see under the bill.

The American Bittern nests in the marsh on a platform of rotting vegetation. It seldom leaves the marsh except to take mice and grasshoppers in a meadow and rarely alights in trees. The bird is brown, striped and spotted in lighter lines. The top of the head is dark, the throat white, and there is a black streak from behind the eye down the side of the neck. This pattern is similar to the immature Black-crowned Night Heron, but the American Bittern's wings are much darker and it does not fly to trees. It feeds on frogs, small fish, insects, mice and snakes.

Waterfowl
Family Anatidae

WHISTLING SWAN
Olor columbianus
LENGTH 36 INCHES, WINGSPAN 85 INCHES

Two species of swan are native to North America, the Whistling, which we are likely to see in the east in small numbers, and the Trumpeter. The latter, the largest swan, is a western bird and is seen only in Alaska, parts of British Columbia and Wyoming. Until recently it was close to extinction. A third species, the Mute Swan, was introduced from Europe as an ornamental bird and is now breeding in the wild in small numbers in the eastern United States.

The Whistling Swan winters on the coast, with the largest colony in Maryland on Chesapeake Bay. On migration it flies northwest via the Great Lakes and can be seen on marshes en route.

This marvelous bird, once the target of gunmen, nests on the open tundra in the Arctic from Alaska and the Mackenzie Delta across to Baffin Island. The breadth of its territory and the fact that it usually does not concentrate, but spreads its nests across uninhabited areas, has probably saved it from extinction. One marked concentration is in the islands at the mouth of the Mackenzie River where a nest can be seen every mile or so. From the air the white backs are visible against the tundra from a considerable height. It is doubtful if the species would long survive in other than the complete protection it has now.

Birds pair for life, and the young of one year remain with the parents until the next spring. The winter is spent on both the Atlantic and Pacific coasts, with a large colony in Maryland on Chesapeake Bay.

All mature swans have entirely white feathers, dark bills and long necks which are carried straight out in front during flight. When swimming the Whistling and Trumpeter Swans hold the neck in a straight vertical and the ornamental Mute Swan swims with its neck in an S-curve over its body, outlining its arched secondary feathers. Young birds, cygnets, are pearl gray, darker on the head. Swans feed on aquatic plants in shallow water, which they take by extending the neck. Nests are built on low mounds close to the water.

On migration they fly in long V's with a slow wing beat but a remarkably fast flight — faster than ducks. The body appears slim. They land gracefully without splashing and take off into the wind by pattering along the surface using feet and wings, for about twenty feet.

Geese
Sub-Family Anserinae

The habits of swans and wild geese are quite similar. Both mate for life and keep their young with them until the following spring. Geese do not mate until the third year which invariably means a large population of non-breeders. The female incubates the eggs while the male remains close to the nest, standing guard. When feeding in the water both "tip" for roots under the surface, and on land graze on grass and grain. All water fowl lose their flight feathers after the eggs are hatched and are flightless for a period.

In the northeast we see only three species with any regularity, the Canada, the Brant and the Snow. Others such as the Barnacle and the White-fronted are seen on rare occasions.

CANADA GOOSE
Branta canadensis
LENGTH 16-25 INCHES, WINGSPAN 50-68 INCHES, WEIGHT 2¼-18 POUNDS

When most people think of a wild goose, the Canada is the bird they have in mind. In spring and autumn, in North American skies, flocks are seen almost always after they have been heard, for the honking of this large goose carries a great distance. They fly in an undulating V-formation, periodically changing the leader, for the lead position requires the greatest energy. Migrating flocks usually consist of several families traveling together. Moving both by day and night, these birds make flights of hundreds of miles between stops, which they reconnoiter with great care. After they land some birds remain as sentinels while the others rest and feed. When alarmed they do not always take flight, but may lie with their necks stretched out on the ground or water. Pairs mate for life and are very solicitous with one another. If one dies it appears that the remaining bird will take another mate.

There are about ten recognized sub-species of the Canada Goose which range in size from three pounds to eighteen pounds. All have differing voices and all have long black necks with the familiar white chin strap going almost to the top of the head, pale brown underparts and darker brown backs and wings. They breed throughout the northwestern United States, the whole of western Canada, northern Quebec and Ontario, Newfoundland and into the Arctic Islands. Nesting is on the ground in a wide variety of habitat, but always near water. The Canada Goose is easy to tame and adapts to urban surroundings and association with man. As an example, large flocks of free birds nest in parks in a number of eastern cities.

Whistling Swans

Red-breasted Merganser

Black Duck

Greater Scaup

Canada Goose

A typical formation of Whistling Swans in flight (note how necks are carried straight out) and representative members of the geese and duck sub-families.

31

At the risk of being lyrical, we shall just say that the sight and sound of migrating flocks in April and October is one of the great thrills of the wild — worthy of the time to stop and watch.

BRANT

Branta bernicla
Length 17 inches, wingspan 48 inches

The Brant is smaller than but similar to the Canada Goose with a black head and neck, but in the Brant, the black extends to cover the breast. Adult birds have a narrow white band at the top of their fairly short necks. The back and wings are quite dark, the flanks and belly pale and the underside of the tail is white. This is a small goose which is graceful on the water riding high like a gull and pivoting as it feeds. The tail is carried high. The similar, but much darker Black Brant (*Branta nigricans*) is a western bird which winters on the Pacific coast.

Brants are essentially salt water geese although on migration they may occasionally be seen inland. They breed across the northern Arctic from the Mackenzie Delta to Baffin Island and in most of the Arctic Islands. Migration is via the east side of Hudson and James Bays, the Great Lakes and the Maritimes to the wintering grounds which are in salt water bays from Massachusetts to the Carolinas. The number visiting the Maritimes used to be very large until a blight in 1931 virtually wiped out the eel grass, which is their principal water food.

When passing over land they fly quite high, and their call, like that of the Canada, carries for some distance. It is a hoarse *r-r-r-ronk* and *ruk-ruk*. When over water they stay a few feet above the surface. They are distinguished in flight from Canadas by their relatively short necks, their voices, the black breast and the loose formations or lines of their flight. They do not adopt the familiar V of most geese and ducks.

SNOW GOOSE

Chen hyperborea
Length 19 inches, wingspan 59 inches

Perhaps the greatest experience in bird watching is to see the flock of Snow Geese in the St. Lawrence River, about thirty miles east of Quebec City. More than 100,000 birds, the entire eastern migration, stop to feed for about six weeks starting in late March and again for six weeks in September and October. They fly back and forth from the north shore at Cap Tourmente, near St. Joachim, to the muddy islands off the opposite south shore, feeding mostly at low tide in the marsh grasses. In the evening one can walk far out into the marsh before the birds arrive and stay to watch them settle for the night. They come in, wave after wave, with wings set and feet down, landing close by, for at times they are entirely unsuspecting. Walking back to shore in the semi-dark, one can move through the flock of thousands of birds, only to have them waddle aside.

The eastern flock winters on the coast from Maryland to Carolina and, after its stay on the St. Lawrence, flies on to breed in the northernmost Arctic Islands. The sub-species, the Greater Snow Goose, is slightly larger than the related Lesser Snow and Blue Goose which migrate through the western and central parts of North America respectively, and breed somewhat farther south. The population of Greater Snows has varied considerably depending on both shooting pressure and the availability of food on its St. Lawrence visits. At the turn of the century the flock numbered 3,000 and was protected for many years. The flock has grown to some 100,000 birds and shooting is now permitted.

Mature birds are entirely white, with the exception of the wing-tips which are black. The bill and legs are pink and the bill has a black patch running horizontally between the mandibles. Young birds have much pale gray on the back of the head and neck, back and flanks. The voice in flight is an unbeautiful high pitched *kowk*. When heard from a large flock it can be very exciting.

Ducks
Sub-Family Anatinae

Ducks can generally be divided into two classes, those taking their food on or from the surface of the water, and those taking their food under the surface. The first rely largely on plant food and some of the latter principally on animal matter. The surface feeding ducks either skim the surface for floating vegetation or, by up-ending, tails and feet in the air, feed on plant-life with their heads on or near the bottom. They also feed on land. Grain is an important part of the diet of surface feeding ducks, particularly in the west, for birds resident in the prairies and for others migrating to and from the Arctic. Large flocks of surface feeding ducks can do considerable damage to early plantings in the spring and to standing crops before harvest in the autumn, but most of the grain taken is waste left in harvested fields. Most have broad flat bills with a "nail" or hard down-turning projection at the tip. The legs of the surface feeding ducks are placed near the center of the body, making them only adequate swimmers, but making them well balanced and effective while walking. Diving ducks rely more heavily on animal food than do the surface feeders, but most consume vegetable matter as well. They dive from the surface of the water with a little hop upward. The legs of the divers are set near the rear of the body making them more effective under the surface, but clumsy on land. Some are only capable of pushing themselves along on their breasts. Most of the surface feeders, or pond ducks, have a brightly colored iridescent speculum, that area of secondary flight feathers at the trailing edge of the wing nearest the body. The primary flight feathers of all birds are those supported by the bones outside the bend, or wrist, of the wing (furthest removed from the body).

All ducks require open water and are therefore migratory in northern

North America. Some remain in the northeast in winter, feeding in open water of the Great Lakes and at the warm water outlets from industrial and power plants.

The pond ducks especially suffer heavily from lead poisoning, as the bottoms of marshes are increasingly polluted with pellets from shot guns. The pellets are taken in feeding and are not expelled.

Unlike swans and geese, ducks do not mate for life, but only for a brief period from late winter until the eggs are laid and incubation begun. Most pairs are formed in the wintering area before migration starts, but the male deserts as soon as his job is done and the female is left to incubate the eggs. The males then band together in open water in preparation for the moult which renders them flightless for a period in late summer. During the moult the male loses his nuptial dress and assumes a pattern quite similar to the female and to the juveniles of both sexes. Breeding plumage is recovered gradually during the autumn and winter.

MALLARD
Anas platyrhynchos
LENGTH 16 INCHES, WINGSPAN 36 INCHES

The Mallard is probably the most readily recognized and most numerous of all ducks. It is common in Europe and Asia as well as North America, for the Mallard is circumpolar. It is also one of a few ducks easily domesticated and thus provides the stock for domestic barnyard breeds as well as for those populating the park lagoons, the semi-domesticated, but free birds.

In North America, the Mallard is primarily a western bird, and although it breeds throughout the northeast, its main range is from Alaska to New Mexico. Its eastern abundant counterpart is the Black Duck, the female of which is indistinguishable from the female Mallard. In the extensive area where both occur, there is some cross-breeding. It is apparently up to the females to distinguish between Black and Mallard males, and to reject the wrong suitor which, according to some authorities, is the reason for the Mallard's bold markings.

The distinctive feature of the Mallard, as in many ducks, is the bright iridescent speculum. The speculum is the area of the secondary flight feathers nearest the body that can only be seen effectively in flight. In the Mallard, in both sexes, this is violet-blue, outlined top and bottom, in white. The rest of the female is pale mottled brown with an orange bill. The male's bill is yellow and the iridescent green head is separated from the brown breast by a narrow white band around the neck. The underparts are white, the back pale, the rump black, and there are two saucy turned-up or curled tail feathers.

The Mallard has perhaps the most impressive take-off of any duck. It literally leaps from the water or land, rising vertically for several feet before flying off. It feeds principally on pond seeds and grain, but some animal matter may be taken. In the west, for example, it feeds on the

34

carcasses of rotting salmon. It also consumes vast quantities of larvae and is sometimes used for mosquito abatement.

Like other ducks, Mallards take a new mate each year. As soon as incubation starts, the male deserts for the company of other males for the start of his moult, leaving the female alone to finish the incubation and raise the young. One set of eggs each season is customary, but if the first is destroyed, a second is usually started.

The Mallard is prized by hunters above other ducks for its size (a good three pounds) and taste.

BLACK DUCK

1983174

Anas rubripes
LENGTH 16 INCHES, WINGSPAN 36 INCHES

The Black is the most abundant surface feeding duck in the east. The same size as the Mallard, the Black is also prized by hunters. It appears more majestic than the Mallard, but actually is not an elegant bird. Its color varies considerably with age and season, young birds being almost as pale as the female Mallard. Older male birds appear black against the sky in spring, but in fact are a dark mottled brown with noticeably paler head and neck. The speculum is purple, bordered in black, and the undersides of the wings are white. The legs vary from red to green, and although some duck hunters still maintain that the red-legged "northern Blacks" of late autumn are a separate sub-species which have bred in the Arctic, the argument that has raged for years was officially settled thirty years ago. Terry Shortt, recognized ornithological expert whose illustrations appear on these pages, proved that leg color changed with age and sex!

Blacks breed from eastern Manitoba to Labrador, including all of Quebec, the Maritimes and the States south to Virginia, but the concentration is in the northeastern portion of this range. The habitat is varied, but the nest is usually built on the ground close to water — sometimes salt. Blacks feed principally on pond weeds, but in their winter range in the United States and southern Canada, a large proportion of their food is animal. The Black Duck is particularly susceptible to lead poisoning; the spent pellets it takes from the marsh bottom effectively paralyze the stomach muscles.

GADWALL

Anas strepera
LENGTH 15 INCHES, WINGSPAN 35 INCHES

The Gadwall is uncommon everywhere but has the widest distribution of any duck, for it breeds in western North America, Asia, Europe and parts of Africa. In the east, small numbers breed in two locations in Ontario and it is seen regularly as a migrant. It prefers fresh water and nests near prairie sloughs in the southern half of the Canadian prairies, locally in central British Columbia and in the northwestern United States. Pairs or single birds are often seen with flocks of Pintails and Widgeons, so it is well to scan flocks closely.

The male Gadwall is an elegant combination of subdued colors. The head and neck are brown, the breast mottled banker's gray, the back dark gray with a reddish mantle, the flanks brown, the belly white and the rump black. In flight, the speculum is a patchwork: white nearest the body, then black on both sides of the white patch, flanked by bands of maroon. It is the only pond-feeding duck with white patches at the rear of the speculum. While swimming, the female is similar to the female Mallard, but in the air it is distinguished by the maroon on the speculum, white underwings and white belly.

The Gadwall feeds almost entirely on vegetable matter and, more than most surface feeding ducks, will dive for its food if necessary. Apart from pond vegetation it takes grain in the fields and acorns and nuts in the woods. Most ducks can handle acorns, for their powerful gizzards wear down the husk, reducing it to tiny pieces.

PINTAIL
Anas acuta
LENGTH 19 INCHES, WINGSPAN 35 INCHES

While the Wood Duck is undoubtedly the most beautiful of our ducks, the Pintail is the most elegant. It takes its name from the two upward slanting tail feathers, several inches long, which extend beyond the black rump. Since the back and flanks of the male are gray and the belly white, this gives the same effect as if spats were worn. The other distinctive feature is a narrow white line which intersects the brown head vertically like a truncated chin strap, rising out of the white breast and long neck.

The male is clearly identified in flight by its dark head, white belly, darkish underwings, long pin-tail and wide reddish speculum, bordered at the rear with white. The female is mottled brown like a Mallard, but the longer neck and tail and red speculum identify her. In flight the wings are longer, slimmer and more pointed than most ducks.

The Pintail breeds widely in Europe and Asia, as well as having the widest distribution of any North American duck. It arrives early in the spring from the southern United States and reaches Alaska and the Canadian Arctic before the end of April. It breeds across Canada, with the possible exception of Newfoundland and in the prairies of the United States west from Minnesota, near fresh water marshes and ponds. The young are hatched early in June while other ducks are just beginning to nest. In the autumn it is among the first of the ducks to migrate through the northeast, and is rarely seen after early October. A few birds remain in the northern United States and southern Canada in winter, but most move south of the frost. Some western birds winter in the Hawaiian Islands, a 2,000 mile flight from Alaska.

Pintails are very graceful, both in the air and on the water. The flight is fast and they are clearly recognizable by their long tails. On descending from a considerable height they come down in a zig-zag rush, causing a roar of air through their wings and then land in a long braking glide.

GREEN-WINGED TEAL
Anas carolinensis
LENGTH 11 INCHES, WINGSPAN 24 INCHES

This smallest of our ducks is among the first to arrive in the spring — it is in the Arctic by early May (the Pintail is there by April), and the last to leave in the autumn. It breeds as far south as California in the west, in the northeastern United States, and in all Canadian provinces, but the main population is in the prairies. It prefers to winter in fresh water in the western and southern States and in Mexico.

The beautiful breeding plumage of the male includes a brown head, marked with a broad green eye mask which extends around the back of the neck and is narrowly outlined in white. The breast is pale and mottled, the belly white, the sides gray with a distinctive vertical white line up the side near the front. The back and short tail are dark and the underpart of the tail is pale yelow. The speculum is green nearest the body and black on the outside, outlined in front by a band of white. Following the moult in June and July, the male is much like the pale mottled female with a darker back and green wing patches, until the late autumn when the green face markings again appear.

Teal fly fast with great control, jigging about in tight flocks like much smaller birds. In autumn marshes they skim a few feet over the reeds, appearing so quickly that they are able to put down on the water before being seen. The hunter must then content himself with watching them swim among his decoys.

The female's voice is a rather high-pitched *quack* and the male's is a mellow whistling call. Feeding is principally in shallow water on marsh vegetation, but Teal will also take acorns and chestnuts in the forest, far from the nearest pond.

BLUE-WINGED TEAL
Anas discors
LENGTH 11 INCHES, WINGSPAN 24 INCHES

This little duck is slightly larger than the Green-wing but the difference is not apparent. The spring male is very handsome with a dark bluish-gray head and neck and a white crescent around the front of the eye. The back and tail are dark brown, the flanks and underparts light brown speckled with dark. There is a white patch at the side of the tail. When at rest a portion of the "teal blue" on the forward edge of the wing and green speculum are obvious, but it is in flight that one sees the extensive pale blue of the part of the wing close to the body, trailed by a white line and the green of the speculum. The wing markings of the female are similar, but the rest of the bird is a rather drab mottled brown which the male adopts after the summer moult.

The Blue-wing winters in the southern United States, the West Indies and South America, and is the last of the ducks to arrive on the breeding grounds. These extend across Canada north to the 60th parallel, and in the northern half of the United States. Older male birds have often left the north by mid-August and are followed by most of the females and juveniles in late September. In large marshes with many hunters on the opening day of the season, the entire population will move out overnight. The Blue-wing prefers fresh water ponds, marshes and sloughs where it nests on the ground close to the water. It is rare on the coast except in migration.

When in flight the Blue-wing's underwings show much white with a dark trailing edge. The tight flocks wheel about at great speed, the birds showing amazing agility and control as they twist and turn together. Their lisping peeps are the only noise other than the lovely sound of the wind in the wings.

Unlike most pond ducks the Blue-winged Teal does not tip up to feed with the feet waving in the air, instead it skims the surface for plant life, occasionally ducking only its head. Approximately one quarter of its diet is animal in the form of insects and crustaceans.

AMERICAN WIDGEON (Baldpate)
Mareca americana
LENGTH 14 INCHES, WINGSPAN 34 INCHES

When seen from a distance on the water, the American Widgeon can best be isolated from other ducks by three prominent patches of white: one on the bald pate and neck, one on the forewing, and the third and largest at the base of the tail. There is a broad green eye mask running to the back of the head and curving down the neck. The back is reddish brown, the breast and flanks pinkish, the tail black. The female has a pale head, pinkish breast and sides and dark back. In flight the white leading half of the inner wing is prominent, trailed by the green speculum edged with black. The underparts show much white on the wings, belly and head. A close relative, the European Widgeon, has a red head with a broad yellow central stripe, and is a rare but regular visitor not known to breed in North America.

The Widgeon is essentially a western bird, breeding from Alaska to Colorado in the west, and Hudson Bay in the east. There are a few small local breeding areas in the northeastern United States, in southern Ontario, Quebec and the Maritimes, but they are plentiful in eastern marshes on both spring and fall migrations. The winter is spent in the southern United States and South America.

The Widgeon feeds largely at night in shallow water and on land, and loafs in open water or in the reeds during the day. In deeper water it keeps company with diving ducks such as Canvasbacks and Redheads, pirating the wild celery they bring to the surface. They are restless and nervous, taking flight at the first sign of danger. In the water they sit lightly with tails high, pivoting about in search of food.

NORTHERN SHOVELER

Spatula clypeata
LENGTH 14 INCHES, WINGSPAN 31 INCHES

While the male Northern Shoveler is handsome, its grotesquely large black bill is out of proportion with the body and gives it an ungraceful appearance. The bill is nearly three inches long, longer than the head, and doubles in width near the tip, like a shovel. All ducks have comb-like teeth, but the Shoveler is specially equipped to strain the food which it takes as it moves about on the surface with its bill submerged. It also uses its bill to stir up mud from the bottom, which it strains for minute vegetable and animal matter. The head and neck are dark green, the breast white, the flanks and belly chestnut colored. There is a large white patch in front of the black tail, and a dark center line on the white back. In flight and seen from above, the pale blue of the forward part of the wings, trailed by a green speculum, shows clearly. When seen from below, the Shoveler is identified by the dark head, white breast and chestnut belly. The female is much like the female Mallard when sitting, except for the huge bill and, in flight, the pale blue on the wings.

Like the Widgeon, the Shoveler is a bird of the western and northern ponds and marshes, breeding locally in a few places in the northeast. This interesting species breeds in Europe, the Middle East, Asia and Japan and migrates to Africa and the Pacific. It is closely related to the Blue-winged Teal and, like it, is a late migrant in the spring and makes an early departure in the fall for the southern United States, the West Indies and Central America.

WOOD DUCK

Aix sponsa
LENGTH 13 INCHES, WINGSPAN 28 INCHES

The Wood Duck is the glamor bird of the waterfowl. The crested head is of iridescent green and blue, darkening to purple on the lower part. The head of the male is marked by two parallel white lines, one extending from the base of the bill above the eye to the end of the crest, the other from behind the eye. The chin is white with curling white lines extending upward behind the eye and around the back of the head. The breast is white polka dots on chestnut, and is separated from the tawny flanks by two perpendicular white and black lines. The back and long tail are bronze green, the belly white. The female is more demure, the head and back being a handsome grayish brown with white markings around the eye and under the chin. The breast and flanks are brown, mottled with white and the belly is white. By mid-summer the male closely resembles the female but has more white on the face.

This is the only one of our pond ducks to nest off the ground. It chooses natural hollows high up in rotting trees, but is easily attracted to nesting boxes. It prefers to be near water, but will often choose a site at the center of a wood. In the open it flies directly and fast, but among the trees it dodges about with great agility. When the young hatch, the mother calls to them from the ground. They climb to the edge of the hole and tumble to the ground, often from fifty feet, but are seldom hurt. They feed principally on pond vegetation, but also take acorns and beechnuts which are split in the remarkably strong gizzard.

There is a resident population on the west coast, but the main breeding area is in the east, reaching into southern Canada and the United States from the Arctic. The winter is spent in the southern United States and south to central Mexico.

REDHEAD

Aythya americana
LENGTH 15 INCHES, WINGSPAN 33 INCHES

This was once the most abundant of diving ducks, but the claiming of marshes and prairie sloughs for agriculture and settlement, and the 1930's drought, have had much to do with its decline. It is also one of the finest game birds, and its trusting and inquisitive nature have contributed to its reduced numbers.

Primarily a western and southern bird, its range extends from California to Wisconsin in the United States and in Canada from British Columbia to Manitoba. The nest is built in emergent vegetation close to the water, usually anchored to reeds. On migration, Redheads are found from coast to coast, "rafting" in bays in open water during the day and feeding in about ten feet of water in the early morning and evening. Their diet is almost entirely vegetable in the form of roots and leaves. When rafting, large groups of birds will suddenly take flight or "boil-up", mill about in the air for a few minutes, then quickly re-settle for no apparent reason. They also go for constitutionals or airborne promenades at the beginning and end of the day, flying back and forth over the water at great height in irregular lines. Redheads often associate with Canvasbacks.

RING-NECKED DUCK

Aythya collaris
LENGTH 12 INCHES, WINGSPAN 28 INCHES

At any distance, even in good light, the male Ring-neck, Greater Scaup and Lesser Scaup look very much alike. It is easy to describe the differences, but often difficult to distinguish them with any certainty. If they are quite close, the Ring-neck can be identified by the more triangular tufted head and the black-tipped bill with a white ring. The Ring-neck takes its name from the brownish ring which separates the black iridescent head from the black breast. The back and tail are black, the flanks white with fine black lines, the belly white. In flight, the trailing edge of the wing is gray, much darker than that of either scaup. On the water the female Ring-neck has a white eye-ring and closely resembles the female Redhead. From July until September the male and female are similar, the male being darker.

40

Once a western bird, breeding is now in the northern mid-west of the United States, in New England, and across Canada, in shallow fresh water in standing cattails near open water. The nest, made of vegetation and lined with down, is anchored to the reeds, presumably moving up and down with changes in the water level.

On migration Ring-necks travel in small flocks and, when landing, pitch in without circling. They have a habit of landing in open water and swimming to the feeding area, where plant life, taken at some depth, is the principal diet.

CANVASBACK
Aythya valisineria
LENGTH 15 INCHES, WINGSPAN 34 INCHES

The Canvasback is the largest of the game ducks, weighing about three pounds, and also the most favored for its flavor. As a consequence of this, drought, and the draining of much of its summer habitat, its numbers have been much reduced. In addition, its habit of straining seeds from the bottom mud has exposed it to lead poisoning from spent pellets. For many years it was entirely protected, but limited shooting has been permitted recently.

From its wintering areas in the estuaries of both the east and west coasts of the United States, and south through Mexico, it arrives on its breeding grounds early in the spring, flying fast in V-formation. It breeds from Alaska south to California and east to Manitoba, and is seen in the northeast only on migration.

The nest is built close to deep water at the edge of marshes, lakes and sloughs. It may be on the bottom or floating in shallow water among the rushes or other high plants.

The Canvasback has a bleached canvas back and underparts, a black breast and tail. The head and neck are the same chestnut as the Redhead, but a different shape — flat and long. The bill is dark and slopes upward into the flat face. In flight the head often appears black and one must rely on its silhouette for identification, which includes the whitish back and gray wings and the longish black tail. The female has a dull brown head and neck with pale back and sides.

The Canvasback feeds largely on the roots of underwater plants which it takes in twenty to thirty feet of water, usually leaving the stems and leaves to float away. In the west it will feed with other duck on rotting salmon.

GREATER SCAUP
Aythya marila
LENGTH 13 INCHES, WINGSPAN 31 INCHES

The Greater and Lesser Scaup are almost impossible to differentiate while they are on the water. In good light conditions, when the birds are quite close, and when both seem to be present, I have been able to convince myself that I have been able to do it, but it was probably wishful thinking. The male of each species in spring has a blue bill (the name "Blue Bill" is commonly used), black head, neck and breast, with a gray back darkening toward the tail. The flanks and belly are white. The Greater Scaup has a green iridescent tinge on the head, which is puffy and rounded in shape. The female is brown, darker on the head, and has a distinct white patch around the bill, which marks it from the Ring-neck and Redhead. The speculum of the Greater Scaup is white well into the primaries, while that of the Lesser is white only close to the body.

On migration they raft in flocks of thousands during the day, breaking into smaller groups in the early morning and evening to feed. It is marvellous to watch a large group suddenly take flight, mill about, and then re-settle. The sound of air through the wings is a rustling roar if a large flock flies close.

The North American range extends from Alaska, across the northern tundra, around Hudson Bay to extreme northern Quebec, Anticosti and Newfoundland. Few birds nest south of the 60th parallel. Breeding is also in Northern Europe and Asia. The nest is made on the ground near a pond, lake or sluggish river. We see them in late autumn, for they are the last of the migrants, arriving in the northeast after mid-October when hardy shooters set up floating blinds on large lakes and rivers. The best "flighting" is during windy snow storms. Some Greater Scaup remain in open fresh water for the winter, but most move to tidal estuaries on both coasts where they feed equally on animal and vegetable life.

LESSER SCAUP
Aythya affinis
LENGTH 12 INCHES, WINGSPAN 29 INCHES

This duck is very similar to the Greater Scaup, only three ounces lighter and undiscernably smaller. Both have dark heads, but the Lesser's has a higher dome and is larger, with a purple, not green, gloss. The smaller duck's speculum and flanks are grayer. The name "Scaup" derives from the courtship voice of these usually quiet birds, and probably also from its habit of feeding on molluscs which, in Scotland, are called "scalp".

The habits of the two scaup are similar, but the Lesser tends to favor smaller bodies of water and marshes on migration and in winter. It takes most of its food in about five feet of water, but can dive to twenty feet if necessary.

The breeding range is more southerly, but in Alaska, the Yukon and the western Northwest Territories they overlap. In the United States the Lesser breeds in the northwestern interior to northern Colorado east to

Iowa. It inhabits ponds and lakes from eastern British Columbia to extreme western Ontario with a few small local populations in southern Ontario. It winters on both coasts and inland where there is open water and through Mexico and the West Indies to South America.

COMMON GOLDENEYE (Whistler)
Bucephala clangula
LENGTH 13 INCHES, WINGSPAN 31 INCHES

In 1909 William Dawson wrote "of all wing music, from the droning of the rufous hummer to the startling whirr of the Ruffed Grouse, I know of none so thrilling sweet as the whistling wing-note of the Goldeneye . . ." Even by today's standards, this whistling is still one of the exciting sounds in nature, especially on a pre-dawn autumn morning.

The Goldeneye is readily identified on the water and in flight, for it shows larger areas of white than any other duck, except the Common Merganser. The male's puffy head is black with a large white patch on the cheek below the yellow eye. The neck, breast and belly are white, the back is white with a black streak on the center and another on each side at the base of the wing, which shows large patches of white. The female has a brown head, white throat, gray flanks and back and a white belly. Seen from the top, the wings have two dark bars across the white speculum.

This is a tree nesting duck which chooses a natural cavity or woodpecker hole about sixty feet above the ground, and as close as possible to water. When the young are hatched and acting on a call from the mother, they climb to the opening and tumble to the ground. Goldeneye breed to the tree limits of Europe, Asia and North America, and as far south as the northern central States and New England. They will remain in winter wherever there is food and open water, but most move to the coast where they feed in bays and estuaries, usually resting at sea beyond the surf line. A large part of the diet is animal in the form of crayfish and insects in fresh water and crabs, mussels and snails in salt. In addition, about one-quarter of their food is vegetable.

The closely related Barrow's Goldeneye is a western bird with a small breeding population in northern Quebec and is seen in small numbers on the east coast and occasionally along the St. Lawrence.

BUFFLEHEAD (also Butterball)
Bucephala albeola
LENGTH 10 INCHES, WINGSPAN 24 INCHES

This beautiful bird is the smallest of the diving ducks, little larger than a teal. It is a striking black and white, with iridescent purple and green tints on its head. The male in spring can only be mistaken for the Hooded Merganser, for both have a large white patch on each side of the disproportionately large head. The Bufflehead is puffier, the scallop shaped patch radiating out behind the eye to the black crest. The rest of the bird is patterned like a skunk in reverse, all white except for a broad black stripe down the center of the back. The wings are black-tipped and black close to the body, with white in between. The female has a dark grayish brown head and back with a white cheek patch behind the eye, gray flanks and white undersides and a white speculum on the dark wing.

This is another tree nesting duck, breeding in wooded regions from the southern Yukon and British Columbia, across the prairies to northern Ontario and the northwestern States. It will use woodpecker holes in trees near lakes and ponds and if necessary it will lay its eggs in a tunnel in a mud bank.

In the east it is seen on migration only, somewhat late in the spring and late in the autumn, moving south just ahead of the frost. It travels in small groups, usually flying fast and low over the water. Unlike other diving ducks, it does not run and flap off the water, but leaps straight up, sometimes emerging flying from under the water.

The food is principally animal and the flesh is fat and unpalatable. Buoyant and fluffy-looking, it compresses its head feathers before diving. It winters broadly across the United States and northern Mexico, south of the freeze-up and in open salt water as far north as Alaska and New England on the two coasts.

OLDSQUAW

Clangula hyemalis
LENGTH 15 INCHES, WINGSPAN 30 INCHES

This elegant diving duck with the unfortunate name breeds in the regions of Europe, Arctic Asia and North America, and winters along both North American coasts, in the east from Greenland to Carolina, and in the Great Lakes. On the coasts, where most birds winter, they feed off-shore, resting sometimes in sheltered bays at night. In the Great Lakes, they are usually well out from shore. They are best seen along the St. Lawrence and the shores of Great Lakes in spring and autumn while on migration.

The male is noted for its very long tail, longer than that of a Pintail. In winter the head, neck and belly are white with a large gray patch on the cheek. A wide black band extends across the breast around the front of the wings, meets on the back and extends as a single line to the tail. The wings are dark. The female is darker and lacks the cheek patch. In summer the head and neck of the male is largely dark with a white patch on the cheek. In flight, the long streamer tail and black and white of this flashing bird are unmistakable.

The Oldsquaw feeds almost entirely on animal life — crustaceans, molluscs, insects and fish, which it sometimes takes at great depths. Oldsquaws have been trapped in gill nets set as deep as 200 feet; large numbers of birds perish in this manner, particularly in the Great Lakes, and their bodies are then used in fertilizer plants. In the Arctic the eggs are taken by Eskimo, and both eggs and young by gulls, jaegers and foxes. When a nest is robbed, a second is attempted.

They are noisy, cheerful birds — always a welcome sight on a wild autumn day.

44

COMMON EIDER (formerly American Eider)
Somateria mollissima
LENGTH 17 INCHES, WINGSPAN 41 INCHES

Eiders are large diving ducks which nest in large colonies on the shores of the Arctic and northern Atlantic Oceans and are seldom seen away from the coast. They are heavy and squat and well suited to riding out coastal storms in winter. They build their nests using down from their breasts. The Common Eider is valued by native people in the north for its eggs and for its light colored down which has extraordinary insulating qualities and the capacity to remain soft and resilient. In Europe the eider has been protected for many years and a portion of down is taken from the nest under supervision for a controlled market. The careful husbandry of Norway and Iceland was not practised in North America, and eider numbers were greatly reduced. Vast numbers were slaughtered and the down torn from the breasts. Protection, and the practice of taking only some of the eggs together with part of the down from each nest, not enough to affect the eggs, has led to a revival. It takes thirty five to forty nests to produce one pound of down. The habit of ground nesting in large colonies, usually on low lying rocky islands, makes collection simple.

Nesting extends along the Arctic coast from Alaska eastward, including the islands, to Hudson Bay, Quebec, Newfoundland, the St. Lawrence, and western Nova Scotia. In winter eiders congregate in large flocks off the east coast, south to New Jersey, and in the Great Lakes, feeding in fairly shallow water on blue mussels and other crustacea. The mussels are taken whole, and the shells are ground to dust by the powerful gizzards.

Common Eiders have a distinctive bill, enlarged at the base, making the head look oval. In winter, the male is an impressive black and white. The head, throat, breast and back are white, the top of the head, belly and sides, tips and trailing edges of the wings, black. The back of the head is green-washed, the breast, buff-washed. The pale bill slopes upward in a straight line to the forehead, unlike the King Eider's concave shield. The female is a rich brown, heavily barred. The male and female are similarly marked during the summer. They fly close to the water with the bill tipped downward.

KING EIDER
Somateria spectabilis
LENGTH 16 INCHES, WINGSPAN 37 INCHES

The King Eider is a more northern breeder than the Common and is also more tolerant of fresh water. Its range extends from Prince Patrick and Ellesmere Islands south to Hudson Bay. It accepts the ponds and rivers of the tundra for nesting, although it probably flies to the ocean for much of its food during this season. In winter the center of east coast population is off the coast of Labrador although some birds, particularly juveniles, winter off New England and in the Great Lakes. This species also breeds widely along the coasts of northern Europe and Greenland.

The male is an exceptionally handsome bird due to its unusual bill, which extends like a broad orange shield upright and across the front of the head. It is regally outlined in black. The top of the head and nape are a lovely pale blue, the cheeks white, the breast and upper back are white with the lower breast washed in pink. On the water, one sees a white crescent along the side of the black wings and a white patch near the dark tail. In flight the wings are black on the leading and trailing edges and at the tips, but there is a unique large white triangle on each wing. The female closely resembles the female Common Eider, but is a somewhat richer brown.

Unlike the Common Eider, the King does not nest in colonies and is not much used for its down, which is darker and therefore less desirable. On the feeding grounds, this duck ranks with the Oldsquaw as one of the deepest diving, having been taken in nets set at 200 feet.

WHITE-WINGED SCOTER
Melanitta deglandi
LENGTH 16 INCHES, WINGSPAN 38 INCHES

There are three species of Scoters — Common, White-winged and Surf, all are large blackish ducks with distinctive bills. They spend most of their lives at sea, coming inland only to breed. All dive for their food of mussels, oysters, scallops and crabs which are swallowed whole and ground by the powerful gizzard and chemicals of the stomach. Pebbles and sand are taken as a grinding agent.

The White-winged is the most common and also the most widely distributed during the nesting season. It nests on the ground in scrub and woodlands close to fresh water, from Alaska across British Columbia and the Prairie Provinces into the northern United States. The male has a distinct knob on the upper part of the bill, a white patch below the eye and a white fleck on the wing which can sometimes be seen when the bird is sitting. In flight the speculum is white; the other two Scoters have entirely dark wings. The female is browner and has two white spots on the face, one at the base of the bill and the other behind the eye and also has the white speculum.

This duck migrates to both coasts in winter and to the Great Lakes. In eastern waters it is found from Newfoundland to South Carolina, usually remaining quite close to the shore. Non-breeding birds remain in salt water during the summer and can be seen in bays and from the tidal shores.

Scoters were once heavily shot off the New England coast in the autumn and winter. They come readily to decoys and, despite their fishy flavor, were once much prized as game birds.

SURF SCOTER
Melanitta perspicillata
LENGTH 14 INCHES, WINGSPAN 33 INCHES

Surf Scoters are well named for they are smaller and more agile than the other Scoters and do, in fact, take much of their food at the surf line.

They dive into the rising front of a wave and can be seen swimming with their wings through the smooth, almost vertical front of the rollers before they break. In flight the exciting sound of the wings can be heard for some distance. They fly quite close to the water in irregular flocks and, on landing, have the characteristic habit of hitting the water with wings extended upward as they skid to a stop.

This duck breeds from Alaska to Hudson Bay across the northern edge of the Prairie Provinces and in northern Quebec and Labrador. Migration to both coasts is more northerly than with the White-winged, and consequently few birds are seen in the Great Lakes and upper St. Lawrence.

The seldom-found nest is built on the ground, well hidden in a clump of small trees or scrub, close to a lake or marsh. While nesting, Scoters rely heavily on vegetable matter for their food, but at times aquatic insects make up the bulk of the diet.

The male Surf Scoter is black with three white patches on the head, one at the base of the sharply rising orange bill, another on the forehead and the third down the back of the head. At any distance the white patches cannot be readily distinguished and the bird appears to be entirely black. The female closely resembles the female White-winged while sitting, but lacks the white speculum.

The third of these large, black, diving birds, the Common Scoter (*Oidemia nigra*) is circumpolar, breeding sparsely in the northern States and Canada. It is seldom seen, but a few winter in the Great Lakes and pass up and down the St. Lawrence. The male is entirely black with a large orange knob on the bill.

RUDDY DUCK

Oxyura jamaicensis
LENGTH 11 INCHES, WINGSPAN 23 INCHES

In the east the Ruddy Duck is seen mostly on migration, and then only irregularly. It is essentially a western duck, breeding in ponds, lakes and sloughs, but small, local populations are present in the northeastern States and Ontario and Quebec. In winter it migrates to both coasts and to the southern United States and Mexico.

While swimming, this elegant little duck with the ruddy plumage and bright blue bill habitually cocks its stiff, narrow tail upward, or carries it low in the water. Ruddy Ducks perform much like Grebes — they sink without a ripple and are agile divers with legs set far back, making them almost incapable of walking on land. Instead they push themselves along on their breasts and on taking off, paddle furiously along the water for some distance. Courtship is elaborate. The breeding plumage is reddish chestnut colored on back, breast and sides. The upturned bill and legs are blue, the top of the head black and the cheeks white. The wings and tail are plain rich brown and the belly whitish. In winter the male loses its ruddy color, becoming dark brown above and pale brown below, much like the female.

This tiny duck, which weighs under one pound, lays enormous eggs for its size, some two and a half inches long. The usual clutch of about fourteen eggs, laid one per day, weighs three pounds, or three times the weight of the female. When hatched, the young are well developed, capable of diving for their food within hours of birth. Other species must feed on the surface for some weeks. Most male ducks desert the female as soon as incubation begins, but the Ruddy remains close to the nest and assists in raising the young.

HOODED MERGANSER
Lophodytes cucullatus
LENGTH 13 INCHES, WINGSPAN 26 INCHES

Mergansers are fish-eating diving ducks. They have thin bills, serrated on the sides, for capturing and holding fish. All fly fast with the head, neck and body in a straight line.

The Hooded Merganser is the smallest and least common of the three merganser species and one of the most strikingly handsome of all ducks. The male has a black head and neck with a large fan-like crest outlined in black, making a conspicuous white triangle behind each eye. The crest may be raised or lowered. The breast is white, the flanks brownish and finely barred and there are two parallel black lines perpendicular at the front of the wing. The back is black with a grid of fine black and white lines parallel to and near the tail. In flight the inner parts of the wing show much white. The female has gray flanks and breast, white belly, dark back and brown crested head.

The Hooded Merganser breeds in a broad band across North America in ponds, lakes and streams close to secluded woodland. Nesting is in cavities in trees, old stumps and fallen logs which may be up to half a mile from the nearest water.

As with Wood Ducks, with whom the merganser competes for nesting holes, the young leap to the ground soon after hatching.

The diet is almost entirely animal, consisting of small fish, frogs, larvae and insects. The preference is for still water, but in winter this duck is capable of maintaining itself in fast water if that is all that is open. In winter it withdraws southward and to open fresh water near the coasts.

COMMON MERGANSER (formerly American Merganser)
Mergus merganser
LENGTH 18 INCHES, WINGSPAN 37 INCHES

The Common Merganser is a widespread summer resident in fresh water lakes and rivers across the northern United States and Canada. This is the duck you will find when you open your summer cottage, for in early spring it will descend chimneys. It nests in tree cavities, when possible, but will accept other locations such as river bank tunnels, rock piles or abandoned buildings. The habit of using chimneys as nesting holes is almost always fatal to the bird, for it cannot escape, and is unpleasant for the cottage owner. The only way to avoid this problem is to screen the chimney.

This is also the duck much maligned and persecuted for its supposed destructive effect on valuable game fish. Fishermen have debated the role of the merganser for years, and it is clear that in some areas where game fish exist alone, too many mergansers have a destructive limiting effect. Without predation by ducks, lakes and ponds can become over-stocked, limiting the supply of food and oxygen and the result is a vast number of small, underfed and useless fish. In ideal conditions, where game fish and coarse fish appear together, mergansers are beneficial, for they feed principally on the slower moving, coarse fish.

The male in flight, like all male mergansers, is a flash of black and white. The throat, undersides, flanks and inner wings are white, contrasting with the dark green head, dark wing tips, back and tail. This species is unique in that the female has a crested brown head while that of the male is smooth. The female is pale and shows much pale gray on the wings, tail and flanks, white on the speculum, throat and breast. The bill and head are long and thin.

RED-BREASTED MERGANSER
Mergus serrator
LENGTH 16 INCHES, WINGSPAN 33 INCHES

Both the Red-breasted and Common Merganser breed in northern Europe as well as in North America. The Red-breasted breeds farther north than the Common and is seldom seen in the more settled areas inland in New England and Canada, except on migration. Along the coasts however, it is common in summer, and nests close to salt water in bays and estuaries, always on the ground, in rock piles or under fallen logs. In winter most birds move to salt water on both coasts, although some are present in the Great Lakes.

While the Common Merganser seldom forms flocks of more than twenty birds, the Red-breasted on migration, and in winter, is highly gregarious, moving in flocks of hundreds. When feeding, they will often form regular lines, driving schools of fish before them, and diving repeatedly. They will join with flocks of gulls, loons, grebes, murres and guillemots, devastating huge schools of fish. They feed principally outside the surf line.

Mergansers are awkward on land, often standing with their breasts on the ground. They can, however, take off from land if necessary. The Hooded Merganser springs up from the water, but the other two must flap and push with their feet for some distance to become airborne.

Turkey Vulture

Marsh Hawk

Cooper's Hawk

Red-tailed Hawk

Bald Eagle

The vultures, hawks, and eagles are all birds of prey and live entirely on animals, birds, and large insects which they kill or take as carrion.

The male Red-breasted has a long, needle-like bill, black loosely crested head and back, gray flanks, white throat and undersides and white inner wings with dark tips. The reddish band across the breast is quite distinctive. The female and young are similar to the female Common Merganser, but the brown of the head fuses gently into the whitish breast while the Common has a distinct line.

Vultures
Family Cathartidae

Of three species of vultures in North America, the Turkey Vulture is the only one likely to be seen in the northeast, although the more southerly Black Vulture has been recorded on rare occasions.

TURKEY VULTURE
Cathartes aura
LENGTH 25 INCHES, WINGSPAN 72 INCHES

This marvellous but somewhat eerie bird is a scavenger with legs and claws too weak to do its own killing. It relies on its amazing vision and effortless soaring capacity. Rising to great heights on thermal currents, it watches the country below for signs of death. In the south, where vultures are common, they watch one another as well as the ground and when prey is sighted by one and it descends, dozens will congregate from some distance. In the northeast, where few vultures are present, it is unusual to find more than a few on a carcass. Automobiles and garbage dumps now provide the principal food source, although I recently surprised a pair feeding on a dead lamb in a field in southern Ontario.

Turkey Vultures are not beautiful except in flight, when the distinctive lift of the wings above the horizontal when circling, and their control through tilting show their grace. The small naked head is red, the upper sides uniformly dark brown. From below the flight feathers are paler than the body and forewings.

Southern Canada and the northeastern United States form the extreme northern limits of a range extending to the Straits of Magellan. The two eggs are laid on the ground in a sheltered place, sometimes a cave or a ledge or even in an abandoned building. While vultures have no economic significance in the northeast, their value in the south and in tropical countries, where they consume decaying animals, is great.

Hawks, Eagles, and Harriers

Family Accipitridae

One tends to think of all hawk-like birds as belonging to the same family, but the true hawks are only one of several families within the FALCONIFORMES, a worldwide order of birds which includes, besides the true hawks, the kites, eagles, harriers, ospreys, vultures and the Secretary Bird of Africa. All told they number about 260 species, of which thirty five occur in North America. The true hawks are divided into sub-families which include the ACCIPITERS (Goshawk, Cooper's Hawk and Sharp-shinned Hawk) the BUTEOS, which are also called buzzards (Rough-legged, Red-tailed, Red-shouldered and Broad-winged Hawks) the EAGLES (Golden Eagle and Bald Eagle) and the HARRIERS (Marsh Hawk).

All are birds of prey and live entirely on animals, birds and large insects which they kill or take as carrion. The bills are hooked to enable them to rip the food they eat and the legs are strong with curved talons for seizing and carrying their prey. They have keen eyes and hunt with a variety of techniques, attacking from high soaring stations, from positions close to the ground and from perches. The markings of the male and female are similar (with the exception of the Marsh Hawk where the male is gray and the female brown) and the female in all cases is appreciably larger.

Hawks serve to keep the rodent population in balance but have, themselves, been unnecessarily slaughtered in the past because of depradation on poultry and game birds. In the South, and in frontier settlements where most households kept chickens and allowed them the run of the yard, the accipiters, particularly the Cooper's Hawk, took to the easy life of stealing chickens. Few people could distinguish the accipiters from the other hawks and shot at all. There is less temptation toward chicken thievery today when chickens are raised indoors, but accipiters still live by preying on song birds, though they help maintain the balance among small birds by taking the weak.

The use of pesticides — which builds up a high toxic content in insects, worms and rodents — has endangered the continued existence of many species. The hawks themselves are able to tolerate the toxic effects quite well, but tend to lay sterile or thin shelled eggs which fail to produce the next generation.

Most nest in high trees, close to the main trunk, building flat platform nests which are used in successive years with the addition of fresh sprigs and green leaves.

GOSHAWK

Accipiter gentilis
LENGTH 19 INCHES, WINGSPAN 42 INCHES

Three species of hawks, the Goshawk, Cooper's Hawk and the Sharp-shinned Hawk are called accipiters. Similar in character and appearance, they all have short rounded wings and long narrow banded tails, gray-blue backs and dark crowns. They hunt in the forest and are rarely seen except on migration. When they are, they fly with fast wing beats and glide in short intervals rather than soar. They are not particularly popular hawks for they prey on small birds, game birds and sometimes poultry. They nest close to the main trunk of a tree, building large platforms on a horizontal branch, usually a new one every year, unlike other hawks which use the same nest year after year. In medieval times, trained Goshawks were used in hunting.

The Goshawk is the largest and rarest of the accipiters. It is larger than a crow and mainly gray, with a dark crown and black cheek patches. A good point of identification is the white fluffy patch under the tail. The body is slate gray on the back and wings, whitish gray below and finely barred. There is a white line above the eye. Young birds are brown above, light on the head, with alternate dark and light brown tail stripes and whitish below with dark stripes.

The Goshawk is so rare and secretive that in many years in the forests, I have only identified it three times with certainty. Once, on the border of the Laurentide Park in northern Quebec, I managed to follow a family group about for more than an hour as they flew from tree to tree, the young apparently newly from the nest, for they were uncertain and awkward.

The Goshawk feeds on birds as large as grouse and will take chickens when it can. It also takes large numbers of rabbits, squirrels and mice, hunting below the tree top level, usually close to the ground, pouncing on its prey with a burst of speed.

Breeding extends across northern Europe and Asia and in North America to the tree limit in the north, south to Mexico in the west and to New England in the east.

SHARP-SHINNED HAWK
Accipiter striatus
LENGTH 11 INCHES, WINGSPAN 21 INCHES

This small hawk is almost identical to the larger Cooper's; both have very dark blue upper parts, gray and black banded tails, black crown and gray cheeks. The breast, legs and underparts are horizontally barred red and white, like a 1920s bathing suit. The young are brown above and heavily spotted brown on white below. Only the tails are different: the Sharp-shinned's is square at the end while the Cooper's is rounded. Size is the chief distinguishing feature and the Cooper's is much larger. In all hawks the female is larger than the male, and the female Sharp-shinned may be almost as large as the male Cooper's.

This hawk is reasonably common where extensive woodlands remain, from Alaska to Labrador in the north and Mexico and the Gulf Coast in the south.

It can best be seen near forest openings and roadsides where it hunts for small birds, particularly warblers and sparrows. They also take squirrels and mice.

Hawks migrate during daylight, this one flying just over the tree tops early in the day with the characteristic flight — four or five flaps and a glide of a few seconds, but soaring high by noon. Certain well defined migration routes are followed, particularly in the autumn, and in September considerable numbers of Sharp-shins can be seen passing along the northern shores of Lakes Ontario and Erie before moving south. Some birds remain in southern Canada in winter, but most move south of the Great Lakes, some as far as Central America.

COOPER'S HAWK
Accipiter cooperii
LENGTH 16 INCHES, WINGSPAN 28 INCHES

This hawk is intermediate in size between the other two accipiters, the Goshawk and Sharp-shinned Hawk, and its pattern is precisely that of the latter, except the tip of the tail which is rounded rather than square. It is described by some authors as being uncommon and by one as being the commonest of the birds of prey. This is probably because it is often overlooked. Although buteos are much in evidence because they soar above the trees, the accipiters hunt below the level of the canopy, and one must be in the forest to see them. They have a habit of remaining for long periods perched high in a tree, just under the top leaves, seeing without being seen.

The Cooper's Hawk especially tends to favor woodland for hunting, relying less than the Sharp-shinned on openings and edges.

This accipiter feeds principally on birds, up to robin-sized, and to some extent on small mammals, and in earlier times, was the legendary terror of the barnyard. When chickens were allowed to run free, the lure of this easy prey was tempting, although not all individuals were chicken thieves. One reads of cases where Cooper's were known to nest near farms and did not rob them.

The Cooper's Hawk is a more southerly breeder than the other two accipiters, for it nests in a narrow band across southern Canada from British

54

Columbia to southwestern Quebec and sparingly in New Brunswick and Nova Scotia along the Bay of Fundy. In the United States it breeds throughout the country with the exception of southern Florida. It migrates largely from New England and Canada in winter to the southern States and as far south as Costa Rica.

RED-TAILED HAWK

Buteo jamaicensis
LENGTH 18 INCHES, WINGSPAN 48 INCHES

The Red-tail is one of a large family of hawks called buteos, of which four species are present in the eastern part of North America. Buteos have long, broad wings and widely fanned tails when in flight. They hunt principally in open country, watching for prey from a prominent tree or while soaring in large circles high above the earth.

The Red-tail is among the larger of the hawks but at a distance, and against the clouds they, like other buteos, are difficult to identify with certainty, for the coloring and marking of individuals differ considerably. In a reasonable light the pinkish underside and narrow black band near the end of the tail are quite distinctive. In the east, the majority of Red-tails have rich brown bodies with a darker band across the belly, brown feathers at the front of the undersides of the wing and whitish flight feathers tipped with black. When perching, the chestnut colored upper side of the tail can be seen, as well as the brown spotted back. The plumage is soft and, despite its size, the male weighs only two pounds and the larger female under three pounds.

This buteo is common in the open country but is little seen in the dense forests. It nests in open woodlands in a high tree, but in the prairies and deserts of the western United States will settle for a cliff ledge. It hunts rabbits, snakes, frogs and mice which it takes in a pounce from the air. An occasional individual becomes a chicken thief, but generally their shyness keeps them away from farm buildings. The breeding range extends throughout North America to the limit of trees, and south to Panama and the West Indies. It migrates almost entirely from the northeast in winter to the mid-United States and south.

The cry of the Red-tail is an unforgettable downward slurring screech of about two seconds.

RED-SHOULDERED HAWK

Buteo lineatus
LENGTH 16 INCHES, WINGSPAN 40 INCHES

Like the Red-tailed, the Red-shouldered is a buteo and is most often seen soaring over fields and open country in long, slow circles on its large broad wings and widely fanned tail. When seen from below the red-shoulder patches are not visible and the bird is identified by its conspicuous banded tail (five wide dark bands, separated by narrower white ones), uniformly pale brown body and underwings, and the whitish flight feathers, tipped with black. Some hawks, including the Red-shouldered, have "windows" or translucent areas at the base of the primary flight feathers which can be seen in a good light. The extensive reddish shoulder patches are visible when the bird's upper parts are seen while flying, as are the black and white banded flight feathers and tail. When perched most hawks look alike, except when seen clearly and from reasonable proximity. This one shows the red shoulder patches quite distinctly, and much black and white on the folded wing.

The habits of the buteos are similar, but this one does more of its hunting from a perch in a tree, watching the ground for mice, caterpillars, grasshoppers, frogs and small snakes. It favors wet areas such as small marshes and boggy streams to hunt, dropping from its perch to grasp its prey in its talons.

The nest is built in large trees up to about sixty feet, often in small wood lots in farming country. The same nest may be used in successive years with the addition of fresh sprigs and green leaves when the eggs are laid. The cry, which is a piercing scream of *kee you*, is heard mostly in the spring.

The Red-shouldered Hawk is present in summer and winter throughout most of the eastern half of the United States and in a narrow band on the west coast. In Canada it summers in southern Ontario to the north shore of Lake Huron and Ottawa, in southwestern Quebec and, sparingly in southern New Brunswick.

BROAD-WINGED HAWK
Buteo platypterus
LENGTH 13 INCHES, WINGSPAN 33 INCHES

The Broad-winged Hawk is the smallest of the buteos and the most secretive, leaving its forest hunting area only to engage in spectacular mass migratory flights. It is distinguished from the other buteos by its crow size, short tail, chunky appearance and in flight, by its relatively broad wings. The tail, when seen from above and below, shows four bold black and white bands of equal width and a narrow white tip. The underside of the body is reddish, either plain or finely barred with white, and the undersides of the wings are pale. The back, wings and head are a uniform dark brown. Young birds have vertically striped breasts.

It breeds across the eastern United States, the central prairies, Ontario, southern Quebec, and New Brunswick. Within its summer range, where it is quite common, the Broad-wing is often overlooked, for unlike most buteos, it seldom leaves the deciduous woodland which is its hunting and nesting area. There it feeds on snakes, frogs, toads, grasshoppers, crickets and caterpillars, as well as the usual selection of small forest rodents.

In late September it gathers in huge, loose migrating flocks. Great numbers can be seen soaring above the shores of Lake Erie, particularly at Port Stanley, near the beginning of a migration flight which takes them

4,000 miles to South America. Most of this journey is made in drifting circles, along the shore lines and mountain ridges to take maximum advantage of thermals.

ROUGH-LEGGED HAWK

Buteo lagopus
LENGTH 19 INCHES, WINGSPAN 52 INCHES

The Rough-legged is a bird of the Arctic and sub-Arctic regions of both North America and Europe. It is the largest of the buteos, and its shaggy legs and belly are the most heavily feathered. It is seen in the settled areas of the northern United States and southern Canada only on migration — soaring at great heights — passing mostly over open country and, near the coast, marshes and dunes, usually to coincide with melting or new snow which assists in its hunting.

It breeds from northern Alaska across the Yukon and the Northwest Territories to northern Quebec and Newfoundland and in the Arctic Islands. The winter is spent in the United States, sparingly in southern Canada and south to New Mexico and Virginia. Nesting is usually on a cliff, high river bank or boulder, but where there are trees it will use them, keeping the same nest year after year.

In the north the food is almost entirely lemmings and carrion when available. Rough-legs characteristically hover over their prey in the manner of ospreys and kestrels, usually with legs dangling, showing the heavy feathering.

The Rough-leg is a big, shaggy chested, brown-backed bird with a light mottled head and chest, but there is much variation between individuals, some occurring in a dark or melanistic phase which are almost black. In flight, and seen from below, the long broad wings are mostly white, sharply outlined in black, the leading edge being somewhat darker. A conspicuous dark patch at the "wrist" of the wing is an excellent guide to identification. The tail is long, white at the base and banded at the tip. The throat and breast are streaked brown and black and the belly is black.

BALD EAGLE

Haliaeetus leucocephalus
LENGTH 32 INCHES, WINGSPAN 85 INCHES, WEIGHT 13 POUNDS

This great bird, whose wingspan is longer than most humans, is the national emblem of the United States, and one of only two eagles present in North America. Its numbers were much reduced during the 1950s due to the wide use of toxic pesticides, but in recent years it appears to have made a modest recovery. The other, the ràre Golden Eagle, is a bird of remote mountains and desert grasslands and is not likely to be seen in the northeast.

Bald Eagles are invariably associated with water, for they feed almost entirely on fish which they take from the surface, find dead or steal from ospreys. They nest in high trees near the water and the nest, which they recycle, sometimes becomes enormous after years of additions, one reportedly twenty feet high and ten feet wide. The territory is large and one pair may build two or more nests which they use alternately from year to year. Once the young are fledged, the adults wander widely and may turn up in duck marshes and even garbage dumps.

The head of this giant bird is feathered, not naked and, like the neck and tail, is pure white. The rest of the adult plumage is blackish. Immature birds do not gain adult plumage until the fourth year, and are dark brown, somewhat lighter on the leading edge of the underside of the wing, resembling the Golden Eagle. There is little danger of confusion, as the Goldens are now rare in the east.

Bald Eagles fly and soar with stiff flat wings using thermals to patrol their vast territories. The only large concentrations are on the islands and mainland shore of the west coast, but a number of breeding areas occur elsewhere. The main breeding area is in the southern United States and many nests can be seen in the Everglades National Park in Florida. In the east they are present in Quebec along the St. Lawrence and in northwestern Ontario. Bounties were once paid in Alaska for paired feet in an attempt to reduce the inroads being made on the salmon by the Bald Eagle.

MARSH HAWK

Circus cyaneus
LENGTH 17 INCHES, WINGSPAN 42 INCHES, WEIGHT 1¼ POUNDS

This medium-sized long winged hawk is most often seen flying low over marshes and wet meadows and, on migration, anywhere over open ground. The male is a gray bird with a conspicuous white patch at the base of its long slim tail and a distinctive flying style. It alternately flaps and glides, holding its long wings above the horizontal. As it glides, it tilts back and forth to counter the wind, using its tail as a rudder. It feeds on mammals as large as rabbits, some small birds, snakes, insects and frogs. On sighting its prey it pounces quickly, using surprise as a weapon, for it is not a fast flyer. It, like the Rough-legged Hawk which often shares its hunting ground, frequently hovers over one spot while hunting, harrying its prey. The male is slate gray above, pale and somewhat spotted below, while the female is brown above and below, and paler on the flight feathers. The tail is barred with a wide band near the tip, and both birds have owl-like facial discs.

The breeding range extends across the northern part of the United States and Canada, with the exception of the eastern Arctic, northern Quebec and possibly Newfoundland, where it has been seen but is not known to nest. The nest is built on the ground either in, or close to, a marsh, fresh or salt. Because of its low flying, it is vulnerable to thoughtless shooting, but its ground nesting and high reproductive rate (it lays five eggs rather than the usual two or three for other hawks) assures its place as a fairly common bird. It winters casually from southern Canada to Columbia. In Europe and Asia, where it is known as the Hen Harrier, it breeds widely from Scotland to Siberia and south to Portugal.

Ospreys
Family Pandionidae

OSPREY

Pandion haliaetus
LENGTH 22 INCHES, WINGSPAN 54 INCHES

This exciting and beautiful bird with the majestic flight is unusual in that it is the single member of its family. It is widespread, breeding in all continents except South America, but is uncommon everywhere. About 1950, when it nested in Scotland for the first time in one hundred years, the site was kept secret in order to avoid disturbance. In North America one sees the Osprey regularly on the seacoast and on some large lakes and rivers, from Alaska to Newfoundland and New England, and south to Central America along the coasts.

Ospreys live entirely on fish which they take from the surface after a spectacular dive of up to a hundred feet. They half-close their wings and land with a great splash, sometimes submerging completely, to grasp a

American Kestrel

Peregrine Falcon

Osprey

The exciting and beautiful Osprey is uncommon everywhere, although it breeds on all continents except South America. Falcons can be distinguished from hawks by their long, pointed wings and by their long, narrow tails.

two or three pound fish in their talons. The soles of the feet are horny, aiding in the grip. The bird then flies off the water, arranging the fish fore and aft, and carries it to the nest or feeding perch. The nest is usually built in a tree or crag, but platforms on poles in suitable locations are accepted, the same nest being used year after year.

Ospreys rise with ease to great heights by extensive circling and by mere inclinations of tail and wings. When seen flying, Ospreys can easily be mistaken for immature gulls at a casual glance. They fly with easy flappings when hunting, almost listlessly. The body is largely white, the wings streaked dark and white, but the key distinguishing feature is the dark patch at the wrist of the wing. The wings and tail are long, the tail banded. When perched, the upper parts are brown, the top of the head, face and throat white with a dark line extending through the eye to the back of the head. The legs are white and long, feathered only to the knee. When on the wing they call frequently with a series of loud clear whistles.

Falcons
Family Falconidae

The falcons are fast flying birds of prey which rely on amazing bursts of speed to overtake and kill other birds. The sport of falconry, or the use of falcons and other hawks trained to kill birds and animals and return with their kill to their master, was established in China as long as 4,000 years ago, and in Persia by 1700 B.C. In England and Europe it became a sport for nobles by the middle ages, and flourished as a royal sport until the 17th century. The class structure of the period extended to falconry, thus only royalty could fly the Gyrfalcon, noblemen the Peregrine, noble ladies the Merlin, and so on to the squires and clergy who were restricted to Goshawks and Kestrels. In Asia, eagles are still used commercially to take foxes and wolves.

Falcons can be distinguished from other members of the hawk family by their long wings which come to a sharp point and by their long narrow tails. They use powerful rowing strokes, sweeping back the outer part of the wing as they fly. They seldom soar, but when they do, the tail is opened in a fan to increase the lifting power of thermal currents.

GYRFALCON
Falco rusticolus
LENGTH 20 INCHES, WINGSPAN 48 INCHES

This is the largest of the falcons. It is a great, powerful bird with a four foot wingspan and is seldom seen south of the Arctic circle. During winters when the lemming population is low, some birds wander south as far as the northern United States where they may be found in open country. It is hard to identify with certainty other than by its size and pointed wings, for it varies in color from white to black, most birds being grayish. In its southern range, the Gyrfalcon usually associates with flocks of gulls on which it feeds.

In the north in summer it takes murres, duck and shore birds, and usually nests near sea-bird colonies. In winter it feeds on ptarmigan, following the flocks to their wintering areas, but the chief food is the lemming.

PEREGRINE FALCON
Falco peregrinus
LENGTH 15 INCHES, WINGSPAN 40 INCHES

The Peregrine Falcon, or Duck Hawk, is one of the world's fastest flying birds and has been timed in its dive, or stoop, at 180 miles an hour. Unfortunately, although it still nests on the west coast and in the western Arctic in small numbers, it has not been seen in eastern North America in the wild for some years. Always rare in the east, it is now actually endangered. Attempts are being made to save the Peregrine from extinction in North America through controlled breeding programs of captive birds in the United States and Canada. Released birds are now breeding on elevated platforms and it is hoped that they will re-establish in their natural state. Thirty years ago a pair bred successfully for several years on a ledge of the Sun Life Building in Montreal, feeding on the city's vast stock of pigeons and House Sparrows.

Peregrines feed almost entirely on birds which they strike with their powerful talons in mid-air, at the end of a stoop. Their prey is usually killed by the first blow and may be grasped immediately, or retrieved from the ground. They also appear to harass flocks of ducks and smaller birds for practice or fun, without intent to kill.

Peregrines are relatively small and streamlined, and the distinctive black and white facial markings can be seen for some distance. The flat top of the head, the cheeks, back and wings are bluish black, the underparts barred. In flight thc forepart of the under-wing is spotted, the after part barred. The wings are long and pointed, and in flight the long lightly barred tail is compressed and narrow.

Peregrines breed from Alaska to southern South America and from northern Europe and Asia to South Africa and Australia.

MERLIN (renamed from Pigeon Hawk in 1973)

Falco columbarius
LENGTH 12 INCHES, WINGSPAN 23 INCHES

This falcon takes its former name from its resemblance in flight to the pigeon, for it flies with the same powerful rowing strokes as the Mourning Dove. It is the same size and has similar pointed longish wings. It can quickly be distinguished from the pigeons by its heavily barred tail, the widest bar being near the tip. The back and wings are dark blue, usually appearing black, the underparts and underwings mottled brown and white. In poor light it resembles the Kestrel, but lacks the Kestrel's reddish back and tail and distinct facial markings. The Merlin is widely distributed, but uncommon in its nesting territory, which spreads over all of the northern United States and Canada, except the eastern Arctic, extreme northern Quebec and southern Ontario. Nesting is usually in open woodland but sometimes in barrens and bogs, and hunting is done close to marshes, lakes and ponds. Much of its time is spent ineffectively badgering crows and gulls, for the largest prey it can handle is a small bird — Flicker or Robin-sized. It takes large insects such as dragonflies, butterflies and grasshoppers in and about the marshes.

The Merlin migrates to its winter range from southern Canada to northern South America in company with the main concentrations of small birds, on which it feeds as it travels.

Nesting habitats are varied, including cliffs, old crows' nests, natural tree cavities, old woodpecker holes or a hollow in the ground.

AMERICAN KESTREL (renamed from Sparrow Hawk in 1973)

Falco sparverius
LENGTH 9 INCHES, WINGSPAN 21 INCHES

This is our smallest (Robin-sized) falcon and certainly the most common. Along roadsides in open farming country one can see the Kestrel every mile or so perched on wires, fence posts and branches, or hovering over its prey. It has become quite common in cities and towns where it helps to control the population of House Sparrows, and nests in crevices in buildings. Larger insects such as grasshoppers, crickets, beetles, spiders and dragonflies are the principal or sole diet during the summer; in autumn and winter, if the bird remains in the east, these are replaced by mice and small birds, particularly sparrows.

The American Kestrel is a beautiful bird, with a barred red back, plain red tail tipped with a black band and blue wings. The head is strikingly marked, dark on top with vertical black lines behind and in front of the white cheek. The breast and belly are buffy to white, spotted with black. In flight the underwings are barred brown and white and are long and pointed. This falcon frequently hovers when hunting, but spends most of its time perched in a prominent position on the top of a dead tree or on a wire or post.

The nesting range extends from Alaska across Canada and to the southern tip of South America. Most birds withdraw from the northeast in winter, but a few remain. They return early in the spring and can be heard calling their sharp *killy, killy, killy* cry. In the wild they nest in woodpecker holes, natural tree cavities, crevices in cliffs and sometimes in old nests.

Grouse and Ptarmigan
Family Tetraonidae

This small family of seventeen species of chicken-like birds which lives throughout the northern hemisphere of North America and Eurasia is largely non-migratory, although some tend to wander irregularly in winter. The more northerly breeders will drift southward from the open barrens of the Arctic to areas of better cover and food, some traveling long distances over water from the islands. Although they nest on the ground, they survive the winters because of their ability to feed in trees above snow cover.

They are chicken-like land birds with small heads and bills and long legs, for they walk and run much of the time. They are brown, with the exception of the Ptarmigans which turn white in winter. The females are almost identical, the males have a ruff, or display feathers of some kind, including fan-shaped tails. The Willow and Rock Ptarmigans breed in eastern Canada but are not seen south of James Bay and Labrador, except in Newfoundland where both breed.

SPRUCE GROUSE (also called Franklin's Grouse)
Canachites canadensis
LENGTH 13 INCHES

This handsome grouse is so ridiculously unafraid that it has not survived inhabited areas. For example, it occurred formerly in the forests of southern Ontario, but now occurs only north of Algonquin Park, and there only distant from settlement. I can recall seeing a family group in late summer near the Rouge River, some 200 miles north of Montreal, feeding in a thick stand of spruce, and so tame that they could not be induced to fly even when threatened with shouts and waving branches. Despite their poor flavor, they have been eliminated by thoughtless slaughter

64

Spruce Grouse

Ruffed Grouse

Bobwhite

Ring-necked Pheasant

The grouse and ptarmigan and pheasant families are chicken-like land birds with small heads and bills. They have long legs, for they run much of the time.

from areas where they provided a glimpse of wildlife to many who cannot travel to the wilderness. It would appear the colloquial name "fool hen" is well deserved.

Where it survives, the Spruce Grouse is quite common across Canada to the treeline (except in Prince Edward Island and Newfoundland), in the northwestern United States from Oregon to Wyoming and in New England. There it is permanently resident in coniferous forests, in muskegs and in open barren land, where it feeds on berries, buds and insects in summer, and on the needles and seeds of conifers in winter.

The male has a brown back, black throat, breast and belly, pale spotted flanks and a black tail with a suggestion of chestnut at the tip. At close range a bare red patch above the eye is quite apparent.

RUFFED GROUSE

Bonasa umbellus
LENGTH 14 INCHES

Many people refer incorrectly to this large chicken-like grouse as a "partridge". Our only partridge is the Gray Partridge which was imported many years ago from Europe and is now well established in several parts of North America. The Ruffed Grouse is a native bird of the open woodland and small wood-lot — able to survive severe weather and human encroachment.

The spring mating display of this grouse is a remarkable feature which is often not seen but frequently heard. The hollow sound of the drumming male is familiar in woodlands from coast to coast, from Alaska to the central States. The bird stands on a fallen log, thrusting the wings forward and upward, beating slowly at first, then gradually increasing the tempo to the speed and sound of a distant chain saw motor, and as suddenly dying away — all lasting for a few seconds. The dark ruff on the neck is extended and the tail held vertically in a fan — peacock fashion.

The Ruffed Grouse is remarkably hardy and survives because of its ability to feed in the trees above the snow cover. The partridge, on the other hand, has never adapted to feeding above ground level and consequently suffers much during heavy snows. From spring to late autumn, the Ruffed Grouse feeds in open places in woodlands and on the edge of meadows, bursting from under one's feet with a whirr of wings, usually flying only far enough to be out of sight. It will alight in the dense cover of cedar or spruce, or on the ground, after a gliding flight just when it appears that it must smash into the trees. When the hen is with chicks, it sends them to cover and then, to distract the intruder, will walk about, dragging its wings, flushing only when the young birds are safe. The best way to watch a family under these circumstances is to sit down and remain perfectly still. The hen will then collect the young and continue to feed.

Both birds are speckled brown, the tail of the male being barred chestnut black with a broad black band near the tip. The female's tail lacks the reddish color of the male and is smaller.

It nests in a hollow on the ground. In winter it moves to cover and feeds on cedar and spruce buds. During heavy snows it may dig in for protection and is sometimes trapped if ice forms above it.

SHARP-TAILED GROUSE
Pedioecetes phasianellus
LENGTH 15 INCHES

Although this brushland and prairie grouse is essentially a western bird, it is also quite common in Minnesota, Michigan, northern and western Ontario, as far east as Manitoulin Island. In the west it is commonly referred to as "prairie chicken" or just "chicken", but it is quite distinct from the Greater Prairie Chicken, which is in the same family and has almost disappeared from much of its former area. All of the chicken-like birds are confusing in the field, for they are usually seen only when they flush, and it is difficult to see them for long enough to distinguish their differing features. This one is of medium size and has a short pointed tail which is white with two longer brown feathers at the center — a good distinguishing mark as the bird flies away. Most grouse have barred breasts, but that of the Sharp-tail is covered with V-shaped spots. The legs are covered with white feathers to the knee. The Sharp-tail may be found in the same country as the Ruffed Grouse whose tail is wider and banded.

In spring, males congregate on their dancing grounds and as part of the mating ritual, stamp their feet with the head held low, feathers ruffled and their short tails erect. They nest on the ground and, in summer, feed heavily on insects, switching in autumn to waste grain and other seeds, berries and nuts. In winter they feed in the trees on twigs and buds of birch, willow and alder. Roosting at night is on the ground, often under the snow.

Sharp-tails are permanently resident in areas of hard winter, but the more northerly birds (they nest as far north as Alaska) migrate irregularly southward. The breeding range extends through the northwestern United States. In the past they have erupted as far east as southern Quebec, so it is not impossible that they may be seen again in more southerly areas.

Quails, Pheasants, and Partridge
Family Phasianidae

There are some 174 species in the Phasianidae family, ranging in size from tiny quail to the peacock. Most have short necks and short thick bills and all are remarkably beautiful birds.

Of the nine species represented in North America, the five in the west are probably the most exciting visually. Three, the California, Gambel's and the Mountain Quail, have long topknots and facial stripes. In the east only the Bobwhite is native to North America, and its range and numbers in the northeast are limited. Two species have been introduced from Europe, the Ring-necked Pheasant and the Gray Partridge, and are reasonably common in some areas.

All family Phasianidae are chicken-like birds which nest and take their food on the ground, suffering in winter because they have never adapted to feeding in trees above the snow cover.

GRAY PARTRIDGE (also called Hungarian Partridge)
Perdix perdix
LENGTH 10 INCHES

This little partridge, the only true partridge in North America, was introduced about 1900 from Europe where it is common south from the British Isles, southern Scandinavia and central Russia. It was brought here as a game bird and, despite serious odds, has thrived in New England and south of the Great Lakes, the central prairies, southern Ontario, Quebec, and the Maritime Provinces (except Newfoundland). In flight it can be recognized by its chestnut colored fan-like tail, barred dark, and brown in the centre. It is smaller than the Ruffed Grouse with which it is often confused and lacks the ruff. The face is brown, the crown dark, the flanks barred reddish and white, and there is a distinct chestnut patch on the belly. The breast and upper back are gray, the wings and back brown.

Like the pheasant, the partridge has not adapted to feeding in trees or bushes in winter and, as a consequence, the numbers decrease greatly in winters with heavy snow. They then frequent farm yards, seeking grain around the barns, many of the farmers leaving grain out for the birds in heavy weather. The high reproductive rate (they lay as many as twenty eggs) helps them to survive, but their choice of nesting sites does not, for the nests are often destroyed by plowing, early mowing of hay, the burning of stubble and predators, both domestic animals and foxes.

When they flush, these partridge take off in a flurry of wings with a rapid cackle, flying only a short distance, low to the ground, with alternate flapping and gliding. In summer and autumn they appear at the roadsides in the late afternoon to scratch for gravel, the grinding agent for the seeds they eat. In summer they rely heavily on insects. They spend the day in fields, usually grain fields, and are seldom found far from open land.

BOBWHITE
Colinus virginianus
LENGTH 8 INCHES

This little quail exists precariously near small woods in extreme southern Ontario along the shore of Lake Erie. Although it was once widespread, when the land was newly-cleared and plenty of brushy cover existed, only small numbers remain. Today it thrives in unforested land with plenty of briar tangles and a proximity to cultivated land, because it feeds on waste corn and other crops during the winter months. In summer it feeds almost entirely on harmful insects. Modern practices of clean farming (plowing fields to the edge and clearing the leafy thickets) have eliminated the Bobwhite from its earlier range. In the southern and central United States it is abundant in many areas and is valued as a game bird.

Pairs form in the spring and become territorial during the nesting season. During autumn and winter they form coveys of about thirty birds, often roosting shoulder to shoulder in order to keep warm. A few birds even perch atop their neighbors. If disturbed when so compactly grouped, they explode upward and outward like a small bomb. These coveys remain quite stable, however, even when shot at. They maintain their own identity by refusing to accept additional members. Attempts to introduce Bobwhites into new areas have not been successful, nor have attempts to bolster an existing stock with more southerly birds, for the progeny lack the strength of the hardier existing stock.

The Bobwhite is a ruddy brown, hump-backed little bird with a dark crown, conspicuous white face and throat which is divided by a broad dark line extending from behind the eye making a necklace of black, and fusing into brown on the upper breast. The flanks and belly are spotted brown on white. The female is paler and shows yellow on the face instead of white.

RING-NECKED PHEASANT
Phasianus colchicus
LENGTH 27 INCHES

The long-necked cock pheasant is the glamor bird of the game species, a beautiful blend of color. Its dark head of iridescent green, splashed brilliant red around the eye, is separated from the contrasting multicolored orange-brown-green body by a white neck ring. The long narrow barred tail is half the length of the bird. The modestly dressed female is spotted brown with a pale face patch, but is unmistakable with its long tail.

Ring-necks are native to central Asia, China and Japan, and were introduced into Europe and North America. Reasonably sized local populations exist in the east. In the west they are quite common on the prairies of the United States and Canada. They have been introduced into many urban areas, enhancing the surroundings as they feed and nest in gardens and semi-wild parks.

In the country pheasants feed in grain fields and meadows, but require fairly extensive shrubby cover for protection and nesting. In summer, insects form a large portion of the diet. They are easily taken by foxes, and their obvious color and the frequent *kok-cack* call makes them a prime target for hunters. Many birds are bred in captivity and released on game preserves for shooting. For most of these birds their first flight is their last.

70

Rails, Gallinules, and Coots
Family Rallidae

Rallidae are all marsh birds. The rails, although capable of swimming, seldom do so, while the gallinules and coots are in the water most of the time.

The rails are skulking birds, always hesitant to fly when disturbed, preferring to run through the marsh to hide. When they arrive at water too deep for wading, they climb about in the reeds with their long legs and large feet. Their bodies are remarkably narrow, making it easy for them to squeeze through a tight growth of reeds, and giving rise to the common expression "thin as a rail". When they do fly it is only for a short distance before they drop abruptly back into the reeds. Despite the apparent weakness of their flight, they migrate long distances, some to South America, always at night. All have short tails, long legs and large feet.

The gallinule and coot are more aquatic and therefore more visible, indeed both are quite common in marshes within their range. They take much of their food while swimming and diving, but also feed on land.

KING RAIL
Rallus elegans
LENGTH 14 INCHES, WINGSPAN 24 INCHES

This rail breeds almost exclusively in fresh water marshes from Massachusetts southward throughout the eastern half of the United States, and in Canada only along the shores of Lake Erie and Lake Ontario, although there is the possibility of encountering non-breeding birds in marshes somewhat further north.

It is the largest of the rails with broad rusty colored wings and back and somewhat darker flight feathers. The bill is long, the throat white, the face and breast plain reddish brown, the flanks and abdomen show vertical zebra stripes ending with a stubby white-bottomed tail. When it flies, the long legs and large unwebbed feet dangle behind. The Clapper Rail, similar in size and design, but grayer, is a rare visitor to the coastal marshes of New England. The Virginia Rail, which is quite common in the northeastern United States and Canada, is almost identical in marking and color to the King Rail, but half the size.

Nesting is in, or close to, a fairly extensive marsh, often adjacent to grain or hay fields. When the bird roams from the marsh to feed on seeds and grasshoppers it is sometimes possible to have a reasonable view for more than a few seconds. In the marsh a sighting is a matter of considerable luck, for it prefers to hide. The voice, the best method of identification, is a series of deep *ump-ump, ump-ump, ump* sounds, all in the same pitch, usually slowly and deliberately uttered, but sometimes run together.

Coots in flight

American Coot

Common Gallinule

Virginia Rail

Sora

Rails, gallinules, and coots are all marsh birds. Top: American Coots in flight. Above: Typical habitat of the Sora and Virginia Rail.

72

VIRGINIA RAIL
Rallus limicola
LENGTH 8 INCHES

This little rail is an almost exact replica of the King Rail, and is the only small one with a long slim, slightly decurved bill. It nests in fresh water and slightly brackish marshes of cattails, bulrushes or sedges. The woven nest is fastened to reed stalks up to a foot above the water or mud. Most of its summer feeding is on aquatic insects and small fish, but in the autumn it visits harvested fields for seeds and berries. All rails are hard to find, and this one runs quickly through the heavy vegetation at the first sign of intrusion, only rarely fluttering a few yards before dropping back into the marsh. It is hard to believe that the night migration flights of these flutterers may take them hundreds of miles.

The voice is an elaborate mixture of grunts, *wak, waks* and *kiddick, kiddicks*, all descending in tone and volume.

The breeding range extends across the northern two-thirds of the United States and southern Canada, north in the west to northern Alberta. North American birds winter from the southern United States into South America, south to the tip of the continent.

SORA
Porzana carolina
LENGTH 7 INCHES

The Sora is the most common of the rails and also has the broadest breeding range: most of British Columbia to the Maritimes, south to the central United States. It does not require the extensive marshes of other rails, accepting small reed patches, fresh water marshes and bogs even in, or close to, cities. Again it is seldom seen unless one is patient. Upon establishing its presence by its call, a watcher is best to sit quietly at dusk when this rail will come to the edge, or even leave its marsh to feed. If you suspect the Sora is present, a hand clap or stick thrown in the water will often start it calling, *keek, keek*. The spring courtship call is a whistled *ker-wee*, rising at the end and often repeated. The usual summer call is a rapidly descending whinny which can be heard for a considerable distance.

The Sora is easy to identify for it has a yellow chicken-like bill, black face at the front and black throat. The sides of the head, breast and front flanks are gray, the abdomen barred black and white, the back and wings olive brown with fine black and white stripes. The tiny stubby tail is black on top and white below. The longish legs are yellow.

On migration Soras gather in suitable marshes in large numbers, particularly wild rice marshes, for in autumn they change from an animal to vegetable diet, including waste grain. Migration is at night and so close to the ground that many birds perish against buildings. Migration is usually simultaneous, for every Sora will desert a marsh the night of the first frost. The winter is spent from the extreme southern United States to Columbia and Peru, a distance for some of three thousand miles.

YELLOW RAIL
Coturnicops noveboracensis
LENGTH 5 INCHES

This tiny rail is rare everywhere, but is known to breed locally from Alberta to New Brunswick, north to Hudson Bay and central Quebec and south to North Dakota, Michigan and Massachusetts.

Unlike the other rails which nest in dense cattails and bulrushes, this one prefers wet meadows and shallow marshes where the vegetation is no higher than a foot. The nest may be a few inches over the water or on a mat of dead grass in the mud. Of all the rails, this is probably the hardest to flush, for it seldom takes to the air. Ornithologists seeking specimens have used trained dogs which capture the birds on the ground. Yellow Rails are best located by their call which is a long series of *ticks*, rather like the sound of tapping two small stones together.

This bird rather resembles a very young chicken, yellowish beige about the head and breast, white on the throat, with a brown and dark barred back with white feather edges. The belly, as with other rails, is barred dark brown and white.

The Yellow Rail feeds only on small snails, and remains in northern marshes later than most of its family, retiring in winter to the Gulf States, and in the west to California.

COMMON GALLINULE (also called Florida Gallinule)
Gallinula chloropus
LENGTH 11 INCHES, WINGSPAN 21 INCHES

This duck-like bird with spidery feet has a world-wide distribution with the exception of Australia. Its North American range extends from extreme southern Ontario to Ottawa and Lac St. Pierre in Quebec, south to Florida and west to Nebraska and Arizona. It is quite common in fresh water marshes having a mixture of heavy cattails and similar cover and some open water, for the Gallinule spends much of its time feeding along the edge of the reeds, up-ending and diving like a duck, but also walking about on the lily pads and in the marsh. It feeds largely on plant life, but also on insects and snails.

The adults, when seen clearly, cannot be mistaken for any other bird. They are small-headed blackish birds, with short, bright red bills and frontal shield. There is a brown hint at the back, a horizontal white line on the flank and white underside to the short tail. The Purple Gallinule, which occurs along the Gulf Coast and in eastern Florida, is similar, but its brilliant purple coloring and white forehead patch differentiate it. The Common Gallinule has yellow legs and large, thin, unwebbed feet. When swimming the head moves back and forth with each paddle of its feet.

Nesting is in loose colonies, the nest usually being built over the water near the edge of a reed bed, attached to growing vegetation. It consists of a platform of dead reeds, with a sloping walk to the water. A number of platforms are usually built nearby, presumably for caring for the young. The sound of gallinules in the marsh is always entertaining for they seem to chatter to one another with loud and eerie *kik, kik, kik* noises, sometimes complaining, and always rather harsh.

AMERICAN COOT
Fulica americana
LENGTH 12 INCHES, WINGSPAN 25 INCHES

The American Coot is remarkably noisy and is constantly uttering a bewildering series of grunts, cackles, groans and croaks. All of these sounds are grating and harsh and have probably given rise to the expression "as crazy as a coot".

The bird itself is slate gray, but slightly darker on the head. From a distance it resembles the Common Gallinule because both are blackish, duck-like birds with small heads, but the coot lacks the white line along the upper flank of the gallinule. At close range, however, immatures are especially confusing.

The coot's chicken-like bill, which extends high on the forehead and over the eye, is white with a thin chestnut colored band near the tip. Its long toes have large pads which are an aid in swimming, and are quite unlike the spidery ones of the gallinule.

Even in the breeding season coots associate in groups, and nest in loose colonies. The nest is usually built on a floating mass of decaying vegetation, but sometimes is fastened to growing reeds. Acceptable habitat varies widely, from enclosed marshes with open water to ponds and rivers. Most feeding and resting is quite close to the edge of the reeds, the principal food being aquatic plants and some insects. On land it takes grass, sprouting grain and in the autumn is often found in grain fields after harvesting. The coot flies fast and close to the water, but to take off, must flap and run along the surface for some distance.

The breeding range in North America is extensive, in the west throughout the United States and north to Lake Athabaska, and in the east around the Great Lakes, southern Quebec, New Brunswick and New England. It also breeds in northern South America, Mexico and the West Indies.

Plovers and Turnstones
Family Charadriidae

The wading shorebirds fall generally into two families, the Plovers and Turnstones, or CHARADRIIDAE, which are relatively easy to remember and to identify, and the SCOLOPACIDAE which include the woodcock, snipe and sandpipers, a larger and more difficult group to learn well. Both families are seen principally as transients in the northeast, for most breed in the Arctic and sub-Arctic, and winter south of the frost line — many in South America.

Plovers are squat, plump, brownish birds with short heavy bills and short necks accordioned into their bodies. Their stance, on spindly legs, is almost horizontal with the short tail sticking out straight and behind. They run like a miniature corps-de-ballet stopping, poised, and then changing direction. The flight is fast and direct on longish, pointed wings which, with the exception of the Golden Plover, show a white line from the tip to the base. With the exception of the Killdeer, they migrate in flocks, feeding on sandy and muddy shores beside bodies of fresh and salt water and in grasslands, where they take insects and tiny marine animals. On an open shore you can approach within fifty yards without disturbing them, and in Florida, in the winter, they run all around your feet.

Plovers nest on the ground, scratching a shallow depression in sand or gravel and lining the nest with bits of shell and sea weed. The nest is usually close to water, sometimes on beaches and dunes and sometimes on gravel ridges. They lay three or four eggs. When the young are only two or three weeks old the adults start their southward migrations, turning up on east coast and inland beaches by late July. The young follow about a month later.

Piping Plover

Semipalmated Plover

Killdeer

American
Golden Plover

Black-bellied Plover

Ruddy Turnstone

*Most plovers and turnstones are transients in the northeast, for they
breed in the Arctic, and winter south of the frost line.*

77

SEMIPALMATED PLOVER
Charadrius semipalmatus
LENGTH 6 INCHES

This common plover breeds across northern North America in Alaska, the Yukon, the Northwest Territories, the southern Arctic Islands, Labrador and Newfoundland, and migrates through eastern Canada and the United States. It winters from South Carolina south to Argentina. The similar Ringed Plover (*Charadrius hiaticula*) which breeds in the Canadian Arctic archipelago and Greenland, migrates to Africa and India, and is not seen in the northeast.

During its migration, the Semipalmated Plover can be found in flocks on mudflats, in wet fields, on riverbanks and in ponds and lakes. It is seldom seen in gravel pit ponds where there are no mud flats. It is a very active bird, running about in search of food, picking at tiny snails and stopping frequently as if to listen. It is distinctly marked like a miniature Killdeer, but with only one broad black line around the neck, curling upward to the nape. The crown and head are brown with a white patch across the forehead which continues as a fleck behind the eye. The breast and belly are white, the back brown and the short tail dark and edged with white. The yellowish bill is short and stubby, turning slightly downward at the end. The spindly legs are orange.

PIPING PLOVER
Charadrius melodus
LENGTH 5½ INCHES

This uncommon little plover is somewhat like the Semipalmated, but paler on the back and head. The neck ring is narrow but bulges at the side of the breast and a dark streak runs over the forehead between the eyes. The side of the face is almost unmarked. Immature and winter birds are very pale and lack the mark across the forehead. The Snowy Plover (*Charadrius alexandrinus*) which is the same size and also pale but with an incomplete neck ring, is seldom seen in the northeast. It is a western bird and winters on the Gulf.

The Piping Plover, although uncommon, may be seen in summer, for it breeds across the southern prairies and north central States, in southern Ontario south from the Bruce Penninsula to eastern Lake Ontario and on the south shores of Lake Michigan and Lake Ontario. In the Maritimes it is a summer resident in the southern Gaspé, the north shore of the St. Lawrence near the mouth, southern Newfoundland, Prince Edward Island and Nova Scotia, and south along the coast to Virginia.

Small flocks form in the autumn as it moves south to the Atlantic coast from South Carolina to around Florida and the shores of the Gulf of Mexico, where it feeds and rests on sandy beaches, often high above the tide line in the dunes.

The call is a melodious *pee - loo,* the second note higher. It also uses a series of a dozen or so whistles, descending in scale.

KILLDEER
Charadrius vociferus
LENGTH 8 INCHES

Vociferus, the scientific name of the Killdeer, is entirely apt for this handsome plover which is always very noisy. When disturbed, or when flying, it constantly screeches its name *Kill - dee.*

The Killdeer is present in the northeast from early spring until autumn, but unlike most plovers it breeds away from water, in pastures, golf courses and even in hedges around suburban lawns where it lays blotched or camouflaged eggs in a shallow scrape. It feeds on insects in short grass and plowed fields during the breeding season, but when the young are grown it chooses stream and lake edges for tiny marine animals. Other plovers tend to form flocks but, although a number of Killdeer may fly together, they tend to be more solitary. In wintering areas, from Long Island southward, large numbers will feed in suitable areas. I recall once seeing thousands feeding in the carefully manicured Civil War battlefields of Virginia.

The Killdeer is the outstanding performer of the "broken-wing act" when a predator (man or animal or another bird) is close to the nest or young. When so threatened, it will flutter about, dragging one wing to distract the intruder. I once saw a mother Killdeer which had nested at the edge of a busy walk leading from a hangar on an airfield in constant distraction because of the traffic.

This large plover can be identified from a considerable distance by two prominent black rings which look as if they had been painted on its white throat and lower neck. The head is as precisely painted and the effect is of zebra stripes, for there are really four dark areas separated by white: dark crown, white forehead stripe extending to the back of the head, a dark line near the bill, white throat and two black rings on the upper breast. The back is brown, and in flight the white on the wings is flashing. The rump is chestnut colored, the tail dark and tipped with white.

RUDDY TURNSTONE
Arenaria interpres
LENGTH 7 INCHES

This dashing little plover is a spring and autumn migrant through much of the eastern part of North America, and the west coast. It breeds from Greenland, eastward on the northern coasts of Europe and North America and in the Arctic Islands, wintering widely from southern Europe, Africa, Asia, Australia, New Zealand to North and South America. It is common on the shores of the Great Lakes and on salt water beaches, although it may turn up on ponds and river banks anywhere for a short stay. It arrives early in August and can be seen until September or October, but is less common in the spring. It prefers pebbled tidal beaches with plenty of seaweed, and runs about turning over stones, appropriately, with its slightly upturned pointed bill, in its search for insects and minute animal life. It is easy to watch and to photograph, for it allows the observer to come quite close, as do many of the sandpipers.

The nuptial plumage which remains, although somewhat frayed, until late summer in adults, is elaborate and handsome — a splendid mixture of black and white below, and chestnut on the back and wings. The chestnut on the back is marked with a diagonal black cross, the wings are a startling pattern of all three colors in lengthwise streaks. The rump has a large white diamond patch, the tail is white with a broad black band near the tip. The face and underparts are white, the breast and upper flanks black with black lines extending upward to the face, making a pattern of white spots. The short legs are bright orange and the bill, unlike the other plovers, is sharp and upturned. The winter and immature design is similar, but the face and back are all brownish olive.

AMERICAN GOLDEN PLOVER
Pluvialis dominica
LENGTH 9 INCHES

The story of the Golden Plover has two parallels with that of the Eskimo Curlew which is now almost extinct. Individuals of both species migrate some 9,000 miles, with a non-stop flight of about 2,400 miles over open ocean, and both were nearly wiped out in the latter part of the 19th century by heavy slaughter. The Golden Plover breeds in the Arctic from Siberia to Baffin Island, and is seen in the east only on migration. It has three principal southbound migration routes, the first over the Pacific as far as New Zealand, the second through the prairies west of Hudson Bay and the Mississippi Valley to central and southern South America, and the third eastward via Labrador and Nova Scotia, south via the Atlantic to northern South America where it rests before continuing to Argentina. Many birds perish on the long two-day flight across the open ocean. The flight northward, is a single route across the Gulf of Mexico, up the Mississippi Valley, through the prairies, to the Arctic in huge vulnerable flocks. Market gunners took a heavy toll of the spring flight eighty or ninety years ago, shipping carloads to market each year. The pressure on the Eskimo Curlew was too great and, although it is still seen periodically, it is doubtful that it will re-establish. The Golden Plover, however, is again a common nester on the tundra. The story of the Eskimo Curlew is beautifully told in Fred Bodsworth's book "The Last of the Curlews".

The spring plumage of the Golden Plover is striking. The dark upper parts are speckled yellowish gold and white, the undersides are black from the eye to the tail, a Z-shaped white band runs from the forehead over the eye and down the face, to the side of the neck and turns back at the side of the breast. After nesting it loses the black and white markings and becomes brownish and mottled.

In the autumn the Golden is seen principally in plowed fields and short grass, but sometimes on beaches in the east. The main flight through eastern Canada stops for a time to fatten for the ocean leg, mainly in Labrador and occasionally in Nova Scotia. In autumn dress it is difficult to distinguish from the Black-bellied Plover which is somewhat paler, however it habitually holds its wings high for a moment after landing and does much head bobbing.

BLACK-BELLIED PLOVER

Squatarola squatarola
LENGTH 10 INCHES

The appearance of the Black-bellied Plover at all seasons is similar to the Golden Plover, but two distinctions mark it — the white rump (the Golden's rump and tail are the same color as the back) and the black patches under the base of the wings. It is lighter on the head and back than the Golden, and in spring plumage the black on the belly ends at the leg, there becoming white. The bill is somewhat longer, but this is not apparent unless one sees the two species together. The Black-bellied is the one more likely to be seen through most of the east on migration, more so in the fall than in the spring when many birds fly non-stop from the east coast of the United States to James Bay and Hudson Bay. In the autumn, small flocks stop inland to feed in short-grass meadows, wet plowed fields, and mud flats on lakes, ponds and rivers. On the coast where it is more common it frequents sand bars and mud flats as well as meadows.

Black-bellied Plovers are easy to attract by imitating the whistling call which is a plaintive *pee - ah - wee* (high, lower, high, slurring from one note to another). Once, when shooting on the St. Lawrence River, I called a single bird, which was obviously looking for friends. It flew around the blind for some time, finally settling on the head of a decoy, for we were some distance from shore. Frustrated, it then flew off.

It nests along the north coast of Russia, Siberia and North America, high into the islands, and winters on the coasts of the United States south to Brazil and in Australia, Asia, Africa, the Mediterranean and British Isles.

Woodcocks, Snipes, Sandpipers, and Curlews
Family Scolopacidae

The seventy-five species of this family are represented in every area on the globe where beaches and marshy areas exist that are suitable for feeding. Of the forty five species present during some season of the year in North America, several are common to both eastern and western hemispheres. Most of those in the western hemisphere breed in the high Arctic and winter in the southern United States or in South America.

All are wading, or shore birds, with the exception of the Woodcock, but even it requires soft, marshy soil when feeding. As a family they have long thin bills, which are often curved, and they vary considerably in size: from the Least Sandpiper which is under five inches long to the Long-billed Curlew of the west which is nineteen inches long. Slimmer than the plovers, and with longer necks, their feathers have pale edges which pattern a spotty design on the upper parts. All have pointed wings except the Woodcock.

In eastern North America there are fifteen species of small and medium sized sandpipers, or "peeps", all of whom are frustratingly similar in their autumn and winter dress. A suitable mud flat or beach is likely to have several species feeding together and the observer must watch for subtle differences, such as length and shape of the bill, general coloration including that of the legs, relative size and behavior.

All sandpipers feed exclusively on animals of varying forms such as insects, both aquatic and terrestial, crustacea, small fish, worms and

Northern Phalarope

Spotted Sandpiper

Least Sandpiper

American Woodcock

Greater Yellowlegs

The Family Scolopacidae have long, thin bills; all are wading or shore birds, but they vary in length from five to nineteen inches. The phalaropes are small and sandpiper-like.

83

larvae, which they take in mud or sand at the edge of salt and fresh water and, with some species, in grasslands. They move south of areas of heavy frost in winter.

AMERICAN WOODCOCK
Philohela minor
LENGTH 9 INCHES

The remarkable mating display of the male American Woodcock takes place almost entirely in the air. In early spring, while patches of snow remain in the woods, this unusual sandpiper arrives in the northeast after having flown singly from the south. It flies at night, quite close to the ground, and many perish by hitting buildings and other obstructions. Brightly lighted tall buildings have a fatal attraction for many puzzled birds.

For nesting and feeding, they choose an area of second growth near marshy ground fed by a stream or spring, and with sufficient clearing for the male's aerial display. Male and female establish separate territories, and the male may mate with one or several females. They nest on the ground and the young are fully grown about a month after hatching.

The male's mating display takes place about thirty minutes after sunset and begins with a long series of calls similar to the *peent* of the Nighthawk. During this initial stage the male is almost oblivious to intrusion, and one can move quietly to within a few feet of the sitting bird. It will then suddenly take off, spiraling upward with its wings whistling, until it is almost out of sight. After a few circles it plunges back to earth in a series of side-slips, uttering a lovely chittering call. If it is undisturbed one can watch it return to its calling spot and begin the process again, *peenting* harshly for two or three minutes before taking off.

The woodcock is a chunky bird with a large head, not unlike that of the Australian Kiwi. It has a short neck and tail and rounded wings. The face and underparts are cinnamon colored and there are three black bars on the top of the head. The back is darker and heavily speckled. Its great round eyes are set forward and high above the ear. The bill is long and straight, the upper mandible flexible at the tip, enabling it to grasp earthworms some three inches below the surface while keeping its bill closed. Worms are the principal diet and, although it will take insects and some grass and berries, will not settle in an area without plenty of worms.

Woodcock sleep during the day and feed at night, bursting into flight only when disturbed. In the autumn they remain until the ground freezes and are often sought as a game bird.

The breeding range extends throughout the eastern United States and north into Canada in southeastern Manitoba, across the Great Lakes, southern Ontario and Quebec and in the Maritime Provinces. It winters in the southern States south of the frost line.

COMMON SNIPE (formerly called Wilson's Snipe)
Capella gallinago
LENGTH 9 INCHES

The snipe may be easily confused with the woodcock and the dowitcher, all of which have long straight bills and are about the same size. The woodcock, however, can be immediately identified by its woodland habitat, and when flushed, by its rounded wings. Both the snipe and the dowitcher have pointed wings, and in the spring there can be no mistaking the rusty colored dowitcher from the heavily striped snipe with its pale undersides. In any plumage the grayish, finely barred tail and white rump of the dowitcher are easy to distinguish from the reddish one of the snipe. My serious interest in birds started from this difference. When snipe shooting one day I nearly fired on a dowitcher, to be stopped abruptly by my companion who pointed out the difference.

The snipe is heavily striped, dark and beige, on the head and back. The breast is pale brown, lightly striped with dark, the belly white and the tail, as noted above, is reddish with a black terminal band.

The snipe breeds from Alaska to Newfoundland, except in the eastern Arctic, and south to the northern United States. It winters from British Columbia south to Brazil. It chooses wet meadows, marshes, streams and lakesides for nesting and feeding. The nest is placed on the ground, usually in a clump of grass or ferns. It relies mostly on insects and larvae, prodding for them in the wet ground with its long thin bill. On take-off, and when flying, the snipe has a distinctive flat *skawp* call, rather like pulling a rubber boot out of thick mud. Its spring display flight consists of a series of dives and climbs while making a *winnowing* sound with the feathers of its tail and wings, like the tremulous whistling of a duck's wings.

In the autumn snipe concentrate to some extent in marshes, feeding close to grassy cover, unlike other shorebirds.

WHIMBREL (formerly called Hudsonian Curlew)
Numenius phaeopus
LENGTH 14 INCHES

The Whimbrel is a large sandpiper or curlew which nests in both eastern and western hemispheres. It has a long downcurved bill, black and white striped head, a long neck, and finely streaked brown breast, back, wings and tail. The underparts are pale, and the long legs trail behind when it flies.

There are two distinct North American populations, one in the western Arctic which migrates up the west coast. The other, which nests along the west shore of Hudson Bay, appears to migrate largely in a circular pattern, coming north in the spring over the Great Lakes, and going south in the autumn through the Maritimes, on its way to the southern United States and Brazil where it winters. This suggests that after nesting most birds move east, skirt northern Quebec and Labrador, and migrate southward by way of the Maritimes.

On migration Whimbrel may be seen feeding with other shore birds in marshes without too much cover, on mud flats and in pastures and meadows. Migration is in flocks. They fly in V-formation and lines, frequently setting their wings and sailing for a few moments. A migrating flock may first appear to be duck, but the slower wing-beat and frequent gliding of the Whimbrel soon differentiate them.

UPLAND SANDPIPER (formerly called Upland Plover)
Bartramia longicauda
LENGTH 10 INCHES

This grassland sandpiper is not common anywhere. It is a small-headed, long slim bird with a short straight bill. The neck and tail are long, and it is spotted medium brown on the upper parts, neck and breast. The outer wings are much darker. It flies about its nesting territory with stiff downcurving wings after the fashion of the Spotted Sandpiper, but on alighting holds its wings vertically, momentarily revealing its pale spotted underwings.

This sandpiper is found in pastures and hay fields where it feeds on insects such as grasshoppers and crickets, and is sometimes seen in the grass at airports. The call is rich, liquid and mournful, often a rolling trill, which it gives while flying near the nest.

It breeds north to Alaska, in the prairies, in the northeastern United States and in southern Ontario and extreme southern Quebec. It has a long migration to southern South America. The Upland Sandpiper was much more common one hundred years ago, but was heavily shot for food before being brought under protection.

SPOTTED SANDPIPER
Actitis macularia
LENGTH 7 INCHES

There is hardly a lake, river, stream or pond in North America, outside of the eastern Arctic and the deep south, that does not have this plain gray-brown bird with the spotted undersides feeding at its edge. In winter it loses its spots and is then white below with a tawny area at the side of the breast. The flight of the Spotted is distinctive. It flutters, or vibrates, with down-curved wings held stiff, revealing white bars on the top of the wings and the dark tail. On land it characteristically stands with the head lower than the tail. It constantly teeters, bobbing its tail up and down. The call is a repeated *peet, weet* or a series of *weets* and sometimes a loud whistle.

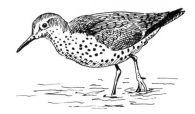

It does much of its feeding at the edge of the water taking tiny fish, insects and larvae and can often be seen working over fallen or floating trees. The nest is usually placed some distance from water, sometimes in the open but more often hidden in the grass or under a log.

SOLITARY SANDPIPER

Tringa solitaria
LENGTH 7 INCHES

This bird is similar in looks, habits and habitat to the much more common Spotted Sandpiper and, as a consequence, is often overlooked. It is much the darker of the two and lacks the white wing and eye stripe of the Spotted. It is also a bobber, but the Solitary bobs its head rather than its tail, and in flight it uses full wing beats instead of a flutter. The longish neck is pale and marked with buffy lines, the tail white with black bars and two dark central feathers. The conformation is similar to both the Greater and Lesser Yellowlegs, but the Solitary has dark green legs.

Unlike most sandpipers, it nests in trees, using abandoned nests of other birds such as Robins, usually close to woodland streams, ponds and lakes. It breeds in the Arctic from Alaska and the Mackenzie River, across the northern prairies, northern Ontario and Quebec, and winters from the southern United States to Argentina.

WILLET

Catoptrophorus semipalmatus
LENGTH 14 INCHES, WINGSPAN 27 INCHES

The Willet is among those species of large shorebirds brought to the brink of extinction early in the century by heavy shooting, and it is still seen only rarely in the northeast. It is a southerly nester breeding in the west, north only to the southern prairies of Canada and the northern United States, and in the east along the seaboard south from Nova Scotia. It was thus under more pressure in settled areas than those species of shorebirds which nest in the Arctic, and by 1915 was thought to be extinct in the east, north of Virginia. With protection, it has re-established and is fairly common once again in most of its former territory. It is seen only on rare occasions in Ontario and Quebec, for the Nova Scotia population appears to migrate to the West Indies and South America over the ocean.

Willets move about in small numbers and call loudly on the ground, *pill-will-willet*. They have a habit of raising the wings high while standing, a useful point of identification, especially on the coastal marshes in summer where they are an unspectacular gray, speckled above and below and with a long straight thickish bill and gray legs. In winter they are white below and uniformly gray-brown above. In flight the wings are strikingly marked with black and white, the trailing edge black with a wide band of white in front and a black patch at the wrist. The short tail is white with a gray tip. On the ground it can easily be confused with the Greater Yellowlegs, but the leg color and the heavier bill are quite different. In the air the difference is apparent, for the Yellowlegs have plain dark wings.

The western population breeds inland in the wet meadows at the edge of sloughs and lakes and migrates both southward and west to the coast.

GREATER YELLOWLEGS
Totanus melanoleucus
LENGTH 11 INCHES, WINGSPAN 25 INCHES

The habits and appearance of the Greater and Lesser Yellowlegs are almost identical. Both are slim grayish-brown shorebirds with long thin bills, small heads, whitish tails, dark unstreaked wings and long, thin, bright yellow legs. They feed for the most part in the shallow water at the edge of ponds, lakes, rivers and marshes, chasing about after small fish, crustacea and aquatic insects, but seldom probing in the mud. The bill and even the entire head are submerged while feeding, and sometimes they swim after their prey. The Greater is some two inches longer than the Lesser, and its bill is longer and slightly upturned.

The cry is a sharp whistle, down slurring and repeated three to five times. It is easily imitated and single birds, and even small flocks, can be decoyed.

The Greater Yellowlegs is an early spring migrant in the northeast from its wintering area, which extends from the southern United States to Argentina and Chile, arriving earlier and leaving later than the Lesser. It is then quite common in suitable habitat, feeding with the Lesser and other shorebirds. Wary and elusive, it is the first to give alarm, and flies off crying, and taking other species along, frustrating the observer.

It breeds in sparse woodland, usually close to bays or ponds from southern Alaska, south on the coast to central British Columbia and eastward across the northern prairies, northern Ontario, central Quebec, Labrador, Newfoundland and on Cape Breton Island in Nova Scotia.

LESSER YELLOWLEGS
Totanus flavipes
LENGTH 9 INCHES, WINGSPAN 20 INCHES

The Lesser Yellowlegs is similar in appearance to the Greater Yellowlegs, and has a markedly shorter bill; if the two species are seen together the Lesser is somewhat smaller, but unless other known shorebirds of similar size are available for comparison, size is not a reliable point of identification. The call of the Lesser is a less strident, more nasal, down-slurring *whew*, seldom repeated more than three times.

The winter range is similar to the Greater Yellowlegs, but the arrival in the northeast in spring is a little later, and the autumn migration starts and ends earlier. The breeding range is more northerly and further west, from Alaska, the Yukon and western Northwest Territories, northern prairies and Ontario around James Bay.

RED KNOT (name changed from Knot in 1973)
Calidris canutus
LENGTH 9 INCHES

This sandpiper, which breeds in the North American and Eurasian Arctic, has a migration route of some 9,000 miles each way for some individuals. The North American breeding range extends from Alaska and the northernmost Arctic Islands south to Victoria and Southampton Islands. Most birds winter in South America, south to Tierra del Fuego. Birds breeding in Alaska migrate along the west coast, most eastern birds by way of Hudson Bay and the Great Lakes to the Atlantic coast. Migration takes place in dense flocks which, in spring, are a remarkable sight, for the Knot is then robin-red below and gray above. As the flock wheels in unison, there is an abrupt color change. The spring colors are Dowitcher-like, and the two species can be confused. The notable difference is in the bill: the Dowitcher's is long, while that of the Knot is straight and short. In flight the wings of the Red Knot show narrow white and black bands on the inner parts, plain dark on the outer parts. The legs are short. In autumn the red is replaced with white and the back is paler. The rump is whitish, the tail pale gray.

The Knot is named for its call which is a hoarse, grunt-like *knut*. It also uses a double-noted call.

PURPLE SANDPIPER
Erolia maritima
LENGTH 8 INCHES

This is the darkest and also the most northerly wintering of the eastern sandpipers. It breeds across northern Europe and Asia, Greenland, Iceland, and the islands of the Canadian eastern Arctic, and winters on the coast from Greenland south to South Carolina. In this winter range it is almost invariably associated with rocky shores, jetties and breakwaters where it feeds in small flocks in the seaweed and windblown tide-wrack along the edge of the shore. At low tide it moves to the edge of the water, constantly fluttering about to avoid incoming waves. It is seen occasionally inland.

The Purple Sandpiper is a chunky, short-necked bird with a fairly long, slightly down curving bill which is yellow at the base. In winter the head and breast are dark gray, the back purplish black, the tail dark, the wings dark with a white band near the trailing edge. The throat and belly are white and the short legs dark yellow. In summer it is more mottled and paler.

PECTORAL SANDPIPER
Erolia melanotos
LENGTH 8 INCHES

This sandpiper is seen rarely in spring and fairly commonly in the autumn in the eastern United States and Canada, its main spring migration being to the west of Hudson Bay. The North American breeding grounds are in Alaska, through northern Canada close to the Arctic Ocean, in the Arctic Islands and on the west side of Hudson and James Bays.

This is a bird of the grassy marshes, pond edges and mown hay fields near water, although it is seen occasionally on mud flats feeding with other sandpipers. When approached it crouches, or "freezes", then at the last moment it moves off in fast zig-zag flight like a snipe. Although the Pectoral is an uncommon bird, it seems to favor specific areas on migration, returning habitually to the same patches each year in flocks of up to thirty birds. The voice is not unlike a snipe and when flushed it flies off with a *crrrick*-like sound.

The main distinguishing feature is the dark mottled breast which ends in an abrupt line at the white underparts, far less suffused than most of the other small sandpipers. Baird's Sandpipers' breast markings also end in an abrupt line, but are more ochre colored. The Pectoral's bill is as long as its head, straight and slim, the crown is dark, the back quite dark with a reddish tinge. The wings are dark and lack the white stripe of other peeps, the tail shows a black central line with surrounding white at the rump and dark at the tip.

LEAST SANDPIPER
Erolia minutilla
LENGTH 4¾ INCHES

This common sandpiper is the smallest of its family, but the observer cannot confidently rely on size for identification. It is better to remember that this is the only small peep with yellow legs, the others are all much darker. The breast is buffy and streaked, the back and wings uniformly dark with only a suggestion of wing streaks. The crown is dark, the bill thin and straight.

On migration, both spring and fall, the Least is seen in fresh and salt marshes from coast to coast, mostly in muddy areas, but also on sandy beaches, both probing and feeding from the surface. The breeding area is sub-Arctic, from Alaska and the Yukon, across the central Northwest Territories, around southern Hudson Bay to Labrador and Newfoundland. Wintering is from the southern United States to Brazil. Breeding begins late in May, but as early as July we begin to see small flocks of adults moving south through northeastern marshes.

Least Sandpipers are easy to watch, for they are quite tame and allow close approach. When they fly they zig-zag off like a snipe, usually settling again close by.

WHITE-RUMPED SANDPIPER
Erolia fuscicollis
LENGTH 6 INCHES

Of the small, short-legged sandpipers, this is the only one with an all white rump. The uncommon Stilt Sandpiper is similarly marked, but its legs are very long and greenish, trailing behind as the bird flies and it lacks white wing streaks which the White-rumped has. Otherwise it is similar to the other small peeps; slim bill, breast speckled brown, back medium dark brown and mottled, but turning plain grayish in winter.

Many shorebirds have a clockwise migration route, flying north in the spring in the west and returning south in autumn by way of the Atlantic coast. The White-rumped is one of these, for its spring passage is between Hudson Bay and the Rockies to extreme northern mainland Canada and the islands, its autumn passage, farther east where it is uncommon but is seen feeding with others peeps on most beaches and mud flats. There are exceptions to this pattern, and the bird can be a rare spring migrant in the east and a rare autumn migrant in the west. It winters from Paraguay south to the tip of South America.

BAIRD'S SANDPIPER
Erolia bairdii
LENGTH 6 INCHES

This little peep is a rare to uncommon migrant in the east for its main migration route takes it north and south to the west of Hudson Bay through the central plains of the United States and Canada. It should be seen, however, with some regularity in southern Ontario and the east-central States in the autumn, less so on the coast. It appears only very occasionally in spring in the east. When feeding it tends to keep apart from other sandpipers, seeking rather drier ground, above the line of wet mud which the others prefer, often in short grass and even dry fields. It does not probe for its food, but runs about picking up tiny animal forms on the surface.

It is buff colored, almost ochre, across the breast and on the scaly back and crown and has short dark legs. The Least, which it closely resembles, has yellowish legs. The length of the wings is extraordinary, for it has a sixteen inch span, and when the bird is standing, they extend noticeably beyond the end of the tail. In flight the wings are buff to the primaries, which are dark, and the wing stripe is obscure. The tail has the black central stripe of most of the peeps.

Baird's breeds from Siberia, east across Arctic Canada to Greenland and winters in southern Chile and Argentina. In winter it often occurs at considerable elevations, having been recorded in Chile at 13,000 feet.

DUNLIN (Red-backed Sandpiper)
Erolia alpina
LENGTH 7 INCHES

There can be no mistaking the handsome spring Dunlin with its distinctive black stomach patch, reddish mottled back, dark crown and finely streaked white breast and flanks. The bill is quite long and hooks downward near the tip. It is a chunky bird with a short neck and short black legs. Winter dress is almost all gray, unspeckled slate gray above, with suffused gray on the breast and flanks, the wings gray on the foreparts, white streaked then black behind. The winter Sanderling is similarly marked, but the area of white on the wings is much larger and the gray of the back and wings paler.

The winter range in the east extends south from Massachusetts and around Florida to the Gulf Coast. This habit of remaining in North America in winter, and the fact that shorebirds were shot for food in the 19th century, led to a steep decline in the Dunlin's numbers. Combined with a low reproductive rate and heavy natural mortality, it is likely that, without complete protection, the Dunlin would have disappeared by now. It is again a common bird on the coast, but less so inland on migration, although many are seen going through the Great Lakes. During the inland spring migration they should be sought in flooded grassy areas in fields, or often lawns, for they are tame and unsuspecting. Dunlins do not move with the same alertness of other sandpipers, but tend to be deliberate, almost sluggish in their feeding, chiefly digging with their bills.

Breeding is in the United Kingdom, northern Europe, Greenland, Iceland and northern North America from Alaska to the west shores of Hudson Bay, both on the tundra and on salt marshes.

SHORT-BILLED DOWITCHER
Limnodromus griseus
LENGTH 10 INCHES

The two Dowitcher species, the Short-billed and the Long-billed, are so similar, particularly in autumn, that only in the last thirty years have the separate species been officially recognized. Visual identification is unreliable. Both have heavy snipe-like bills twice as long as the head, are solid chunky looking birds, with long greenish-yellow legs and, in flight, distinctive white backs and rumps. In the marsh, Dowitchers may easily be mistaken for Snipe when they flush, except for the extensive white patch on the back which then shows clearly. The Snipe's back is dark. In spring the breast and neck are medium brown, finely spotted with dark, the back dark, somewhat streaked, but not as heavily as the Snipe, the wings dark with a pale trailing edge.

The breeding range of the Short-billed is poorly known, but includes the southern Mackenzie River and the northern prairie provinces and another area in northern Quebec. Migration from the wintering areas, which extend from the southern United States to Brazil, is mainly through the prairies, but fairly commonly through the eastern States and Canada.

Feeding is mainly in shallow water, but also in soft mud in marshes and on beaches. Roger Tory Peterson writes that the Dowitcher "feeds like a sewing machine" as it prods vertically up and down in the mud.

The Long-billed Dowitcher (*Limnodromus scolopaceus*) has a slightly longer bill, and in spring, is distinctly more rust colored on the underparts, although there is much variation. It breeds in Siberia, Alaska and in the Canadian Arctic east of the mouth of the Mackenzie River.

SEMIPALMATED SANDPIPER
Ereunetes pusillus
LENGTH 5 INCHES

The Semipalmated is the most abundant of all our shorebirds and in the spring migration is seen widely across central North America but uncommonly in the Maritime Provinces of Canada. By mid-July adult birds are already moving south in large numbers and are then seen on the beaches and mud flats of coastal areas as well as inland. The northern breeding range extends from Alaska to northern Labrador and includes the shores of Hudson Bay. The winter range is from South Carolina to Brazil. Early autumn migrants leave the nesting grounds when the young may be only two weeks old and still unable to fly. The young follow about a month later.

Semipalmateds so closely resemble Western Sandpipers (rarely seen in the east) and Baird's, particularly in autumn, that certain identification is often doubtful. Baird's is more buffy on the breast than the other two, and the bill of the Semipalmated is shorter than that of the Western and is straight, while the longer bill of the Western turns downward slightly at the tip. Both of the latter have blackish short legs; the Least Sandpiper has yellow legs when seen closely.

The term semipalmated indicates that the toes are partially webbed, an unusual feature in sandpipers.

The Semipalmated moves about in large flocks in company with other shorebirds, feeding in wet mud flats and sandy beaches. On the coast they stay close to the tide line to feed, and at high tide rest in large groups, standing on one leg, the other drawn up to the body, the head tucked against the back. Away from the coast they stop briefly to feed and rest on mud flats on the shores of lakes, rivers and ponds.

HUDSONIAN GODWIT
Limosa haemastica
LENGTH 13 INCHES, WINGSPAN 26 INCHES

Godwits are large members of the sandpiper family, and three species — the Bar-tailed, Marbled and Hudsonian — nest in North America. Only the Hudsonian is seen regularly in the east, although the Marbled Godwit, which breeds on the prairies, has been seen on rare occasions.

From its winter range near the Straits of Magellan and the Falkland Islands, the Hudsonian Godwit migrates north in spring through the Mississippi Valley, spreading across the Canadian prairies to two separate breeding areas, one near the mouth of the Mackenzie River and the other on the west side of Hudson Bay (near Churchill, Manitoba and in northern Ontario). After nesting, adult birds gather in flocks in the marshes of James Bay and in early August leave on a non-stop flight of some 3,000 miles to northern South America. They over-fly the Maritime Provinces and the Atlantic Ocean, probably a sixty to seventy hour flight. Strong easterly winds on the Atlantic sometimes blow the flocks to the eastern seaboard where they rest and feed, otherwise few birds are seen in autumn.

The Hudsonian Godwit is larger than the Greater Yellowlegs with long gray legs and a slim, slightly upturned bill twice as long as its head. The main distinguishing feature, on the ground and in the air, is the large area of white on the rump and the wide black tip on the tail. The spring bird has reddish-brown underparts, finely barred with black, and dark brown mottled wings and back, the wings show a white band which becomes obscure in the primary feathers. In flight the long legs trail behind. By autumn the underparts and face are pale gray, the back and wings gray-brown.

Godwits feed on muddy shores of salt and fresh water, probing with their long bills, sometimes in water so deep that the head disappears entirely.

SANDERLING
Crocethia alba
LENGTH 7 INCHES

The Sanderling is the palest of the small sandpipers, in autumn and winter being pure white below and pale gray on the back — somewhat darker on the wings. In spring the head, back and flanks are tinged with a rusty color, and immature birds in autumn are buff on the breast. The bill is somewhat stouter than that of other small "peeps" and is black, as are the legs. In flight one should look for the gray back, wide white wingstripes and a black patch at the bend of the wing on top.

Preferring sandy beaches, on the coast and inland, it always seems to be the sandpiper closest to the water, running about in small groups at the edge of the waves, always just ahead of the advancing water. In the spring they advance through North America from coast to coast, but are not much seen east of the Great Lakes. They breed in the islands of Arctic North America and Eurasia, and in autumn prefer to return south along the coasts, although many birds are seen along the Great Lakes and St. Lawrence River. Sanderlings may be seen in small numbers all summer on some beaches, for not all birds return to the Arctic to breed. They winter on the shores of the United States, south from Massachusetts to the Gulf, and in the west from southern British Columbia southward — through the West Indies to the southern tip of South America. European birds winter south to South Africa and New Zealand.

Phalaropes
Family Phalaropodidae

Phalaropes are small, sandpiper-like birds, elegantly patterned in spring, with slim straight bills, lobed toes and slightly webbed feet. There are only three species, the Red, Wilson's and Northern Phalaropes, all of them breeding in North America, but all rare migrants through the east. The Red and the Northern also breed in Europe. These tiny birds are unusual for shorebirds in that they obtain most of their food while swimming, and the Red and the Northern spend most of the winter at sea in the southern hemisphere. Phalaropes are buoyant and ride high in the water, constantly spinning about as they search for food. They feed mainly on insect larvae which they stir up from the bottom of the shallow tundra pools and prairie sloughs where they breed. The habit of spinning continues at sea.

In another unusual turnabout of the family, the female is larger than the male and more strikingly patterned. The unobtrusive male is the first to arrive at the nesting site where he proceeds to build the nest. He is then courted by the flamboyant female which lays the eggs and then departs. The male then incubates the eggs and cares for the young.

Wilson's and the northern Phalarope are seen with some regularity in the interior and on the coasts of the northeast, but the Red Phalarope, which breeds in the Arctic Islands and the most northern mainland of Canada, migrates almost entirely by sea and is rarely seen inland. A few have been recorded in the northeastern States and in Ontario and Quebec.

WILSON'S PHALAROPE
Steganopus tricolor
LENGTH 8 INCHES

Of the three phalarope, Wilson's is the only one which feeds regularly on muddy shores. It is also the only phalarope to spend both summer and winter on land, although many do winter at sea. The main breeding area is in the sloughs and marshes of eastern British Columbia, the southern half of the prairie provinces, south to California and Indiana. Migration is through the western States, south to Argentina where it winters on ponds and lakes. A small breeding population exists in southern Ontario at the Luther Marsh, west of Orangeville, the Holland Marsh, north of Toronto and in a number of other marshes further south. Migrating birds are seen regularly but uncommonly.

The female is the more vividly marked and is especially striking. The pale crown and throat are slashed with a heavy black line which forms a Z from the eye to the back of the head and down each side of the long neck, then broadens, becoming chestnut colored and curves over the back, parallel to a second chestnut stripe on the wing. The bill is straight and as thin as a conductor's baton. The smaller male is similarly but less clearly marked. In flight the tail and rump are whitish and the bluish-gray wings unmarked by the white bar of most shorebirds, including the other two phalaropes. The white wing stripes are retained by the Northern and the Red Phalaropes in fall plumage, but the wings of the Wilson's remain plain and quite distinguishable from most other shorebirds.

NORTHERN PHALAROPE
Lobipes lobatus
LENGTH 6 INCHES

The Northern Phalarope is a rare migrant through the interior of the northeast, although it is sometimes seen on lakes, ponds and sewage lagoons when it stops briefly to rest and feed. It is more common in the New England and Maritime Provinces. The North American breeding range extends from Alaska, across the eastern Arctic, around Hudson Bay to northern Quebec and Labrador, and includes the southern part of Baffin Island. Migration from this area is mainly in a southwesterly direction, across the plains to the Pacific, and along the coast to the Atlantic. It winters at sea, mainly south of the Equator, but some birds turn up on beaches and close to land, mainly after storms.

The Northern is generally seen in the east in its autumn plumage when it resembles the Sanderling and, to a greater degree, the Wilson's Phalarope. The back and wings are darker than the Sanderling, the black eyestripe is much more pronounced and the undersides are pure white. The breeding plumage of the spring female which we are unlikely to see in the east, is truly handsome. The head and nape are dark gray, the throat white, the sides of the neck and lower throat chestnut. The back is striped gray and brown, and the undersides are white.

At sea in winter the Red and Northern Phalarope form large flocks which feed on tiny fish, often in association with whales. When they come to land, they do so in small flocks.

Gulls
Family Laridae

One tends to think of gulls as "seagulls" as indeed many are. Others are equally at home on land, feeding in fields and garbage dumps, for they are largely scavengers. All have strong hooked bills, long pointed wings, webbed feet and all swim. On the water they take most of their food from the surface (except the Kittiwake which can swim below the surface), seldom diving from the air in the manner of terns.

They fly with slow deliberate strokes, strongly, but at no great speed. Some soar like hawks over both land and water while searching for food.

Immature birds are generally mottled gray or brown, and some species take three years to attain adult plumage and the ability to breed. During this period, the variation in color and pattern is enormous, making identification difficult. The sexes are alike.

For ease of description, we have divided the gulls into two categories, those with white heads and those with dark or black heads. Of the latter,

Common Tern

Black Tern

Herring Gull

Bonaparte's Gull

Both gulls and terns are water birds with slender, pointed wings. Terns have straight bills; gulls have hooked bills.

only the Bonaparte's is commonly seen in the northeast. The cries differ considerably between species and each bird has a wide vocabulary — the feeding cry which we hear about fish wharves on the coast is the best known.

GLAUCOUS GULL
Larus hyperboreus
LENGTH 24 INCHES, WINGSPAN 60 INCHES

This large uncommon white-headed gull breeds in the Arctic mainland of North America, Europe and Asia and migrates south on both coasts of North America, as far as New York in the east. It also winters sparingly in the Great Lakes and on the Ottawa and St. Lawrence Rivers. It usually stays close to shore, in bays and harbors, occasionally visiting off-shore fishing banks.

The Glaucous Gull is highly predatory, feeding in summer on the young of other nesting birds, such as murres, ducks and other gulls, and also taking flying birds the size of plovers, swallowing them whole. At all seasons it robs ducks and gulls of their catches and feeds on carrion.

The mature bird is all white below and on the head and tail. The mantle of the wings is pale gray, lighter on the primary feathers. The legs are pink and there is a yellow eye-ring, not easily discernible. Birds of the second winter are almost entirely white, and those of the first winter speckled pale brown. The bill is long and heavy, the only useful difference in appearance between the Glaucous and Iceland Gulls.

GREAT BLACK-BACKED GULL
Larus marinus
LENGTH 24 INCHES, WINGSPAN 65 INCHES

This is the largest gull seen in North America. It is white-headed and the mature bird is white on the neck and underparts, and black across the back and wings, which have white trailing edges. The heavy long bill is yellow, the legs pink. Immature birds closely resemble the more common and smaller Herring Gull, but the head and underparts are generally paler and the dark tail has a white band at the tip.

The predatory habits of the Great Black-backed are similar to those of the more northerly nesting Glaucous Gull. In summer it feeds mostly on the eggs and young of ducks, terns, other gulls and cormorants.

A dominant bird in many ways, it chooses the highest ground to nest in any locality, whether on an island, sea cliff or lake close to salt water, driving other nesters to inferior positions. It usually nests close to the seabird colonies which it predates. Occasional breeding takes place in Ontario, on the Bruce Peninsula in Lake Huron and at Presquile on Lake Ontario, but the main breeding range is the sea coast from northern Labrador to New York, including the lower St. Lawrence and the Maritime Provinces. In late summer, after the nesting season, this large gull appears commonly on the coast associating on sand bars and mud flats with Herring Gulls and terns. Wintering is from Newfoundland to South Carolina, normally close to shore, or along coastal marshes and beaches. Inland it is less common, but some numbers are seen along the St. Lawrence and in the Great Lakes.

ICELAND GULL
Larus glaucoides
LENGTH 19 INCHES, WINGSPAN 55 INCHES

The Iceland Gull is smaller than the Glaucous, but its wings are proportionately longer. The coloring is similar, but the yellow bill is much shorter and smaller. The eye-ring is red and the head is small in relation to the body, much smaller than that of the Glaucous Gull.

The Iceland, not unnaturally, breeds in Europe. The North American range is southern Baffin Island and extreme northern Quebec. In winter small numbers are seen in the Great Lakes and St. Lawrence River and more commonly on the coast, south as far as Virginia. It feeds at sea and also around fishing wharves, garbage dumps and sewer outlets.

HERRING GULL
Larus argentatus
LENGTH 20 INCHES, WINGSPAN 55 INCHES

The Herring Gull is a large white-headed gull with a heavy yellow bill and flesh-colored legs. The body and neck are white, there is a gray mantle over the wings and back, and black on the wing tips. Seen from below, as it usually is, soaring like a hawk, it is white with darker wings. The heavy bill has a red spot on the lower mandible. It is similar to the equally common but smaller Ring-billed Gull, which has a black ring on the bill and yellow legs.

This gull is largely a scavenger, feeding on dead fish along the shoreline, at garbage dumps, sewage outlets and lagoons and in the wake of ships fairly close to land. It also feeds on marine worms, shellfish (which it opens by dropping), insects in plowed fields, berries and the eggs and young of other birds.

The North American breeding range covers most of Alaska and Canada to the Arctic Ocean and the northcentral United States. On the coast it nests in colonies, often with terns and other gulls. In the interior, it usually chooses small islands on remote lakes, and some large colonies exist along rivers. A colony of 50,000 mixed terns and gulls was destroyed when Expo '67 was built in Montreal.

Migration is across the continent and on the coasts south to the West Indies. European breeding birds winter from Africa to the Philippines.

First winter birds are a ragged brown with dark flight feathers and tail, brown legs and a black bill. Young Ring-bills are much paler, with white tails tipped with dark and, at that age, pink legs. As the Herring Gull advances to its second winter, it is paler and similar to the young Ring-bill, but the area of white on the tail is much smaller. There is a great deal of variation among individuals and at different ages, and certain identification is not easy.

RING-BILLED GULL

Larus delawarensis
LENGTH 16 INCHES, WINGSPAN 49 INCHES

Although common, the Ring-bill is probably more scarce now than before the settlement of North America, for it will not tolerate much interference in nesting and its range is much reduced, particularly in the eastern United States. The largest conjunctive nesting area is on the western plains of Canada and the United States. In the east it includes a number of separate areas: western Lake Superior, most of southern Ontario and southwestern Quebec, eastern James Bay, the north shore of the Lower St. Lawrence, northern New Brunswick, southeastern Newfoundland, and northern New York. Nesting is in colonies usually on islands.

The Ring-bill has the scavenging habits common to other inland gulls. In addition, one sees large numbers feeding on insects such as grasshoppers on golf courses or similar green areas. They are famous for finding and feeding on insects stirred up by the plow. Within an hour of beginning to break a field from pasture, we found seventy five birds circling and feeding behind the tractor. This in an area of southern Ontario where we had not seen a gull for weeks. The next day, all were gone.

The mature Ring-bill is similar to the Herring Gull, but is smaller and the legs are yellow rather than flesh-colored, and the yellow bill has a black ring near the tip. (For a comparative description of immature birds, see Herring Gull).

101

DARK-HEADED GULLS

Six species of dark-headed gulls appear regularly, or from time to time, in the waters of the northeastern United States and eastern Canada. They are:

Black-headed Gull (*Larus ribidundus*) — a wanderer which breeds in Iceland and northern Europe, and is seen on the east coast fairly regularly and on Lake Ontario occasionally.

Laughing Gull (*Larus atricilla*) — a coastal bird which breeds from Nova Scotia south to Venezuela, and is seen in the Maritime Provinces occasionally and in Quebec and Ontario rarely.

Franklin's Gull (*Larus pipixcan*) — breeds in the northcentral United States and the prairies of Canada. It appears regularly around the Great Lakes.

Little Gull (*Larus minutus*) — a tiny nine inch gull which was a rare straggler from Europe until 1962, when it was found nesting at Oshawa, Ontario. It is seen rarely, but with some regularity on the east coast.

Sabine's Gull (*Xema sabini*) — the only forked-tail gull to be seen in Canada. It has a dark gray head and breeds in the Arctic Islands of Canada, in Greenland and Siberia. It migrates to the Pacific coast, but has been seen in the east.

BONAPARTE'S GULL
Larus philadelphia
LENGTH 11 INCHES, WINGSPAN 32 INCHES.

Bonaparte's Gull is the only dark-headed gull to be seen in large numbers in most of the northeast. In its spring plumage it has a black or slate gray head, white body and tail, the wings and back have a mantle of pale gray and the wings are tipped with white. The outside edge of the outer primary feather is edged with black, and all the primaries are tipped with black. The Black-headed Gull, which is so common in Europe, is very similar, but lacks the black edge on the outside primary. The bill is short and black, the legs red. In winter the dark head feathers disappear and are then white with a dark spot behind the eye. Young birds also have this spot, the gray back is marked with brown, and there is a black sub-terminal tail band. The legs are then flesh-colored.

Bonaparte's is a tree nesting gull, choosing a coniferous forest close to muskeg or lakes, and usually placing the nest fifteen to twenty feet above the ground. The range includes the western part of the Northwest Territories, the northern part of British Columbia and the prairie provinces and Ontario north of the Great Lakes to James Bay. Many non-breeding birds remain south of this range in summer and, as a result, Bonaparte's is seen in the Great Lakes all year, for the wintering range, which extends to the Caribbean, starts in the Great Lakes.

The flight is buoyant and tern-like, and feeding birds fly just above the surface with legs dangling, bills taking what they need from the surface. On the water it rides high, with tail and head perked up at a sharp angle.

BLACK-LEGGED KITTIWAKE
Rissa tridactyla
LENGTH 14 INCHES, WINGSPAN 36 INCHES

This ocean-going gull, which may be the most common of all gulls, is rarely seen inland, but has been known on Lake Ontario. It breeds in the Arctic regions around the pole, and in eastern Canada near the mouth on the north shore of the St. Lawrence, in Newfoundland, Anticosti, Bonaventure and Percé. It breeds in colonies on cliffs, usually at the edge of the ocean, but sometimes inland. It favors ledges and projections of the cliff face and therefore does not interfere with the gannets and other species which nest principally on level ground at the top.

Once nesting is finished, the birds are seldom close enough to be seen from the shore, preferring to remain well away from land where they feed on small fish and plankton. This is the only gull to dive from the surface to seek its prey like a duck, while swimming below the surface. In winter it wanders widely through the oceans of the northern hemisphere, in the Atlantic moving as far south as North Carolina.

It is white-headed and in appearance quite similar to the larger Ring-billed and Herring Gulls, white underparts, neck and tail, gray on the back and wings. The wing tips are black, without the white edges and flecks of the other two, the legs are black, the bill yellow and the tail straight across the tip, not rounded as with most other gulls.

Terns
Sub-Family Sterninae

Terns are medium sized water birds with long, slender pointed wings, forked tails, sturdy straight bills, generally with pale coloring and a dark cap extending to the back of the neck. They fly buoyantly, almost as if the body moves up and down, pivoted on the wing-tips, with the bill pointed downward, appearing always to be hunting. They dive into the water for their food which consists of insects and small fish. They divide into two categories: pale-backed and dark-backed. Ten species of pale-backed terns are known in North America, all remarkably alike both in flight and on the water. Although only three of these are likely to be seen in the northeast, we nevertheless list all ten, so that the observer will be aware of what not to look for. The Black Tern is dark-winged and is described separately.

Gull-billed Tern	(*Gelochelidon nilotica*) A southerly bird which is now rare in the east, nests from New Jersey southward and in many parts of the world. It has only been recorded once in Canada.
Forster's Tern	(*Sterna Forsteri*) Breeds in the western plains of the United States and Canada, and has been seen only rarely in the east.
Common Tern	(*Sterna hirundo*) Present in the northeast. Description follows.
Arctic Tern	(*Sterna paradisaea*) Present in the northeast. Description follows.
Roseate Tern	(*Sterna dougallii*) Breeds sparingly in Nova Scotia and south to Venezuela; also in the United Kingdom to Africa, and in the Pacific. Not seen inland.
Bridled Tern	(*Sterna anaethetus*) A tropical bird which has been seen occasionally on the coast.
Least Tern	(*Sterna albifrons*) of world-wide breeding range, in the United States south from Massachusetts. Seen on rare occasions in New Brunswick and Nova Scotia.
Royal Tern	(*Thalasseus maximus*) Breeds south from Virginia and recorded twice in Nova Scotia.
Sandwich Tern	(*Thalasseus sandvicensis*) Breeds southward from Virginia, recorded once in southern Ontario.
Caspian Tern	(*Hydroprogne caspia*) Appears in the northeast. Description follows.

COMMON TERN

Sterna hirundo
LENGTH 14 INCHES, WINGSPAN 31 INCHES

The pale terns are so similar that you can hardly tell them apart, even in pictures or when seen through binoculars. The differences are rarely apparent to most observers, and concern mainly the concentration of color on the wings and feet for, with the exception of the tiny Least (nine inches) and the larger Royal (eighteen inches) and Caspian (twenty inches) they are all about the same size. The Common Tern, one of three pale terns seen regularly in the northeast, is a slender bird with a fairly heavy, dark-tipped red bill and reddish legs. The crown is black, the back and wings pearl-gray, the underparts and the long deeply forked tail white. In winter the forehead is white. The call is a rattling *kee-urr*.

The Common Tern breeds in pairs or in colonies in the more temperate areas of the northern hemisphere, in the northern United States, east from the plains and in Canada from Alberta eastward. Nests are on the ground, usually in the open on beaches and rocks. The colonies are subject to heavy predation, by domestic animals, raccoons and other wild animals, humans and predatory birds. In coastal areas storm tides do much damage. If the nest is destroyed, another attempt is made either in the same location or in another colony. The usual clutch is three eggs and, as terns breed only at three years of age, the maintenance of suitable nesting areas is crucial to survival. The Common Tern may be expected to live eighteen years.

The wintering area extends from the southern United States to the southern tip of South America.

ARCTIC TERN
Sterna paradisaea
LENGTH 15 INCHES, WINGSPAN 31 INCHES

This tern is Arctic in the sense that it breeds around the Pole and winters in the southern hemisphere, some birds going into Antarctica. Migration is by sea, and the main route takes birds bred in northern Canada across the Atlantic and south along the coasts of Europe and Africa. It is likely that some individuals of this species have the longest migration route of any bird, and in the course of a year see more daylight than any other species.

The Arctic Tern is pale-backed and so similar to the Common Tern in appearance that the differences are not readily discernible, except perhaps in spring when they are seen together in large numbers. The Arctic's bill is redder and usually lacks the dark tip of the Common Tern. The legs are shorter, noticeably so when the bird perches on the ground, and the tail more deeply forked. A white line running across the face, which can be observed, separates the black cap from the pale gray undersides, leaving a whiter area between.

This almost white bird with the deeply-forked tail is circumpolar. Its breeding range extends south to about the 60th parallel, except in eastern North America, where it summers as far as Massachusetts, including Labrador and the Maritime Provinces. Here one can usually distinguish between the Common and the Arctic Terns, for they are often seen together.

Following nesting, the long migration is by sea and the Arctic Tern cannot be expected to be seen inland after the summer. Terns are long-lived — one Arctic Tern banded in Norway died there twenty-seven years later.

CASPIAN TERN

Hydroprogne caspia
LENGTH 20 INCHES, WINGSPAN 53 INCHES

This large tern has a habit of soaring like a gull, often at a considerable height, but when fishing it flies close to the water with its bill depressed, like other terns. It dives into the water for most of its food, but also feeds on the surface like a gull. It is noted, too, for its habit of robbing other terns of their catch and of eating their eggs. It is often found nesting with Ring-billed Gulls or resting with them on bars.

This tern is a large bird, the size of a gull, with a heavy, deep red bill, black legs, wide gull-like wings and a white, slightly forked tail. The black crown is crested and becomes mottled in winter. The undersides of the primary flight feathers are quite dark.

The Caspian Tern breeds in many parts of the world, from Europe to New Zealand, and in several parts of the United States and Canada, American birds wintering from the southern United States to Mexico. It is reasonably common in its nesting areas, and in the east it can be found in summer around the shores of Lakes Huron, Erie and Ontario where it nests on the ground in colonies and pairs, often with other terns and gulls. In the west it nests on Great Slave Lake and Lake Athabaska and on prairie lakes.

BLACK TERN

Chlidonias niger
LENGTH 9 INCHES

This delightful little tern is darker than the others described here, and feeds mostly on insects in summer as it flies erratically about the marsh and adjacent fields and meadows. It dives very little for fish and tadpoles, taking dragonflies and other flying insects on the wing. Nesting appears to be precarious, for the eggs are laid in a mass of damp vegetation loosely scraped together, sometimes floating, sometimes on a muskrat house and one, which I found, on a small floating board held by cattails.

The head, neck and underparts are blackish, the back, wings and tail a pleasantly contrasting uniform dark gray. In late summer the underparts and head become mostly white but the upper parts retain their summer gray.

The Black Tern breeds in shallow lakes and marshes across inland North America from British Columbia to southwestern Quebec and from California to New York. While it is far more common on the prairies, most eastern marshes have some Black Terns. On migration quite large numbers can be seen feeding on the Great Lakes and the St. Lawrence River. In the winter they move to the two coasts and feed in bays, marshes and at sea, south from Panama.

Auks, Murres, and Puffins
Family Alcidae

Auks, murres and puffins are the northern equivalent of the penguin family with whom they are allied. They are all stout-bodied, with short tails, wings and legs, and breed north of the Equator only. All twenty-one species are seen off the shores of North America, but they are primarily birds of the north Pacific Ocean where they range in size from the five-inch Least Auklet to the fourteen-inch Razorbill. The five species resident in the North Atlantic are of a more uniform size. They are heavily built and, as fliers, lack great maneuverability, for they have short narrow wings which they use for swimming underwater. (The wings of the Great Auk, extinct since 1844, were so modified through lack of use as to make it flightless.) These birds get airborne on the up-drafts on cliff faces, and fly with short, rapid beats. Their feet are webbed and their short legs set far back on the body like diving ducks but, unlike ducks, the short-tailed Alcids sit upright on land like penguins.

All are black and white, some with brightly colored bills and feet. The feathers grow densely and the insulation they provide permits these species to winter in Arctic waters. The white undersides reflect the chill of the water to some extent, while the black upper parts tend to absorb heat from the sun.

They pursue small fish underwater, carrying large mouthfuls back to the nest in their large bills. In winter, they move further out to sea where

Black Guillemot

Common Puffin

Common Murre

Razorbill

Auks, murres, and puffins are the northern equivalents of the penguins. They are primarily seen in the north Pacific Ocean — only five species are resident in the north Atlantic.

they live entirely except in the breeding season. Nesting is in colonies, sometimes vast, on remote abrupt cliffs and islands where little nesting material is available. Eggs are usually laid on the bare rock on ledges or in crannies and, with some species, in burrows. Incubation is by both sexes.

Most are silent except for a croak, purr or wheezing whistle.

RAZORBILL (Razor-billed Auk)
Alca torda
LENGTH 14 INCHES

This large bird with the somewhat grotesque bill most closely resembles the flightless Great Auk, extinct since 1844, after professional hunters slaughtered it for its thick feathers and oil.

It is stout-bodied with short wings and a long deep bill which looks as if it had a sizeable wart on the end. An inefficient flier, it uses its razorbill to carry large numbers of small fish to the nest. Like most Alcids, it is black on top, and white on the underparts. The Razorbill's neck is so short and thick that its head seems perched on its body when it swims. The bill is ringed in white, as is the speculum which shows as a white line near the end of the wing when the bird is at rest. In flight the bird appears hump-backed, and the short legs trail behind.

The Razorbill breeds in Greenland and remote islands off the coast of Europe, as well as in Labrador, Anticosti, Gaspé, eastern Newfoundland, Cape Breton Island in Nova Scotia, near Grand Manan in New Brunswick and in Maine. The single egg is laid in deep crevices and over-hangs on cliffs which it shares with other seabirds. Unlike the murres, which incubate in an upright position, the Razorbill crouches low over the single egg.

After nesting, it is unusual to see the Razorbill from land, for it winters well offshore from Labrador south to about Long Island, although on occasion, birds have been seen in Lake Ontario and in the St. Lawrence River.

COMMON MURRE
Uria aagle

THICK-BILLED MURRE (formerly Brunnich's Murre)
Uria lomvia
LENGTH 14 INCHES

These two species, which in Europe are called Guillemots, are so similar in habit and appearance that they can be treated as one. Both are duck-like seabirds and resemble the much larger Common Loon, having long, rather slender pointed bills, short necks and large black heads. The upper-part of the heavy body is black, the underparts white. The bills of both Murres are black, but that of the Thick-billed is somewhat heavier and has a white slash along the side. Among the Common Murres some individuals have a white eye ring with a narrow white streak extending back from the eye and were once considered a separate species.

The Murres breed in close association in dense colonies on islands and cliffs. Suitable nesting sites are limited to high cliffs with ledges, where a single egg, of exaggerated pear-shape so it will not roll off the exposed bare rock ledge, is laid.

Incubation, by both sexes, is in an upright position like the penguin, with the birds standing almost shoulder to shoulder. It is the competition for nest sites which limits the population, for the available food supply would support many more. They live on fish, crustacea and sea worms which they take while swimming below the surface. They use their wings under water and have been taken in nets to depths of 180 feet.

Both murres are common, but their numbers are reduced since they were formerly much used as a food source and for their eggs. In the Arctic, Gyrfalcons and other predators nest in close proximity, feeding on the murres and their young.

Murres breed on the islands and mainlands of Europe, Asia and North America, and winter generally to the limit of the continental shelf. In eastern North America, the Common Murre has the more limited breeding range from the central Labrador coast to Cape Breton Island in Nova Scotia, including eastern Newfoundland, the north shore of the St. Lawrence, Anticosti and Gaspé. The Thick-billed nests in Newfoundland, Labrador and north to the Arctic Islands, and numbers sometimes wander to the Great Lakes and southern Quebec in winter.

BLACK GUILLEMOT
Cepphus grylle
LENGTH 11 INCHES

This is the most duck-like of the Alcids, having a longer neck than the others and a more slender longish pointed black bill. It is teal-sized, black above with a large white patch on the wings and white below. As with others of the Alcid family, it feeds under the surface on small fish and crustacea. It is uncommon everywhere, breeding in single pairs or small colonies on islands and mainland shores in crevices in the rocks, in colonies with other seabirds. The two eggs are laid on bare rock, always near the water. The breeding range is from the high eastern Arctic Islands and Hudson Bay to Nova Scotia.

The Guillemot is less migratory than the other Alcids, for it does not stray far from its nesting area, even in the Arctic where it feeds under the ice as long as leads remain open for air. It also breeds in northern Europe and Siberia.

110

COMMON PUFFIN
Fratercula arctica
LENGTH 11 INCHES

Most people will recognize the stocky little Puffin with its huge triangular bill and jaunty black and white plumage, for it has become familiar from the countless television and book illustrations. Its spring and summer plumage resembles a dark-haired man in tail coat, wearing a multi-colored face-guard. The outsize bill, which is compressed laterally, extending high on the forehead and well under the chin, is striped in red and blue, and heavily outlined in yellow. The large head, short neck, stout back and short wings, are black and the underparts white, but the clearest markings are its large white face patches. In autumn, the outer layers of the bill are shed, leaving it smaller and darker for the winter, and the face patches become gray.

The Puffin walks on land in an upright position more easily than other Alcids. Breeding is in colonies on remote cliffs on islands and the mainland, but its preferred habit of nesting in burrows in the earth at the top of the cliff leaves it much exposed to rats and domestic animals in the more southerly areas. There it has deserted many former mainland colonies, remaining only on uninhabited islands. They use their short legs and powerful claws to dig the burrows although some birds lay their single egg on the ground or in a crevice in rocks.

Unlike others of the Auk family, which call their offspring into the sea, the Puffins abandon their young chick after six weeks, when it is grossly overweight and unable to fly. The young live off this fat during final development of feathers, deep in the burrow.

Puffins feed at sea on large schools of small fish, stacking up to forty crosswise in their large bills before returning to the nest. The Puffin is inquisitive by nature and almost fearless.

The main colonies are on the coasts of Labrador, the north shore of the St. Lawrence, Anticosti, Newfoundland and Maine. It also breeds on the coasts of Europe from Portugal to Russia.

It winters at sea, diving for fish, generally remaining in coastal waters close to the nesting colony.

Black-billed Cuckoo

Yellow-billed Cuckoo

Mourning Dove

Top left: Black-billed Cuckoo and Yellow-billed Cuckoo. Note how the tails differ. Above: male and female Mourning Doves in flight and male, showing typical markings.

Pigeons and Doves
Family Columbidae

All in this family are small headed, fast flying birds with small bills and short legs. They have long and pointed wings which flap audibly together on take-off; the tails are either rounded or pointed. All make a cooing sound.

Most feed on the ground on seeds, usually weed seeds, and also waste grain.

Pigeons are prolific, and the 285 species breed in all parts of the world, with the exception of the northern parts of Eurasia and North America and, of course, Antarctica.

ROCK DOVE (Domestic Pigeon)
Columba livia
LENGTH 11 INCHES

In its original wild state in Europe, Asia and Africa, the Rock Dove is mostly pearl gray with a luminous green and pink sheen on the head and throat. There is a diamond shaped white patch on the rump, two black lateral bands on the wings and a black band at the tip of the tail. Interbreeding with other species of domestic doves produces odd markings in the young, from black to white, in many designs. In succeeding generations the dominant genes of the Rock Dove prevail, and the pigeon we see in the streets gradually assumes the pearl gray markings described above.

In North America the Rock Dove lives in both cities and the country, nesting in barns, abandoned buildings and in the supports of bridges and other structures. City-dwelling birds which are usually coated in grime, rely on garbage dumps and hand-outs, now that the horses have left the streets. The bill is too soft and weak to open the shells of most seeds, although on farms grain is an important item of the diet.

MOURNING DOVE
Zenaidura macroura
LENGTH 11 INCHES

This is the common dove of the United States where it breeds throughout the country and winters in all but the coldest parts. In Canada it is a common summer resident in the west and in southern Ontario, far less so in southern Quebec and rare in parts of New Brunswick and Nova Scotia. Breeding also occurs throughout Central America and the West Indies. It is a slim, light brown bird with dark gray wings and a very long pointed tail. The wings have a number of black spots close to the body which are visible when the bird is at rest.

In summer, especially early in the morning, the voice is heard in the suburbs, in farming country and open woods, a mournful but not unpleasant *oooah-ooo-oo-oo*, the first note of a slightly higher pitch, the whole repeated two or three times.

Nesting is principally in coniferous trees, but often in lilacs and other garden trees, usually more than ten feet from the ground. The clearing of the dense pine forests which signaled the end for the Passenger Pigeon actually meant more suitable nesting sites for the less congested Mourning Dove. The nest is a loose platform placed on a horizontal branch, frequently built on top of an old nest of another bird, most often that of a Robin. Nesting starts early in the season when two eggs are laid. In southern areas of the United States it starts as early as February, and three or even four broods are raised by October.

In winter a few birds remain in British Columbia and in southern Ontario where they feed on weed seeds and occasionally come in small flocks to feeding stations. The main population moves much farther south.

Cuckoos
Family Cuculidae

In North America the cuckoo is essentially a southern bird and, of the five species which occur, only two are found in the northeast, the Yellow-billed and the Black-billed. The others have more regional ranges: the Mangrove is restricted to the Florida coastline, the Ani is an occasional visitor from the West Indies and the crested and terrestrial Road Runner is limited to the southwest, particularly Arizona and Texas. Cuckoos are long, slender, almost flat looking birds with narrow tapering tails which make up half their length, and with the exception of the zany Road Runner, they are not reminiscent of the bird which pops out of a clock. In fact, cuckoos are sluggish birds.

European cuckoos (there are 125 species in the world) invariably lay their eggs in the nests of other birds. The two species described here occasionally do so, but usually build their own nests and raise the young. If they happen to leave an egg in another nest, generally that of a sparrow, the parasited host absurdly continues to feed the young cuckoo, even though it is twice her size, and even when it pushes the host's young out of the nest.

They are birds of the thickets and tangles, usually found at the edge of open woods, in the brush at the edge of fields and in dense willows near streams. They feed principally on hairy caterpillars and do much to control crop damage.

YELLOW-BILLED CUCKOO

Coccyzus americanus
LENGTH 11 INCHES

The two species of cuckoos which occur in the northeast are almost identical, the only apparent difference is in the markings on the long slender tail. The tail of the Yellow-billed is alternately patched with black and white — the white patches being larger; the tail of the Black-billed, by contrast, is more ladder-like and paler. Both can be seen clearly as the bird flies overhead. The body is slender and unmarked, brown on the upperparts, dusky white on the underparts. The flight feathers are chestnut colored and the tip of the tail is black. The long bill is downcurved, almost sneering. Only the lower mandible is yellow. The song is a rapid series of clucks, slowing and becoming lower in pitch toward the end.

In Canada the Yellow-billed Cuckoo breeds locally in extreme southern British Columbia, in southern Ontario and in southwestern New Brunswick. Breeding in the United States covers almost the whole country except the northern strip. In winter it moves to South America as far south as Argentina.

BLACK-BILLED CUCKOO

Coccyzus erythropthalmus
LENGTH 11 INCHES

The Black-billed Cuckoo is similar to the Yellow-billed, except that the bill is all black, the brown wings lack the chestnut coloring and the tail is less distinctly marked, being gray and white on the underside. Adult birds have a bright red eye-ring of bare skin, but this is not always easy to see.

The breeding range is quite extensive in Canada — from central Alberta in a narrow band eastward to Nova Scotia. In the United States it is general east of Wyoming and south to South Carolina in summer, and winters in the northwest part of South America. The Black-billed Cuckoo is seen in woodlands as well as in thickets and underbrush.

It, like the Yellow-billed, feeds almost entirely on caterpillars, and will take large numbers of the tent and hairy varieties which other birds will not. During periods of caterpillar outbreaks the number of cuckoos present seems to increase.

The song is a series of short, low-pitched whistled coos, either regularly spaced or in a series of two or three. The whole song may run to hundreds of notes, all at the same pitch.

Owls
Family Strigidae

There are two families of owls in North America, the TYTONIDAE, of which the Barn Owl is the only member, and the STRIGIDAE of which there are seventeen species — nine of which are seen in the northeast and are discussed here. We omit the Barn Owl which is a southern bird seen only seldom in the Atlantic States and sparingly in extreme southern Canada.

Owl watching requires a great deal of patience and tenacity. During the day they roost, usually in coniferous trees close to the trunk, and consequently are well hidden. Sometimes they roost in the same tree for weeks — allowing you to stake out a find and pass the word to others.

Owls seen either in flight or at rest have a distinctive shape. They have large heads and short legs and are feathered to give a neckless appearance. Their unique mark is a feathered facial disc or pattern radiating out from each large eye and enclosing the base of the bill. There is usually a dark area around the eyes and white at the throat. The flight feathers are soft and formed in a way which prevents the air from passing through, permitting an almost silent flight. The wings are large in relation to the size and weight of the body, making the flight buoyant and light with remarkable control in dense forest.

The face is flat across the front, and the eyes face forward, fixed in their sockets, so that the head must be turned to obtain the view required. The head can swivel in 180 degree turns. Contrary to popular opinion, owls have excellent vision in daylight and are able to contract the pupil in bright light and to expand it remarkably in the dark.

One thinks of owls as being nocturnal. Most are, but a few species — the Hawk Owl, the Short-eared and the Snowy — feed principally during the day. All are predators, striking their prey with their claws, the prey ranging from mice and frogs to rabbits and game birds. Their small kills are often swallowed whole, the bones, fur and feathers later being expelled

Screech Owl

Saw-whet Owl

Long-eared Owl

Barred Owl

Great Horned Owl

Snowy Owl

Contrary to popular opinion, owls have excellent daylight vision. They are able, to a remarkable degree, to contract the pupil in bright light and to expand it in the dark.

through the mouth in the form of pellets which pile up at the base of the roost tree. The Great Horned Owl has a bad reputation as a chicken stealer but, on balance, even he contributes to the enormous economic value of this family in the number of harmful rodents it destroys.

Most owls build nests in cavities in trees and lay their eggs much earlier in the season than other birds, some as early as February when they have little competition for their food supply. Incubation is lengthy and the young may spend two months in the nest. Some species do not migrate while others move south of the areas of hard winter.

SCREECH OWL
Otus asio
LENGTH 8 INCHES, WINGSPAN 22 INCHES

This is the only small owl with tufts or "ears". It is usually the easiest to locate for it is fairly common and perches by day, dozing in holes in trees in deciduous woodlands, often in parks in urban areas. It is best found by the pellets of hair and bones which it expels during the digestive process and which accumulate at the base of its tree. It may also be found near bird boxes, where it nests.

The call, which is a mournful whistling wail, lower in scale toward the end, can be imitated, and the bird can be lured from its cavity during the day.

The color of adult birds may range from gray to reddish. The eyes are yellow and the facial disc is marked by a large white cross. The breast is pale with regular dark spots. The tail is finely barred.

It is permanently resident in the whole of the United States and southern Canada east to Quebec. It eats any animal food it can obtain, hunting at night. Mice form the bulk of its diet which includes birds, frogs and even worms, but in summer a great many flying insects are taken.

GREAT HORNED OWL
Bubo virginianus
LENGTH 18 TO 25 INCHES, WINGSPAN 55 INCHES

This great bird is a permanent common resident in its vast breeding range which extends from the tree limits of northern Canada to the southern tip of South America. It reigns supreme in the bird world, and is feared for its strength and ferocity. Fifty years ago P. A. Taverner described it as

118

"the evil genius of the woods". Its food consists principally of rabbits, but it also takes birds, duck, chickens, snakes, mice and animals as large as skunks, hunting in the early evening and at night. During the day it sits in a crevice or tree. In winter it is usually found in evergreens where the cover is heavy, sitting close to the trunk. Crows appear to be the only birds to harass it successfully for they set up a startling clamor, diving at the owl, which usually flies to another tree and eventually is forced to move away entirely.

This owl does not build its own nest, using old ones abandoned by hawks, herons, eagles and squirrels. It also nests in tree cavities and caves. Nesting is early, usually in February, as incubation takes thirty days, and the young are unable to fly for about two months.

The night call of this owl is deep and lovely, a haunting *hoo, hoo, hoooo, hoo, hoo*. The appearance is ferocious, with yellow eyes, two widely spaced "ear" tufts, and a scowl produced by white lines running like eyebrows from the "ear" tufts and converging at the beak. There is a white collar at the throat and the front is finely barred horizontally. The flight is powerful and silent for the wings are large in relation to the weight of the bird.

SNOWY OWL
Nyctea scandiaca
LENGTH 16-20 INCHES, WINGSPAN 92 INCHES

This beautiful large white owl lives in the Arctic and is seen in southern Canada and the northern United States in winter, and then only every fourth year or so. The life cycle of the lemming, which is its principal food, determines its occasional movement to the south. In normal years it is sustained in the Arctic, but in those years when the lemming population declines abruptly, the Snowy Owl wanders south in search of food. It is then easily seen in open places, perching on haystacks or posts, but not in trees like other owls. I have seen as many as a dozen in a day on the banks of the canal of the St. Lawrence Seaway in Montreal. It is a diurnal or day-time owl and is quite easily approached by the observer. When it flies, its flight is rather jerky for the upward wing-beat is slower than the down-beat. It also glides for short distances.

When present, this owl is easily seen because of its stunning appearance and its habit of perching in exposed places. It is mostly white with a round head. Females and young birds display varying degrees of black horizontal bars on back and front. The Snowy Owl's eyes are yellow and it is heavily feathered on the face and legs, indeed to the tips of its claws. The voice is a deep croak, somewhat like the raven's. It also utters a piercing whistle.

It lives principally in the tundra of the northern hemisphere surrounding the Pole. In Canada it breeds north of the tree-line and throughout the Arctic Islands.

HAWK OWL
Surnia ulula
LENGTH 14-16 INCHES, WINGSPAN 33 INCHES

The Hawk Owl has always been a mystery to me, probably because I have seen it only a few times, and then only briefly. It is a medium-sized dark brown and white owl with a long hawk-like tail. The front is horizontally barred, the back and wings brown with many white spots, the long tail tapering and rounded at the tip. The head is covered with white spots and the face is outlined with a dark line or "side burns". It has a dark patch under the bill like a goatee and a whitish collar. It perches at the top of trees, often flicking its long tail, then swooping close to the ground. Rising abruptly, it moves to another tree. It inhabits open, mixed woodland, brushy places in forest openings and muskegs. It hunts during the day and is very agile, using its long tail as a rudder and as a brake.

The breeding range extends through the woodlands of northern Canada, Asia and Europe and in winter it wanders in small numbers to southern Canada and the United States.

The cry is rather melodious, a series of whistles sounding like *keeeee-ip*. The nest is built in a broken tree stump, a woodpecker hole or natural cavity in a tree, or in the old nest of some other large bird.

BARRED OWL
Strix varia
LENGTH 17-20 INCHES, WINGSPAN 44 INCHES

Roger Tory Peterson has aptly described this nocturnal owl as the "eight hooter". Its call, which goes unnoticed during the day, can be heard at night in two groups of four calls — *hoohoo, hoohoo* — *hoohoo, hoohooaw*. The final phrase is emphatic, but the rest of the notes are at a single level and pitch. The call is not as deep as the haunting *hoo-hoo, hoohooo* of the Great Horned Owl.

The Barred Owl is quite common in heavy forest and sometimes in small woodlots of mature trees. It is inquisitive and, when its call is imitated, the bird can be tempted to perch close to the observer. It can also be attracted by "squeaking" on the back of one's hand with the mouth.

The early literature describes the Barred Owl as "a bird of gentle nature" but this, of course, is not so. All predators survive by killing weaker

120

animals. This owl's feet and claws are weaker than those of the other large owls and it has not gained the reputation of being a poultry killer. It feeds principally on mice, frogs, insects and small birds.

The Barred Owl has an op-art look to it. Generally grayish-brown in appearance, the head, throat and breast are finely barred horizontally, the abdomen vertically and the wings are spotted. Even the eyes are dark brown, whereas almost all the others have yellow eyes.

It breeds in woodlands across Canada from British Columbia to Nova Scotia, throughout the United States east of the Rockies and in mountainous country south to Honduras. It is resident within its range.

LONG-EARED OWL

Asio otus
LENGTH 14 TO 16 INCHES, WINGSPAN 39 INCHES

This owl is about the size of a crow, much smaller than the Great Horned Owl but larger than the tiny Screech Owl. All three have "ears" or feather tufts, but those of the Long-eared are close together near the center of the head. The face is a distinct light brown, the eyes yellow. The breast and throat are grayish-brown and heavily mottled. The belly is white with both vertical and horizontal stripes like rough bark. In flight the wings are long, giving the bird the appearance of being larger than it is.

When perched, the long ears are dominant. Otherwise it is a master of camouflage, being almost silent and able to compress its feathers, making it look particularly slim, almost like part of the tree in which it is sitting. This owl is nocturnal, and almost impossible to flush during the day. It usually chooses a roost close to the trunk of an evergreen at the heart of a dense clump of trees. The best way to locate it is by finding the pellets of undigested fur and bones at the base of the tree. In winter groups of up to twenty-five birds roost together.

This owl is violent in defense of its nest and young. It uses the "broken wing" act which so many species adopt and will flutter to the ground, hobbling about with one wing outstretched. It is then very noisy for an otherwise quiet bird. It is enormously widespread in its distribution, and breeds throughout Canada to the tree line, except west of the Rockies. It is also present in the northern half of the United States, Europe, Asia and in southern and north-west Africa.

121

SHORT-EARED OWL

Asio flammeus
LENGTH 13 INCHES, WINGSPAN 41 INCHES

This owl is one of the easiest to find, for it feeds in the open in the daytime and, except in the breeding season, congregates in fairly large flocks. It is tawny in color, the underside of the wing showing a black patch at the wrist. In this regard it may be confused with the Rough-legged Hawk which also frequents open country, but the flight differs, that of the Short-eared is irregular, rather suggestive of an over-sized butterfly. There is much white on the face. The yellow eyes are outlined with dark rings. The head, back and front are pale brown with a number of dark soft vertical streaks. The large head and neckless appearance are quite obvious points of identification.

The range in North America extends from the Arctic Islands, south throughout Canada and the northern third of the United States. It is also present in South America, Asia and Europe. Throughout its range it nests and feeds in open grassland, marshes and dunes, where it flies low over the ground searching for small rodents. When the prey is spotted, the owl thrusts its feet forward and plunges to the ground catching and carrying with its feet. It also takes insects and small birds, but mice form the great bulk of its diet.

Nesting is on the ground. During the breeding season the male puts on a spectacular mating display, climbing to a considerable height then folding its wings and diving toward the earth — much in the manner of the Woodcock. During the dive the wings are rubbed together producing a rattling sound, accompanied by a number of hoots.

BOREAL OWL (also called Richardson's Owl)

Aegolius funereus
LENGTH 10 INCHES, WINGSPAN 24 INCHES

In settled parts of the northeast we see this small owl only in winter as it wanders south in varying numbers from the northern forests. It can be found by patient searching of coniferous groves, often close to buildings. It perches by day in low branches and is so tame that, even when touched, it will not fly. This is also true of the much similar but smaller Saw-whet Owl. The Boreal is an attractive combination of rich brown and white. The face is mostly white with a dark brown border, the eyes are yellow. The head is dark brown, finely spotted with white, the back and wings chocolate with larger white spots and the front light brown with irregular white streaks. The head is smooth without ear tufts.

The Boreal breeds in the forests of northern Canada, Europe and Asia and nests in cavities in trees and also in abandoned nests of squirrels and of other birds.

The casual observer is lucky to find this little owl. During the past twenty years I have only seen one.

122

SAW-WHET OWL
Aegolius acadicus
LENGTH 7 INCHES, WINGSPAN 17 INCHES

This tiny bird is the charmer of the owl family. Although somewhat similar to the Boreal, it is smaller and paler. The facial disc is pale brown except over the eyes and bill, where it is white. Darker lines radiate from the center toward the dark facial outline. The head is brown, finely barred with white, the back and wings reddish brown with some white spots. The breast is light brown turning to streaks on the abdomen. There are no ear tufts. Young birds are almost entirely rich brown.

The Saw-whet is more likely to be seen than the rare Boreal Owl. It breeds throughout the northeast and migrates south of its breeding range in hard winters. The range extends across Canada north to about the 55th parallel and into the United States to California. It prefers moist woodlands and nests in holes in trees. It can be found in tamarack bogs and in thickets of alder and willow.

The Saw-whet is extraordinarily tame and inquisitive. It can be attracted by whistling at dusk, but during the day is difficult to discover for it is nocturnal and remains motionless when approached closely. It can sometimes be found when chickadees set up a clamor.

The name Saw-whet comes from its most unusual call which is not unlike the noise of the filing of a saw. There is also a whistling call note, repeated monotonously.

The Saw-whet is entirely nocturnal and is then very active seeking its food of small rodents, insects and small birds. In severe winters when the snow is deep many of these small owls die of starvation.

Goatsuckers
Family Caprimulgidae

This family of night-flying, soft feathered birds is represented in North America by six species. Two of these, the Whip-poor-will and the Nighthawk occur in the northeast. They are rather drab gray and brown birds with tiny bills and huge mouths, which feed entirely on flying insects. They have weak legs and feet and must crouch, rather than perch, lengthwise along the larger limbs of trees or on other flat surfaces. They spend much of their time in flight, and are noted for amazing control in the air.

"Goatsuckers" were originally thought to feed on goats' milk in the pastures in Europe. They were, in fact, feeding on flying insects stirred up by the animals while grazing, just as swallows are attracted to fishermen in northern rivers who, in turn, have attracted mosquitoes and black flies.

Chimney Swift

Common Nighthawk

Whip-poor-will

Top left: Chimney Swifts in flight. Top right: Nighthawks in flight. This family, the goatsuckers, were originally thought to feed on goats' milk, hence their name.

WHIP-POOR-WILL

Caprimulgus vociferus
LENGTH 9 TO 10 INCHES

This nocturnal bird is well known for its distinctive *whip-poor-will* call which it often repeats more than one hundred times from the same position. The accent is on the first note which is a little higher than the other two and the final note is more drawn out. It calls principally in the spring and early summer, occasionally until late August, starting at dusk and continuing into the night, calling from the ground, a horizontal branch or from a rock.

The Whip-poor-will has a tiny bill but an enormous mouth which extends beyond the eye and is suitable for taking insects in flight. It is a grouse-colored pudgy bird at rest. The head is dark brown with a thick fuzzy white line above the eye and a clear white line around the throat. The back is speckled gray and black, the large rounded wings chestnut colored with black stripes. The tail is long and the three outer feathers are white for the final two-thirds of their length.

Flight is remarkably agile, for the soft large wings are superbly suited for the purpose of chasing insects. The legs and feet are weak and the bird does not walk or hop to any extent and will crouch along a horizontal branch rather than perching across it as do other birds.

The eggs are laid on the ground or in dead leaves in a partially open area close to deciduous trees either of mature or early growth. The diet consists entirely of insects.

The breeding range extends across southern Canada from central Saskatchewan to Nova Scotia and in the United States throughout the eastern half as far south as northern Texas. The winter range extends from the southern United States to Central America.

COMMON NIGHTHAWK

Chordeiles minor
LENGTH 9 INCHES, WINGSPAN 23 INCHES

The Nighthawk is badly named for it is not a hawk, but a member of the family of Goatsuckers. In flight however, it is remarkably similar to a falcon, except that the tail of the nighthawk is slightly forked whereas a falcon's tail is square.

The aerial display is familiar, wittingly or unwittingly, to anyone who has looked up into the summer dusk in almost any city or town in North America. The flight is erratic, jerking from one direction to another as it hunts for insects. The wing beats are slow and purposeful like an oarsman's. Its courting flight is more spectacular, for it climbs to a considerable height, then, as it heads almost straight down, the wings produce a booming sound as it comes out of its dive. The call when flying is a harsh cry sounding like *peeeent*.

Like the Whip-poor-will, the Nighthawk has extremely weak legs and feet, and it lies rather than sits. The markings of the two birds are somewhat similar. The Nighthawk's chin and throat are white, the wings are longer than the tail when at rest, and there is a distinctive white patch near the tip of the wings, which can be seen clearly from below. It feeds mostly at night, but unlike other goatsuckers, may be seen at any time of the day.

The eggs are laid on the ground, on a rock in the forest or on a flat roof. In the country the bird rests by day on fence posts, stumps, or on the ground. In towns it rests on flat roofs.

The range extends from southern Mackenzie River, across North America and in the West Indies. In autumn birds congregate in loose flocks which seem to move in waves, ten birds passing every minute or so. The winter is spent in South America.

Swifts
Family Apopidae

CHIMNEY SWIFT
Chaetura pelagica
LENGTH 5 INCHES, WINGSPAN 13 INCHES

There are four species of swifts in North America of which the Chimney Swift is the only one likely to be seen east of the Mississippi. Its range extends from central Saskatchewan to Nova Scotia and south to the Gulf States and Florida. It winters in the Amazon basin, mixing with other species of swifts.

Originally in North America swifts built their nests and rested at night in hollow trees. When houses were built with chimneys the swifts became much more numerous, as suitable nesting places multiplied many-fold. The nest is formed as a shallow bracket inside the chimney. It is built of twigs which are snapped off a tree by the bird with its feet while flying, and cemented together with saliva. Dozens of pairs may use the same chimney for nesting, and, on migration, hundreds of birds may choose the same night resting place. At dusk great numbers may be seen circling a prominent chimney and then pouring in where they will hang vertically to the sides for the night.

These little birds are short and cigar shaped with long scimitar-like wings. Swifts are sooty gray in color. The tail is short and the spines extend beyond the end of the feathers.

Flight is erratic with rapid wing beats followed by a short glide, and unlike swallows with which they are often found, Swifts seem to expend a great deal of energy. The voice, which is almost constant on the wing, is a staccato series of chittering notes. Swifts rely on flying insects for their food and are seldom seen other than high in the air. Indeed it is hard to imagine them other than charging about *chittering* on stiff wings.

Hummingbirds
Family Trochilidae

RUBY-THROATED HUMMINGBIRD
Archilochus colubris
LENGTH 3 INCHES

More than 300 species of hummingbirds occur in North and South America, the family being restricted to the western hemisphere. The family TROCHILIDAE boasts the world's smallest bird. All have iridescent feathers and have the ability to fly forward, backward and to hover. The wings beat so fast that they are seen only as a blur — the Ruby-throat's beat is between 3,500 and 4,500 times per minute. The long thin bill reaches deep into the heart of a flower and the extendible tongue laps up the blossom's nectar, the bird's principal food.

The Ruby-throat is the only hummingbird present in eastern North America. It breeds as far west as western Alberta and east to Nova Scotia and south throughout the eastern United States. It winters from Mexico through Central America. The back and head are iridescent green, the underparts whitish, the male's throat is bright red, the wings are pointed and stiff. The voice is a curious chatter of squeaky notes and short squeals.

When moving about a garden the flight is direct and rapid and, as a bird passes, the hum of its wings can be heard. When it pauses at a flower it hovers, then backs away, moving from blossom to blossom. It also takes insects in flight and is easily attracted to feeders containing a solution of sugar and water. The nest is about one and a half inches across, and is usually built on the narrow horizontal limb of a tree, often in alders as it prefers to nest over water.

Kingfishers
Family Alcedinidae

BELTED KINGFISHER
Megaceryle alcyon
LENGTH 12 INCHES

The large head and bill, blue and white appearance, ragged crest and rattling call identify this bird. The head and crest, back, wings and tail are bluish gray. The throat and neck are white, as is the abdomen and the throat and abdomen are separated by a wide blue band across the chest. The female has an additional reddish band below the blue one, separated by a band of white.

Belted Kingfisher

Ruby-throated Hummingbird

The Belted Kingfisher is our only kingfisher, and the Ruby-throat is the only hummingbird present in eastern North America.

This is our only kingfisher and is identified with water, for it feeds principally on small fish, although it may also take frogs and insects. In Africa some kingfishers live miles from water and feed entirely on insects. The Belted Kingfisher seeks its food in streams, ponds, lakes, rivers and coastal marshes, but requires a series of high perches from which to watch for its prey. It may dive headlong from its perch or after hovering in one spot over the water. The wings are folded back, and it plunges straight into the water, catching fish under the surface and carrying them with its bill. The kingfisher is often thought to be harmful to game fish, but on the contrary it is almost always beneficial, for it preys mainly on sluggish fish which take young trout.

It is unusual to see more than one pair of kingfishers in the same area, for in its quite large territory it will not tolerate another bird of its species. Both birds of a mating pair will excavate a tunnel up to seven feet long in a bank to use as a nest hole. The eggs are laid on the earth in a small chamber at the end. Nesting may be some distance from water, the presence of suitable banks being the limiting factor.

The breeding range extends across North America from the high Arctic in the west, across central Canada to Labrador and Newfoundland and south to the Gulf Coast. It winters from southern Ontario to Central America, the West Indies and Trinidad.

Woodpeckers
Family Picidae

Woodpeckers can cling to the vertical, or near-vertical, when they feed. They dig in with well-hooked claws on four-toed or three-toed feet, braced against the tree on short legs and a stout spiny tail, generally frayed from rubbing against the bark. Flickers alone of the 213 known woodpeckers, feed also on the ground. Woodpeckers are insectivorous and look for their food either under the bark or deep inside the tree in channels hollowed out by wood-borers. Using their chisel-like bills, they chip away at the bark and drill into the trunk then, with a flick of their extensile tongues (twice the length of their head), impale the larvae on the serrated tip. Woodpeckers are cavity-nesters, excavating holes in trees which, when vacated, become homes for other cavity-nesting birds incapable of making their own holes.

Woodpeckers are essentially non-migratory and, unlike the fly catchers, or birds of prey, are not hunting food when in flight. The flight is undulating, like a quick roller coaster. Instead of ending the wing flap in a soaring hold, woodpeckers, like many finches, close their wings against the body for a moment.

Woodpeckers are found wherever there are trees. Their economic value is immense, for they feed almost entirely on harmful wood-boring insects and on the larvae of many flying insects.

Of the twenty-three species of woodpeckers found regularly in North America, nine are present in the northeast and are described here.

Hairy Woodpecker

Pileated
Woodpecker

Downy Woodpecker

Yellow-bellied
Sapsucker

Black-backed
Three-toed Woodpecker

Common Flicker

Woodpeckers cling to the vertical or near vertical when they feed. Flickers alone of the 213 known woodpeckers also feed on the ground.

COMMON FLICKER
(name changed from Yellow-shafted Flicker in 1973)
Colaptes auratus
LENGTH 11 INCHES

The Flicker is named for its familiar call *wicka, wicka, wicka,* and the more raucous summer *wick, wick, wick,* and not, as might be imagined, for its flickering patches of yellow and white and red. On the wing, it is distinguished by the powerful undulating flight of the woodpeckers, its long bill, yellow undersides to the wing and a large white patch on the rump. On the ground it is a mottled patchwork, largely speckled bird, with a light brown back barred with black. The breast and underparts are heavily spotted with black over yellowish white. The top of the head and neck are pale gray and there is a vivid red crescent cutting the back of the neck. The face and throat are pale brown, ending in a black crescent-shaped collar. The male has a teardrop black moustache from the side of the bill to below the eye.

The principal diet of the Flicker, the only ground-feeding woodpecker, is ants, of which it consumes thousands each day. It will also take berries and wild fruit.

The nest is built in holes in live or dead trees excavated by both birds. In the prairies, the hole may be dug in telephone poles or fence posts. You will hear the flicker sounds of the young birds in the nest if you place your ear against a tree near the nesting cavity. Other cavity-nesting birds, incapable of chiselling out their own tree hole, become largely dependent on the Flicker for a home. The spring courtship and mating spectacle of Flickers consists of both birds leaping up and down on a horizontal branch. This is sometimes repeated on the ground.

The Flicker breeds wherever there are trees in Canada and throughout the eastern United States. In southwestern British Columbia, and along the edge of the Great Plain in the United States where their ranges meet, it hybridizes with the Red-shafted Flicker. It winters from the extreme southern part of Ontario south to the Gulf States.

PILEATED WOODPECKER
Dryocopus pileatus
LENGTH 15 INCHES

The Pileated (meaning capped) is the largest and most exotic of our woodpeckers. A predominantly black bird, the size of a crow, it is distinguished from that bird by its prominent red crest and long powerful bill. When flying, even at considerable distance, it has an unmistakable sweeping flight and flashing black and white markings. The shaggy tail, back and undersides are black, but a flicker of white on the forward edge of the wings can be seen in flight. The white of the face, which runs down the sides of the neck in rivulets, is broken by a wide black bar. The voice is heard only in spring, and is a series of *kuks,* rising in inflection.

131

The Pileated is retiring and not often seen, despite its size. It is a bird of the deep forests, although it will settle in deciduous and mixed woodlots if undisturbed. Wherever it goes, it leaves its mark in the form of a series of rectangular holes, four to eight inches deep. The holes are dug in its search for wood-boring insects, especially carpenter ants, which have eaten into the centre of a tree. It also scatters bark of rotting trees while looking for grubs.

The Pileated is present in all forested areas of Canada and the United States. It does not occur in the sparsely treed central plain of either country. It is resident throughout its range, although it has been known to wander south in winter, when it can be found in stands of mature timber close to habitation.

RED-BELLIED WOODPECKER
Centurus carolinus
LENGTH 9 INCHES

The Red-bellied is badly named, for its underparts are its least distinctive feature, being plain beige from the bill down with a slight suggestion of pink center belly. Instead, the head and neck are bright red, like a balaklava worn round a beige face and neck. It is readily distinguishable from the Redheaded (although similar in size) by its 'ladder-back' black and white barred wings, back and tail. Its white wing patches show in flight.

Identification is almost academic, for this bird rarely moves north of the Great Lakes. It is a rare and local resident in the extreme southern part of Ontario only. Its breeding range is south from Minnesota to western New York. It has been seen occasionally near Ottawa and in southern Quebec, including one I spotted at a friend's feeder one winter in the late 1960s in the Laurentians. This was the first specimen to be sighted in the Province of Quebec for many years, and once the Quebec Society for the Protection of Birds had been notified, observers flocked to see it for the three weeks it remained at the feeder.

In the south its preference is for long-leaf pinewoods and moist woodlands, usually swampy, where the nest is built in a tree-hole excavated by both birds. The food variety is wider than for most woodpeckers and includes corn and wild fruit, besides ants and insects of all kinds.

The Red-bellied is a noisy bird making a great racket with its deep, hoarse call: *chrrrr*, repeated two to twelve times.

RED-HEADED WOODPECKER
Melanerpes erythrocephalus
LENGTH 9 INCHES

This handsome bird, with its crimson-hooded head, neck and throat, is more common in the United States than in Canada. It breeds sparingly in southern Manitoba, southern Ontario, Quebec and southern New Brunswick. It breeds in the north central United States, and is permanently resident throughout the east.

This breathtaking bird is probably the most copied in grade school art classes. Its arresting markings are entirely orderly: crimson head, pure white chest and underparts, black back, tail and upper wings, white patches on the wing tips and rump. The latter are conspicuous in flight.

It is a noisy bird which utters a series of harsh *churs* and *weers*. Preferring fairly open country with small woodlots, it can often be seen flying over fields and, unlike most woodpeckers, it takes flying insects on the wing, wild fruit in late summer, and in winter feeds on acorns. Like others of the family, it relies heavily on insects found under the bark of rotting trees and logs. The nest is built in holes, in dead trees, posts and telephone poles.

YELLOW-BELLIED SAPSUCKER
Sphyrapicus varius
LENGTH 9 INCHES

An uncle of mine once told me that Sapsuckers kill enough trees in New Brunswick to supply ten saw mills. While this is undoubtedly an exaggeration, there is no doubt they do considerable damage. Their offense is to dig a series of parallel pits, at regular intervals, around smooth-barked trees (particularly evident on white birch), then return to feed on the sap which oozes from these holes and on the insects which collect to feed in the sap. The tree usually recovers, but the pitted wood is made useless as lumber. Some woodpeckers drum while excavating but the Yellow-bellied taps irregularly.

The Yellow-bellied looks like a brightly colored Flicker, with two unique features: it has a prominent longitudinal white bar on the black wing, and it is the only woodpecker with a red forehead. Although the throat of the male is red, both have the black collar of the Flicker. The breast is yellowish and the abdomen white. The head is strongly marked with white patches outlined in black and the back is barred black and white.

This bird is generally quiet except for a rather squealing note, slurring downward — and therefore may be easily overlooked. It nests in a deep cavity dug by both birds, in a dead or dying tree, usually near water. It may occur in the forest or woodlots and favors orchards for feeding, where it was once heavily slaughtered as a nuisance.

The breeding range extends from Alaska, across Canada to the Maritimes and New England; to the south, both east and west of the Rockies, and throughout the Appalachians. Wintering is more southerly than for most woodpeckers, throughout the United States, Central America and the West Indies.

HAIRY WOODPECKER
Dendrocopos villosus
LENGTH 8 INCHES

In the field it is often difficult to distinguish the Hairy from the Downy Woodpeckers, for their markings are almost like identical jailbirds. Seen together at close range, the Hairy is much larger. The important difference is in the size of the bill — that of the Hairy is as long as its head, the Downy's is half that length.

This is the only woodpecker with a pure white back. The front is also white, the wing covers black, the wings lined black and white and the short tail is black in the center and white on the outer feathers. The crown and neck of the female are black, but the male has a small red bar across the back of the neck at the nape. There is a single black line through the eye with white ones above and below.

The Hairy is quite common throughout North and Central America and breeds and winters wherever there are trees. In summer it nests in mature forests, in either deciduous or coniferous woodlands, but preferably where they are combined. It feeds close to the nesting cavity, principally on larvae and insects, but occasionally on wild fruit. In northern winters, the Hairy will move close to settled areas, attracted to the suet and occasionally the seeds, at feeding stations.

The Hairy's voice is a harsh rattle, somewhat like that of the Kingfisher, gradually dropping in pitch. It also uses a sharp *peek*. Most birds sing to maintain their territorial boundaries, both the Hairy and the Downy drum loudly on a dead tree or pole. It nests in either dead or living trees, in cavities at varying heights.

DOWNY WOODPECKER
Dendrocopos pubescens
LENGTH 6 INCHES
(see also Hairy Woodpecker)

While the Downy is much smaller than the Hairy Woodpecker, it is almost identical in markings, the only difference is in the outer tail feathers, which are barred black and white in the Downy. Its rattling call starts somewhat higher than the Hairy's, the rattles are more widely spaced and pitch downward at the end.

This is the most common of all woodpeckers in the east, having a tolerance for a wide range of habitat. It feeds in shrubbery as well as open woodland, and is common in farming areas where there are scattered trees. It searches the bark for wood-boring ants and caterpillars, and in winter can be seen in fields working over the stalks of large plants for insect larvae. At feeding stations it becomes very tame and can be approached within a foot or two. It will take both suet and sunflower seeds, feeding in company with chickadees, nuthatches and jays. When both Hairys and Downys are present, the Hairy prevails.

Nesting is in a cavity in dead wood and, on occasion, the Downy will accept a nesting box. The range is extensive: in Canada almost to the limit of trees; in the U.S., throughout, except in the semi-arid southwest. There is some migratory movement, but many birds remain in the northeast in winter.

BLACK-BACKED THREE-TOED WOODPECKER
Picoides arcticus
LENGTH 8 INCHES

This woodpecker is also known as the Arctic Three-toed Woodpecker and, like the Northern Three-toed, has three, instead of the usual four toes. They are the only two woodpeckers with a yellow crown. The head, back and tail are black, but the male has a yellow cap. The front is white and the flanks barred black and white. There is a narrow white line extending back from the eye and a white line around the base of the bill extending to the side of the neck. The outer tail feathers are white.

The range is extensive, although the bird is uncommon. It can be seen across Canada from British Columbia to the Maritime Provinces, but is absent in southern Ontario and southern Quebec. In the northeastern United States it is present in the Adirondacks and northern New England.

Residence in an area is irregular, for these birds prefer to feed on larvae and insects on recently dead trees, or where there is an infestation of Spruce Budworm. Following a burn they may be present for a year or two, removing bark from destroyed trees. When new growth emerges, they disappear. Dozens may congregate on trees flooded by beaver dams. Their presence is often noted by large patches of freshly scaled bark leaving bright patches on dead trees.

The call is a hoarse rattle and in flight there is a sharp cry.

NORTHERN THREE-TOED WOODPECKER
Picoides tridactylus
LENGTH 9 INCHES

The male Northern is almost identical to the Black-backed, but its yellow cap is larger than the Black-backed, and its back is laddered black and white. The yellow cap is separated from a white eye-stripe by a narrow black line. A black patch extends from below the eye around the back of the neck. A further narrow black line extends from the base of the bill. The back and flanks are laddered black and white, the underparts white, the wings black, and the tail black with white outer feathers.

In the east this bird lives north of settled areas but is present in Newfoundland, the Gaspé Peninsula, northern New Brunswick and the Adirondacks, and is rarely seen in the White Mountains. It is more common in the west from Alaska to Arizona, and is also present in northern Europe and Asia.

It breeds and feeds almost entirely in deep coniferous forests and is seldom seen far from its normal habitat.

Flycatchers
Family Tyrannidae

While many families of birds take flying insects as a substantial portion of their diet, the Tyrant Flycatchers, as the name implies, are so dependent on them they cannot live many days without them. As a result, the vast majority of this large family lives entirely within the tropical Americas. Of 364 species, only thirty-two venture north of the tropics, and of these, nine are summer visitors in the northeast.

A number of features are characteristic. All make their living and feed their young on insects which they take in the air. When they have established their nesting territory, they select a series of observation posts on which they perch in an upright position, quite still, on constant lookout for food. They hunt in short flights using quick wing beats, so quick that most of the flycatchers can hover before lunging at an insect. They have great maneuverability and although most of their food is taken near the ground (grasshoppers, tent-worms, beetles and other pests) they are seldom seen on the ground. They prefer to be near water with a reliable fly hatch.

They are fierce tyrants when it comes to their individual nesting territory, which they defend in a noisy but unmusical manner.

The flycatchers which come to the northeast are drab birds, with square tails and a suggestion of a crest, almost indistinguishable one from the other. All have wide bills for scooping in flies. Because it lacks a soft base, the bill appears jammed into the face giving the birds a pinched, mean look.

Flycatchers are business-like birds constantly perched in an upright posture ready for take-off.

EASTERN KINGBIRD
Tyrannus tyrannus
LENGTH 7 INCHES

The Latin name for the Kingbird is apt, for this bird is extremely aggressive in defense of its territory, shouting away at anything that comes within range, be it man or bird. As a small boy in New Brunswick, I was inevitably dive-bombed as I made my way to the beach on a path that led under a prominent spruce, used annually as a nest tree. I have seen Kingbirds give young groundhogs at the base of their tree a bad time. The Kingbird is equally aggressive with any large bird which enters its territory, especially crows, which it pecks at as it chases them away.

It is the most strongly marked of our flycatchers, black and white except for a seldom seen orange flash concealed in the squarish crown. The underparts and a lace-like fringe on the bottom of the tail are pure white. The bill is wide and the head much darker above it than the dark gray upperparts.

Like all flycatchers, its posture is erect and the wing beat fast. In flight, it appears to quiver as if waiting for an insect to get airborne. Kingbirds

Great Crested Flycatcher

Eastern Kingbird

Olive-sided Flycatcher

Eastern Phoebe

Eastern Wood Pewee

Least Flycatcher

Northeastern flycatchers are drab birds with square tails and a suggestion of a crest. All have wide bills for scooping in flies. Top right: two King-birds chasing a crow.

rely entirely on insects and prefer an open habitat where they can dart out in short flights. This sole reliance on insects can be disastrous on migration. A cold spell in May, for instance, can leave hundreds of birds grounded, or clinging to low plants, in a stupor too weak to fly or hunt for food.

The song is a rapid, sputtering chatter heard at dawn. The note used in territorial defense is heard more frequently and may be described as *tzeet*.

Kingbirds prefer an open habitat, nest in either a lone tree or an orchard, and are seldom found in heavy woods. Their perch, or take-off pad, can be an upswinging twig in the middle of a pasture, the branch of a tree at a pond's edge or in a long family line-up on hydro wires.

GREAT CRESTED FLYCATCHER
Myiarchus crinitus
LENGTH 7 INCHES

One of the great joys of birding is reliability. I used to have an early morning rendezvous with the Great Crested Flycatcher on a mountain top in the center of Montreal. Year after year, faithfully between May 6 and May 10, my records show, the loud unmistakable *wheep* of this large, ashy-gray flycatcher would come whistling through the trees, and a few minutes later I would spot it perched in the upper canopy of a big old tree, waiting for insects, in the same open wood where it had been the year before.

The Great Crested is the only flycatcher with a long rusty tail. The head, throat and back are ashy gray, the belly yellow. The wings are also rusty, with two white bars. The crest takes the form of a lump of feathers on the head. The bill is long and, like all flycatchers, wide.

It prefers mature deciduous woodland and builds its nest in a tree cavity, usually an abandoned woodpecker hole, but sometimes natural, and has been known to nest in rural mailboxes. It frequently uses cast-off snake skin as nesting material, and bits of cellophane or onion skins — odd and inexplicable paraphernalia. If the nesting hole is too deep, the cavity is filled with twigs and leaves to provide a platform at the required level. During the breeding season this bird is very aggressive with any large bird in its territory, chasing it off with the unforgettable *wheep*.

The summer range extends from southern Saskatchewan to southern Nova Scotia and throughout the eastern United States. A few birds winter in southern Florida, but most move to eastern Mexico and south to Colombia.

138

EASTERN PHOEBE
Sayornis phoebe
LENGTH 6 INCHES

The Phoebe is the first flycatcher to arrive in the northeast in the spring. The emphatic *pheee-bee* can usually be heard before the end of March, while there is still snow on the ground, and before the final blizzard of the season. Although the principal food is flying insects, the Phoebe can survive for a time on seeds. I suspect that many of the earliest arrivals do not survive to nest.

The Phoebe has two songs. The first is its unmistakable *pheee-bee* which is rather hoarse, the second, which is often alternated with the first, has a broken and rasping second syllable, and sounds like *pheee-blee*.

The Phoebe is a drab gray little household bird, with one redeeming point of identity — it is the only flycatcher to wag its tail consistently when perching. The upper parts are unmarked dark gray with the back somewhat lighter than the rest. The throat and belly are white with a suffused band of dusky olive across the breast. The erect posture is typical. This bird insists on having a roof over its nest, which is why you will find it on struts and girders, tucked under open verandahs, boathouses, abandoned buildings and window sills. It was formerly known as the Bridge Peewee from its habit of nest-building on bridge girders. Before man gave it building props, it nested on rock shelves and on the sides of ravines, provided there was a roof. The nest is made of mud and held together with moss and grass.

In the wild, it prefers to be near water with a reliable fly hatch, and will choose as observation posts such summer cottage appendages as sailboat halyards and other rigging. But barnyards, with their attendant flies, also suit it well.

The summer range extends across Canada from the Mackenzie River and eastern British Columbia to central Ontario, southern Quebec and southern New Brunswick, and the United States south to the Carolinas. It winters from Virginia to southern Mexico.

YELLOW-BELLIED FLYCATCHER
Empidonax flaviventris
LENGTH 5 INCHES

This tiny bird is seen in settled areas of the northeast only on migration, for it prefers the damp cover of the sphagnum forests of the north, where spruce, tamarack and birch prevail. Even during migration it is difficult to locate for it chooses a similar habitat, if possible, or a dense thicket of alder, where it stays close to the ground. One should listen for its plaintive whisperings — two rather sad notes, which may be described as *chur-weee*. The second note is rising and longer. The song is more fluid than those of its EMPIDONAX cousins, the Least and Acadian Flycatchers, and totally different from the Alder's *fee-bee-o*.

Other than song, there is little to distinguish the four flycatchers of the Empidonax family one from the other in the spring. In autumn, when they are wearing their confusing fall plumage and not singing, it is almost impossible. All are small, dark-olive birds with two white bars on their wings. The Yellow-bellied is somewhat easier to identify. Its hues are darker as if they were in focus and, as the name implies, its underparts are decidedly yellowish-gray. (The others are whitish gray.) The head, with its suggested crest, is darker olive than the upper back. The wings are almost black with two white bars, and it has a dark tail and pale yellow eye-ring.

As with all flycatchers, its diet is almost entirely of insects. If these are not available, berries will sustain it for a few days.

It nests on the ground, either beside a concealed lump of moss, or in the roots of a fallen tree.

The range is from the Mackenzie River, across the northern half of the prairie provinces, through central Ontario and most of Quebec and the Maritimes. It also breeds in the northeastern United States as far south as the Catskills, and winters in Central America.

ACADIAN FLYCATCHER

Empidonax virescens
LENGTH 5 INCHES

The Acadian, Alder and Least Flycatchers are so much alike that they are almost indistinguishable in the field. The head is dark gray, the back darker olive-gray, the wings and tail blackish with two white bars on the wings. All three birds have white eye rings, some white on the throat, a grayish olive breast, and a paler abdomen.

The Acadian Flycatcher is a bird of mature deciduous woodland with a strong preference for beech woods. It feeds on passing insects below the leaf canopy and suspends its nest from a thin fork near the end of a branch, usually about ten feet above the ground. It seeks a territory near a stream where there is a constant hatch of flies.

The song is an explosive *spi-chee* and the note on migration and during the summer is a *peeep*.

The Acadian Flycatcher breeds widely through the eastern United States, but in Canada is found only along the shore of Lake Erie in the southernmost part of Ontario.

ALDER FLYCATCHER

Empidonax trailii
LENGTH 5 INCHES

In 1973 the American Ornithological Union ruled that the bird known as Traill's Flycatcher would henceforth be divided into two species: the Alder (singing *fee-bee-o*) and the Willow (singing *fitz-bew*). Writers had been suggesting the move for years and what it does, besides expanding the Empidonax family from four almost identical little birds, to five almost identical little birds, is to divide the Traill's on a geographical and call basis. The Willow Flycatcher, with its distinctive *fitz-bew*, is the more southerly and western bird, being known in southern British Columbia, extreme southern Ontario and southward through the United States.

The Alder is the more northern species, with a vast breeding range extending in an arc across northern Canada from Alaska and the mouth of the Mackenzie River, south to Hudson Bay, the Maritimes and Maine. In winter it moves to Central and South America.

The Alder Flycatcher is browner and darker than its cousin the Acadian, but this feature is not apparent unless the birds are seen together, an unlikely event as the habitats are quite different. The Acadian selects a mature forest, the Alder chooses swampy areas near a stream where alder, willow and shrubs grow in profusion. In some areas it will settle for a drier habitat of old pasture, overgrown with hawthorn and other shrubs.

The nests are unusual, differing from those of most birds, and are loosely woven with a mass of hanging grass. They are built close to the ground in a low bush, but usually straddling a crotch in a branch. The Alder will sometimes nest in a clump of ferns.

The voice is rasping and slurred, the call a hoarse *fee-bee-o*.

LEAST FLYCATCHER
Empidonax minimus
LENGTH 4½ INCHES

The Acadian, the Alder and Least Flycatchers are so much alike that even experienced observers cannot rely on their minor differences for positive identification. The Least is one inch shorter than the others, but this is hard to determine unless they are seen together. The voices of all the Empidonax flycatchers are completely different and this one's is the easiest to learn and remember. It is an emphatic *chebeck*, repeated as often as once per second. With each *chebeck* it flicks its tail and throws its head back.

The Least has a wide nesting range in Canada, from the Mackenzie River Valley and central British Columbia to Nova Scotia, and through the northern United States from Montana eastward. Its choice of acceptable habitat is wider than that of most other flycatchers and it is therefore more widely distributed and more likely to be seen. In unsettled areas it is found in open woodland with scattered coniferous and deciduous trees, at forest edges and in sunny openings in the forest. It is seldom found in dense forest. It is also common in farming country in unsprayed orchards and in parks and gardens of urban areas.

As with other flycatchers, it darts out for flying insects from a series of perches in its territory. The nest is usually five to fifteen feet from the ground and is invariably built in an upward facing crotch, usually in a small tree or shrub.

EASTERN WOOD PEWEE
Contopus virens
LENGTH 5 INCHES

The clear, plaintive whistle *pee-oh-weee* heard early in the morning and evening is the trademark of the Pewee. It is usually found in the wild, away from settled areas in fairly open, mature, deciduous woodland where it chooses a perch on a bare twig, fairly high up, as an observation point. In the morning and evening the song may be heard about thirty times per minute, but during the day, only occasionally as it feeds and then without the same clarity.

This is a medium sized flycatcher, rather darker than the *Empidonax* family. The wings of this species and of the Olive-sided are much longer than other eastern flycatchers and extend half way down the tail when the bird is at rest. It has two white wing-bars and lacks an eye-ring. The head is darker than the back, both being olive gray, the tail and wings are dark. The under-parts are buffy olive, the throat and abdomen are lighter than the breast. The tail is notched.

This bird is fairly common but, curiously, is absent in many areas which appear to be suitable. It breeds from southern Manitoba, across central Ontario and southern Quebec to Nova Scotia, and throughout the eastern half of the United States. In winter it moves to South America, as far south as Peru. The nest is built at varying heights in the form of a saddle on a horizontal limb. Most flycatchers build in a fork.

OLIVE-SIDED FLYCATCHER
Nuttallornis borealis
LENGTH 6 INCHES

The best way to find this bird is by its voice which is a distinctive and far-carrying *hip-threee-beers*. It is a piercing whistling cry, the first note

142

short, the final note slurring downward in pitch. This flycatcher tends to be a bird of remote areas, choosing either open coniferous woodland or openings in the forest near streams and ponds. Its observation perches are usually at the very top of a dead tree, or a high dead branch on a living tree, from which it dashes out for flying insects. In appearance the Olive-sided is similar to the Pewee but the bill is larger and the head more bulky. The throat and central breast are whitish, turning olive brown on the flanks, the head and back are dark olive brown and the tail is short, wide and dark. There are two pale wing bars and usually a patch of white is visible on the upper part of the wings near the center of the back. While the Olive-sided is fairly common in suitable areas, it is aggressive and each pair demands a large nesting area.

From its wintering ground in South America, it moves north to a wide breeding range from Alaska to Newfoundland, and in the west south to Baja California. In the east it is present as far south as North Carolina in the mountains, but absent from the central plains and from the southeast.

Larks
Family Alaudidae

The Horned Lark is the only member of this family native to North America.

HORNED LARK
Eremophila alpestris
LENGTH 8 INCHES

The Horned Lark is found in open areas, plowed fields, short-grass prairie and, in the Arctic, the tundra and high rocky beaches. In settled parts of the country summer ranges include lightly used pastures, golf courses, airports, indeed any open ground where it feeds on weed seeds and insects.

The Horned Lark is a truly delightful bird, especially in winter when it congregates in large flocks. It can then be seen along the gravel edges of roads and in fields, taking seeds from exposed tops of plants. When the

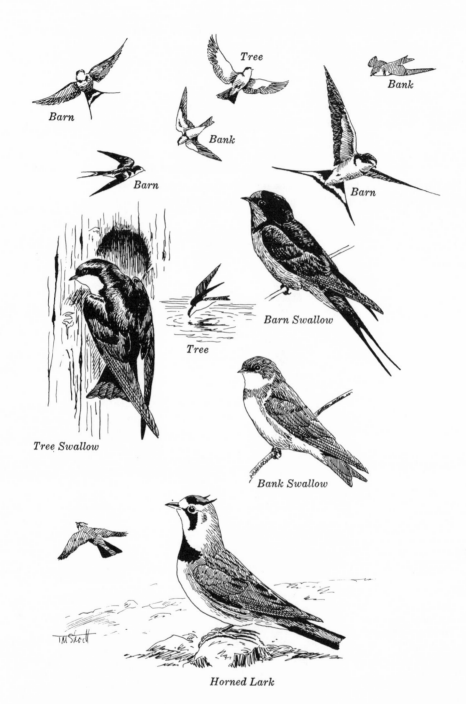

Barn

Tree

Bank

Bank

Barn

Barn

Tree Swallow

Tree

Barn Swallow

Bank Swallow

Horned Lark

Swallows, small birds with long, pointed wings, are aerial wizards whose banking and swooping are often best witnessed at dusk. Above: the Horned Lark is the only member of the lark family native to North America.

flock lands the birds spread out, running about (not hopping) searching for food. When finished they take off in a mass, moving to new ground.

It is a rather long, slim, brown bird. The top of the head and back of the neck are brown, the face yellow and white with a black line extending around the bill, and curving downward like a scimitar below the eye. A tiny tufts of feathers on the sides of the head point up and back, resembling horns. There is a wide black collar across the upper breast. The underparts are white, the flanks light brown, the back and wings lightly streaked brown, the tail is dark brown at the center and white on the outer feathers. The weak, sibilant, highpitched song is heard in flight and when the bird flushes. In winter many faint tinkling notes are heard.

Its range is vast, extending from the islands of the high Arctic to southern Mexico and across the east, with the exception of the extreme southeastern United States, which it does not visit. In winter the Horned Lark withdraws from its northern range to southern Canada southward. Few birds remain in eastern Canada during December and January, but they return in some numbers by early February.

Swallows
Family Hirundinidae

The swallow family is distributed widely in both hemispheres with twenty-three species present in the Americas, of which six migrate north to eastern Canada and the northeastern United States. They rely almost entirely on flying insects for their food, although one or two can survive for a few days on berries when cold weather keeps insects from flying. Their search for food is constant and swallows are in the air for most of the day, resting occasionally on wires or trees. When the young are in the nest or learning to hunt, the parents seldom rest. By midsummer young birds have begun to form large flocks and older birds are rearing a second brood. In the early spring and late summer great numbers of mixed species of swallows can be seen feeding together, perched on wires by the thousands, usually close to water. Swallows, which are all small birds with long pointed wings, are aerial wizards whose banking and swooping are often best witnessed at dusk. They have short wide bills fringed with bristles which help them to capture insects. The legs are short and adapted only for perching, although the Bank and Rough-wings use them for digging their tunnels.

Those species which come to the northeast make long journeys from the Caribbean and South America, returning each year to their birthplace. Only a shortage of nesting sites in a particular area forces them to expand their range.

TREE SWALLOW
Iridoprocne bicolor
LENGTH 5 INCHES

This is the first swallow to arrive in the northeast, usually appearing late in March in small numbers, with the main migration by mid-April. It reaches the Gulf Coast from Cuba and Central America early in March and, except on the coasts, stalls for most of the month in the south until April, when the advance speeds up and suddenly every pond and river is alive with hunting birds. If the weather turns cold and its main food supply of hatching insects is not available for a few days, the Tree Swallow can survive on the few remaining berries left on bushes over the winter. It is quite hardy and can survive a cold spell of several days, unlike other swallows.

Nesting is in the northern half of the United States and in Canada wherever there are trees near a pond, stream or wet meadow. The nest is built in a tree cavity, either natural or an abandoned woodpecker hole. It also accepts nesting boxes readily and, in some areas, a large concentration of boxes may attract enough swallows to reduce crop pests appreciably. Water-killed trees near beaver dams are popular, and colonies sometimes emerge in these areas.

The Tree Swallow is easy to distinguish. It is clear white underneath, with a dark blue-green head and back. The wings and tail are blackish brown. In most lights the upper parts look black. The tail is fairly deeply notched. The song is a delightful liquid chatter.

Two broods are normally raised each year and by mid-summer thousands of birds congregate in flocks, especially on wires where they sit shoulder to shoulder.

BANK SWALLOW
Riparia riparia
LENGTH 5 INCHES

Wherever large numbers of small holes are seen close to the top of a sand or gravel cliff, they indicate the work of Bank Swallows. Sand pits and railway cuttings are man-made additions to suitable habitat which include sea-cliffs and river banks. I grew up watching a colony of several hundred pairs nesting in a sandstone cliff over the ocean. The nest is made at the end of a burrow two or three feet deep. The number of holes in a colony is often deceptive, for many are started and not finished.

The Bank Swallow has the same dark top and pale undersides of most swallows, the top of the head, back, wings and tail are chocolate brown, the underparts white, except for a brown band extending across the upper breast. This band, hard to spot in flight, is obvious when the bird settles. The call is a dry rattle.

The flight is rapid and erratic with twists and turns at full speed when hawking for insects.

The breeding range extends from the Arctic Ocean at the mouth of the Mackenzie River, across Canada to James Bay through the southern half of Quebec and the Maritimes, and south to the Gulf Coast, but excluding the southeastern United States. In winter it moves to South America.

ROUGH-WINGED SWALLOW
Stelgidopteryx ruficollis
LENGTH 5 INCHES

The northern limit of the Rough-winged Swallow's breeding range is the area covered by this book — eastern Canada and the northeastern United States. The southern limit is in Argentina and Paraguay. In most of our area the Rough-winged Swallow is uncommon, but where suitable nesting conditions exist, it is regularly present. Like the Bank Swallow, it requires sandy banks and cliffs for a burrow but, unlike the Bank Swallow, will accept holes in walls or drainpipes and crevices in buildings and bridges. The Bank Swallow nests in colonies of hundreds, but this one nests alone, whether close to water or in arid country.

It is the brownest of the swallows and lacks the sheen of most of the others. The upper parts are sooty brown, the throat and flanks a dingy gray, the belly and central underside of the tail are white. The call is a rasping *chuck*, repeated about twice per second.

The name comes from an unusual formation of tiny hooks on the leading edge of the wing, which are difficult to see even when the bird is held, but which it is possible to feel with a finger.

BARN SWALLOW
Hirundo rustica
LENGTH 6 INCHES

When applied to a gentleman's morning coat, the expression "swallow-tailed" implies a deeply forked tail and this, in the minds of many people, is the typical tail structure of swallows. In fact, the Barn Swallow is the only one with a deeply forked tail. It is a truly beautiful bird, dark iridescent blue above, deep cinnamon on the forehead and undersides. There is a blue ring around the throat, a patch of white at the base of the tail and flecks of white in the fork.

147

This is the common swallow of the barn yard, ponds and suburban areas. It does not require water for flycatching, but does for drinking and swoops along the surface scooping up what it needs in flight. It also requires wet mud for nest building and is usually associated with streams, or at least a small patch of marsh. In the wild the nest is built on rock faces and crevices, but it has adapted so thoroughly to humans that it will nest without disturbance on rafters of verandahs and barns, and against vertical surfaces. Once I counted over twenty nests on the beams of the verandah of a fishing camp in New Brunswick. Bridges are much favored for nesting — look up when you go under one.

Barn Swallows are somewhat messy birds, but should be encouraged to nest, especially where there are animals which attract insects, for they eat huge numbers of flies and mosquitoes.

The voice, both on the wing and at rest, is a bubbly twittering chatter. They are noisy in defense of the nest, and the note becomes more rasping.

In North America the Barn Swallow breeds from Alaska, across the continent to central Ontario, Quebec and southern Newfoundland, and through most of the United States, except the extreme southeast. It is also present throughout most of Europe and Asia to northern Africa and India.

CLIFF SWALLOW
Petrochelidon pyrrhonota
Length 5 inches

This is the swallow which comes back to Capistrano every year (for those who remember the song). Its long migration from South America to the Arctic is astonishingly regular from year to year, but not quite as precise as the legend of Capistrano would have us believe. This regularity is often fatal to vast numbers of swallows, for a late cold spell may keep insects from flying — the sole diet of Cliff Swallows. Early frost in the autumn of 1974 trapped millions of birds in northern Europe, only a small percentage of which was effectively air-lifted south in a unique conservation effort.

The Cliff Swallow has the same cinnamon, white and iridescent blue color scheme as the Barn Swallow, but the tail is short and square. The

148

throat and sides of the head are cinnamon, the forehead white and the top of the head blue. The neck collar and upper breast are buff, the belly is white and the back and wings are dark with a series of tiny white lines down the back. The rump is cinnamon and the tail dark. In flight it soars and coasts more than other swallows.

The nests are built of mud against a vertical surface, like a small gourd pasted to the side of a wall, with a narrow protruding neck at the side for the entrance. Wet mud is required for building, and the gourd nests are therefore usually close to a stream or pond, and always at a place protected from running water when it rains. In the wild, this can be the side of a cliff just under the lip, or if supplied by man, as is increasingly the case, under the eaves of barns and other farm buildings or bridges. They are strangely absent from areas which appear to be suitable, but when present, the colonies of several hundred nests can be seen on the underside of a bridge or on the side of a cliff.

PURPLE MARTIN
Progne subis
LENGTH 7 INCHES

This large swallow has benefited from civilization, so much so as to become almost entirely dependent upon it. In the wild, Martins still nest in woodpecker holes, but competition for these spaces is too intense for a large population to develop. The white man has imitated the Indian in providing nesting houses by hanging gourds for them. Now, houses of up to 100 rooms on platforms fifteen to twenty feet from the ground are the principal summer homes. They will settle in both urban and rural areas and some towns take great pride in their Martin populations. Houses must be removed and cleaned in the autumn and replaced only after the birds have returned in the spring, for otherwise Starlings and House Sparrows will quickly occupy them.

Once established, Martins will return year after year, but it is often difficult to establish them where they have not nested previously, and there are large areas where they do not nest at all, even though suitable accommodation is provided. In their communities the sense of territory is not very strong and they come closer to communal living than most birds.

The Martin is larger than other swallows. The wings are broad and the flight consists of alternate flapping and soaring. The male is dark all over with a bluish sheen, the flight feathers are browner. The females and young birds are grayer and pale on the abdomen and under the tail. The song is a pleasant chirruping gurgle.

The summer range extends across the central prairies of Canada, along the west coast of the United States, and again east of the Rockies to the Atlantic. They winter in South America. Southern migration takes place in vast congregations which frequently suffer many casualties in wet or cold weather due to lack of insects.

Jays and Crows
Family Corvidae

In North America the family CORVIDAE includes seven jays, the magpies, Clark's Nutcracker (common in the Rockies), the Raven and four species of crows. Four of these species occur in the northeast, including the Raven, the largest passerine or perching bird of any kind.

Jays and crows have a number of physical features in common, including a stout long bill and nostrils covered with bristles. They are omnivorous eaters, and tend toward scavenging decayed food. They also feed on grain and the eggs of other birds.

GRAY JAY (also called Canada Jay)
Perisoreus canadensis
LENGTH 10 INCHES

Gray Jays are both a delight and a nuisance at remote lumber or fishing camps in the north woods, where they make themselves entirely at home and are very tame. They act more like pets as they hop about, picking up any bright object which they carry to a nearby tree and stealing scraps of food if a plate is left unattended. Scavenging augments their regular diet of insects, buds and seeds. Inquisitive and friendly, they are the most appealing of the jays, for the feathers are soft and fluffy and the voice is pleasant. They lack the crest and vivid coloring of the more familiar Blue Jay.

The bill is uncharacteristically short and the tail long. The face, head, neck and throat are white with the exception of a dark patch on the back of the head and nape. The back and abdomen are grayish brown, the wings dark brown, the tail is grayish brown and, like the flight feathers, tipped with white. Young birds are sooty brown.

The Gray Jay is resident in most of its range which covers all of Canada where there are coniferous trees south to Michigan and the more remote parts of New England and, in the west, south to California and New Mexico. In winter some birds wander south to the northern States.

Nesting is unusually early, often in late February and the nest is well constructed of twigs and lined with feathers and fur. It is usually built in thick evergreens and sheltered as much as possible.

The Gray Jay has many voices including a whistled *whee-ah*, a scolding chatter and a pleasant chuckling sound and can, at times, be imitative of other birds.

BLUE JAY
Cyanocitta cristata
LENGTH 10 INCHES

It is common to establish prejudices about certain animals. Hyenas are perceived to be bad because they are unattractive and are scavengers, but

150

Blue Jay

Gray Jay

Common Raven

Common Crow

Jays and crows have a number of physical features in common, including a stout, long bill and nostrils covered with bristles.

almost everyone likes Robins because they look gentle and sing beautifully. I confess to a prejudice regarding Blue Jays, for despite their beauty, they are aggressive, rob nests of eggs and nestlings, and have harsh voices. I contribute to the dichotomy by feeding Blue Jays during the winter, but am always disturbed when I see them drive other birds away from the feeding stations. The fact is, if you feed one bird, you feed them all.

Blue Jays are common throughout southern Canada and the United States east of the Rockies where they remain throughout the year. In Canada, they are not much seen in urban areas but in the southern United States they seem quite at home on lawns and in shrubbery. They are spectacular looking birds with brilliant light blue on the wings and long tails which are liberally marked with white patches and horizontal black bars, the crest and back being only slightly paler. The face is white and a black line extends from the crest along the side of the face to form a black necklace across the throat. The underparts are grayish white.

In winter, Blue Jays feed mostly on beech nuts and acorns which they often bury, thereby seeding many oak trees. They will take seeds of all kinds, but favor sunflower seeds which they take in great numbers without troubling to remove husks. They become largely insectivorous in summer.

The common call is a raucous squawk, but in early spring they use a wide variety of quite musical sounds. Curiously, they become almost silent during the nesting season, unlike most birds which sing to maintain their authority over their territory.

COMMON RAVEN
Corvus corax
LENGTH 21 INCHES

The Raven is the largest perching, or passerine, bird in the world and is a constant wonder for its complete mastery of the air. For a bird with a four foot wingspan and fairly heavy build, it executes intriguing twists, turns, rolls and dives. In all areas ravens are wilderness birds, in summer commanding a large territory and in winter moving about in small flocks and sharing a communal roost. In Arctic villages, I have watched them as they scavenge close to houses and feed at garbage dumps. Here they replace the vulture of the south in disposing of decaying carcasses. They

152

seem to prefer the shores of the sea, lakes and rivers in their search for food, and are also found in the mountains where they feed on mice, rabbits and insects.

In appearance the Raven is like a Crow, but much larger and with a heavier bill. The long pointed feathers about the throat give the neck a shaggy appearance. The central tail feathers are longer than the rest causing the tail to have a round look. The voice is a hoarse croak, unlike the familiar *caw* of the crow.

The Raven is a more northerly bird than the crow. Its breeding range extends throughout northern Europe and Asia, through the islands of the high Arctic and Greenland, most of eastern Canada, except southern Ontario, and in isolated areas of the Appalachian Mountains. In the west, it is present as far south as Nicaragua. In winter some birds wander south of the breeding range, but not many.

The nest is usually built on a cliff or in a commanding crevice, but the high branches of a conifer may also be used. The same nest is used year after year and pairs appear to mate for life.

To many, the Raven appears to be a sombre bird of ill-omen, particularly as perpetuated by Edgar Allan Poe. It is also permanently present at the ancient Tower of London which, according to legend, would be lost to an enemy should the Ravens desert it.

COMMON CROW
Corvus brachyrhynchos
LENGTH 17 INCHES

In 1926 P.A. Taverner wrote the definitive description of the crow in "Birds of Western Canada" — "a large, all black bird, too familiar to need much description". Since it is not any less familiar today and, with the larger Raven, is the only big all black bird we see, we shall stay with the Taverner description. The voice needs mention in that the urgency and frequency of its *caws* tell something of its activities.

Much has been written about the economic effect this bird has on crops and its social status among other birds. In Taverner's time the balance of feeling was strongly against the crow because of its habit of feeding on sprouting corn and the eggs of water fowl and other birds in the spring. Later in summer it switches to harmful insects, particularly consuming large numbers of grasshoppers, however the character assassination is complete. No laws protect the crow but, despite considerable persecution, it thrives.

Nesting is across Canada, as far north as Great Slave Lake in the west, but not in the northern half of Quebec or in Labrador, and through the United States except the south west. The nest is built in coniferous and deciduous trees and occasionally on the ground. Most crows migrate in winter, but a few remain in southern Canada where the snow is not too heavy, returning in February in small flocks. It is likely that the crow was limited to the plains of the west before the east was cleared, for despite the fact that it nests in trees, it does not flourish in heavily forested areas.

Black-capped Chickadees

Red-breasted Nuthatch

White-breasted Nuthatch

Titmice are small, busy birds with short, strong bills and short legs. Nuthatches resemble titmice in habits but have straighter and longer bills.

154

Agriculture has expanded the range and population hugely. The winter food is principally waste corn, although carrion and refuse are taken.

In my youth, my family took a young bird from the nest each year, providing us with a summer pet whose name was always "William". We were charmed and the birds grew to trust us. Each morning "William" woke us by scratching on the window. When they could fly they sought their own food and always came when called. At the beach when we swam, they showed great concern and flew about, shouting, until we came ashore. In the autumn "William" joined the other crows as they formed their flocks and migrated with them. None ever returned.

The Common Crow is replaced on the west coast of Canada by the Northwestern Crow which is smaller and has a higher voice.

Titmice
Family Paridae

This family which includes both chickadees and titmice, takes its name from the equally attractive and entertaining Tits of Europe. All are small busy birds with short, strong bills and short legs. They are insectivorous by inclination but feed, particularly in winter, on seeds, nuts and berries. Some sixty-five members of this family are present in all continents, except South America and Australia. Of these, fourteen species are represented in North America and three, the Black-capped Chickadee, the Boreal Chickadee and the Tufted Titmouse, are in the northeast. The sexes of all species are similar. Juveniles resemble the adults but in most cases are paler.

BLACK-CAPPED CHICKADEE
Parus atricapillus
LENGTH 5 INCHES

No bird is more trusting than the chickadee. In the forest they respond almost instantly to a *pshshsh* call, hopping closer branch by branch, until perhaps a dozen birds are within a few feet of one's head. Their *chikadee-dee-dee* call brings in other small birds. They are even more confident at the feeding station and, with patience, will take sunflower seeds from the hand. The easiest way to call birds, or at least to make them hop to an exposed position, is to make a series of *psshhh, psshhh, psshhh* sounds, with the tongue close to the roof of the mouth. Squeaking by sucking abruptly on the knuckles is even more effective.

In summer the chickadee is a woodland bird, but comes readily to gardens and, although territorial, tends to feed in loose groups even while nesting. The diet is chiefly insects, although sunflower seeds are a great favorite in winter. The seed is taken to a nearby branch where it is held by the claw against the bark, and opened by hammering it with the bill.

Chickadees range as far north as Alaska in the west, across the southern half of Canada and the northern half of the United States. It is resident through most of this range, but moves south to some extent in winter.

The nest is excavated in a rotting stump, but sometimes a woodpecker hole is used. From early spring to mid-summer their sweet, whistling call is used, usually three notes of medium length, the second two lower than the first. There is occasionally a bubbling warble.

The chickadee is neatly dressed in gray, black and white. The cap, nape and chin bib are black, the sides of the head are white, the back olive gray, the breast pale olive and the wings and tail gray. The plumage is loose and soft, giving the bird a plump appearance.

BOREAL OR BROWN-CAPPED CHICKADEE
Parus hudsonicus
LENGTH 4 INCHES

The Boreal Chickadee is not seen much in southern areas, in fact not at all in Ontario south of Algonquin Park. It is a permanent resident from the mouth of the Mackenzie River to New England and the Maritime Provinces with the exception of the treeless eastern Arctic and extreme northern Quebec. In winter it moves about the forest with flocks of Black-capped Chickadees and often with woodpeckers, searching for insect eggs and larvae. Small birds must feed for many hours of the day in order to survive the cold nights when they cannot feed. Mortality is highest at night, and it is a marvel that these tiny birds survive at all in the Arctic winter when there is little real daylight.

The markings are similar to those of the Black-capped Chickadee, except that the cap is a rich brown and the flanks are tinged with a chestnut color. The call is similar in structure but higher in pitch, and wiry, almost as if it is saying *sick-a-day-day*. The song is a short warble.

Even in areas where it is reasonably common it tends to be more withdrawn from habitation than the Black-capped, giving one a sense of wilderness.

TUFTED TITMOUSE
Parus bicolor
LENGTH 6 INCHES

This immaculate little bird is non-migratory, common in the southeastern parts of the United States from Texas eastward, but rare in the northern extremes of its range, in southern Ontario and southern New York. It

156

was first sighted in Canada at Point Pelee on Lake Erie in 1914 and has spread slowly since then.

The Tufted is the largest of the four titmouse species in North America, and behaves much like a chickadee with which it feeds in winter. It is predominantly gray and is quickly distinguished from the chickadee by its lack of sharp markings. The large head tuft, or crest, is gray, and there is a black line around the base of the bill. The neck, back, wings and tail are slate gray, the face and underparts are dusky white and there are reddish patches on the flanks. The song is a clear loud whistled *peter, peter, peter,* together with a number of chickadee-like notes, but more scolding and nasal. Unlike most birds, the titmouse sings at all seasons of the year.

It is gregarious, confiding and inquisitive and, like the chickadee, feeds on insect eggs deposited in the bark of trees and shrubs, on caterpillars in summer and on seeds and beech nuts in winter. It nests in holes in rotting stumps as well as in woodpecker holes and, in the nesting season, is best found in moist woodlands and swampy areas. In the south it appears in well treed gardens.

Nuthatches
Family Sittidae

The four nuthatch species in North America are rather like the titmice in habits. They do much of their feeding on insect larvae found in crannies in the bark of trees and shrubs. The bills are straight, longer and thinner than either the chickadee or the titmouse. Nuthatches are less gregarious, but tend to move about in winter with these families.

They are big-headed, streamlined little birds which always seem to be upside down, either clinging to the bottom of a branch or working down the trunk of a tree head first.

We have two species in the northeast, the White-breasted and the Red-breasted.

WHITE-BREASTED NUTHATCH
Sitta carolinensis
LENGTH 5 INCHES

John Kieran is best remembered as the rather homespun genius of the radio program "Information Please" which was enormously popular in the forties. Although he was a sports writer by profession, there was another side to him, and in 1947 he published a splendid book entitled "Footnotes on Nature," in which he describes the circumstances of his first real awareness of birds. Like mine, it came with a realization of ignorance. After graduating from university, he taught for a time in a rural school. In some material provided by the education department he found himself reading ". . . the White-breasted Nuthatch. This bird is known to every farm boy and girl . . . ." He had never heard of the bird, and certainly never seen one. Early the next morning he saw one walking *down* the trunk of a tree close to the porch on which he slept. On his way to school he saw four more Nuthatches and several other species new to him, and realized that he had been walking about with his eyes closed all his life.

The White-breasted Nuthatch moves, head first, down mature deciduous trees, exploring the bark with its long straight bill for insect eggs and hibernating insects. It also searches the underside of large branches, then flies to the top of another tree and starts down again. The nuthatch is somewhat similar in appearance to the chickadee and is often seen with it, especially in winter, but it lacks the black throat. The crown and nape are black, the face and underparts white. The back is bluish gray, as is the center of the short tail. The rest of the tail is black with white flecks. The voice is rapidly repeated *yank, yank.*

The White-breasted is non-migratory and is permanently resident throughout the eastern and western United States, but not in the central plains. In Canada it lives in southern British Columbia, Manitoba, and from southern Ontario to Prince Edward Island. It can be found in mature woodlands, orchards and close to houses, particularly in winter when it feeds on seeds and suet at feeding stations. It nests in tree cavities.

RED-BREASTED NUTHATCH
Sitta canadensis
LENGTH 4 INCHES

It is best to look for this bird in the upper branches of evergreen trees, among the fine twigs and cones, for the Red-breasted, unlike the White-breasted, favors coniferous forests and feeds on the seeds from the cones as well as on insect larvae hidden in the bark.

This nuthatch is smaller than the White-breasted and is distinguished, apart from the obvious difference in color of the underparts and breast, by a black line which runs from the base of the bill through the eye to the nape. There is a white line above this and, again, the crown is black. The throat is white and the underparts a distinctive rust color. The back and wings are bluish gray, the short tail black with white flecks. The call is *nyak, nyak,* higher in pitch than the White-breasted and uttered about twice per second.

The Red-breasted is more northerly, breeding to the northern limits of the spruce forests across Canada. It breeds locally in the northern States, in the Appalachians south to Tennessee, and in the west almost to the Mexican border in the mountains. It is also more migratory than the White-breasted, many birds wandering south to the Gulf Coast in winter. If it remains in winter, it comes readily to suet and sunflower seeds.

Unlike most small hole nesting birds which rely on natural cavities or those excavated by woodpeckers for their homes, the Red-breasted digs his own in a soft decaying stump or post, and for reasons known only to the nuthatch, it usually smears the rim of the nest hole with pitch or spruce gum.

Creepers
Family Certhiidae

This is one of the world's smallest bird families. There are six species, and only one, the Brown Creeper, is in North America. Creepers are limited to the northern hemisphere and most are brown, but the spectacular Wall Creeper of southern Europe has crimson wings and a slate gray back.

They have long, curved claws and bills and, like the titmice and nuthatches, feed on insects and insect eggs, which they find by probing in crevices. Unlike the nuthatch, the creeper works up a tree, not down.

BROWN CREEPER
Certhia familiaris
LENGTH 5 INCHES

Do not look for the Brown Creeper in the branches of trees, for this inconspicuous little bark-like bird prefers feeding on the trunk. It starts near the bottom, working upward in spirals as it pokes in the crevices of the bark for insect eggs and insects. When it reaches the top, it flies down on an angle to the base of another tree and begins the spiraling process all over again.

The Brown Creeper feeds in trees, in gardens and open spaces, but prefers mature forests for nesting, where the cup-like nest is built quite close to the ground in a natural crevice against the trunk. It is usually hidden under a piece of loose bark. It is known to breed in small wood lots where it requires a dead tree. It will accept either a natural cavity or woodpecker hole, and lays its eggs in the dust from the dead tree.

The Brown Creeper is a rich brown, marked with white streaks. The brown tail is rather long with stiff pointed feathers which appear to be braced against the tree. The underparts are white, the feet are large with long curved claws, and the deep probing bill is long and thin and curves downward (decurved). The song is sung only on the breeding ground, and is described as a jumble of musical long and short notes. The call is a single faint note, rather lisping and high pitched.

The breeding range extends across central Canada roughly to the 55th Parallel, except west of the Rockies where it goes somewhat farther north. In the east it breeds in southern Ontario, Quebec and the Maritimes, and as far south as Wisconsin and Massachusetts, in the Appalachians to Tennessee. Some birds are said to winter in Canada, but are seldom seen between November and March.

Winter Wren

Brown Creeper

Short-billed Marsh Wren

Long-billed Marsh Wren

House Wren

Carolina Wren

The Brown Creeper is the only North American creeper. Wrens are energetic, small brown birds with spiky upturned tails.

Wrens
Family Troglodytidae

Wrens are energetic small brown birds with spiky upturned tails which are often cocked up over the back. They are stumpy with short rounded wings and long slender bills which turn down slightly. There are ten North American species of this family of fifty-nine species, of which one member, the Winter Wren, is also found in Europe and Asia. Wrens are found in a variety of habitats from arid country to flooded marshes. All build covered nests, either in cavities and bird boxes or in the open.

HOUSE WREN
Troglodytes aedon
LENGTH 4 INCHES

This is the most common of the wrens in the northeast. Although it still nests widely in the wild, it has adapted comfortably to habitation and nests in a wide variety of situations including nesting boxes, sheds, wood piles, discarded farm machinery, old automobiles — indeed any cavity may be used. It requires a cavity with a small entrance. The nesting box hole should be exactly seven-eighths of an inch wide and should be several inches above the floor level. The nest of twigs is built flush with the entrance hole. Two, or even three broods are brought off each season with an average of about six young per nest.

House Wrens are plain brown birds with fairly long pointed bills. The back and cocked tail are finely barred with black, but this is obvious only at very close range. The undersides are pale brown and at the rump are marked with black and white bars. The song is a bubbling chatter of unmusical notes which rise in tone and then fall abruptly. During the summer this song continues for most of the day, as the birds move about searching for insects.

The habitat is varied, but most feeding is done close to the ground in brushy areas. In woodland areas it can be found in openings and around old burns. In inhabited areas it requires brush and bushes.

The summer range extends across southern Canada east to southern New Brunswick, and the northern two-thirds of the United States. The winter range is from southern Mexico to Florida.

WINTER WREN
Troglodytes troglodytes
LENGTH 3 INCHES

The smaller size and much shorter upturned tail distinguish this bird from the more common House Wren. It is somewhat redder in color, but otherwise the two species are quite similar. The Winter Wren's song is the more spectacular — it is a series of tinkling notes and trills which start high, maintain this unusual range and end in a very high trill. The performance

161

takes about seven seconds and is often repeated. It may sing from its feeding area close to the ground, but often from the highest branches of a mature tree.

The preferred habitat is in mature evergreen woodland, usually in a moist area close to water with a heavy cover of underbrush. The nest may be made under a fallen log, among the exposed roots of an upturned tree or under the eroded banks of a stream, usually in fairly remote areas.

This unobtrusive little bird may easily be overlooked when it is feeding unless it is singing. Then it can be located quite easily.

The Winter Wren is the "Jenny Wren" of Europe, and is the only wren to breed there. In North America it occurs in the west from California to the Aleutians and across central Canada to Newfoundland and the northeastern United States, south to Georgia in the mountains. It is absent from the prairies and extreme southern Ontario, except in migration, which is early. The Winter Wren often arrives on the breeding grounds before the last snow has disappeared. It winters in the southeastern United States and along the west coast.

CAROLINA WREN
Thryothorus ludovicianus
LENGTH 5 INCHES

This wren is common throughout the southeastern United States, but rare in the northeast where its range extends northward to southern Nebraska in the west, and southern Massachusetts in the east, and extreme southern Ontario, north of Lake Erie. It was first recorded to be nesting in Canada at Point Pelee in 1905. Although it has been sighted in southern Quebec and Manitoba, the breeding range has not extended beyond Toronto. Another southern wren, the Bewick's (*Thyromanes bewickii*) also appears to be extending its range northward. It has been observed periodically since 1898 in southern Ontario, but its first nest was discovered as recently as 1950.

The two birds are quite similar, both having a plain brown back and long white stripe above the eye. The Carolina, however, is noticeably larger and is browner below. The breast is cinnamon-beige, the throat white, and the short erect tail is finely barred with black. Bewick's tail, on the other hand, is longer and outlined with white and black dots.

162

The song of the Carolina is a cheerful whistle which has been appropriately described as *tea-kettle, tea-kettle, tea-kettle, tea.* It is loud and is heard throughout the year. Bewick's song is like that of the Song Sparrow, but more wiry. It starts with two or three clear notes, dropping in pitch and ends with a trill.

The Carolina nests in cavities and readily accepts bird boxes close to houses. Care should be exercised in identifying both of these wrens in the northeast, for they are rare and local. Both are common in the southern United States, Bewick's more particularly in the southwest.

LONG-BILLED MARSH WREN
Telmatodytes palustris
LENGTH 4 INCHES

The two Marsh Wrens, the Long-billed and the Short-billed, choose different habitats. The Long-billed is almost invariably found in water-covered cattail marshes, usually fairly extensive ones. They like tall coarse vegetation and build their nests from one to three feet above the water, anchored to upright bulrushes. The nest is a large ball of coarse vegetation with an entrance at the side, the center being lined with fine grass and feathers.

The male, who arrives first on the nesting ground, builds a number of dummy nests, but the female builds the nest which is used. The male is polygamous and may have two or more females nesting in adjacent territories. Long-bills are fairly late nesters, for they must wait till the cattails are quite high before nest building can begin. Despite this, and a thirteen day incubation period, they usually raise two broods of five or six young each season.

The bird is best seen as it sings in the top of the tall grass, straddling the cattails with its feet, or as it flutters stationary in the air. The song starts with a series of rasping notes followed by a rather loud twitter and ends with a whistle. It sings insistently before dawn and in the late evening, but also during the day.

This wren has a dark cap, a triangular patch of black and white lines on the back near the nape, a white stripe over the eye, white underparts, tawny flanks and brown and black barred upturned tail. The bill is long, thin and slightly down-turned. It summers across most of the northern half of the United States, the Canadian prairies, southern Ontario and Quebec, and a further small area of population is in southeastern New Brunswick close to the Nova Scotia border. Long-bills winter in the southern United States and Mexico.

SHORT-BILLED MARSH WREN
Cistothorus platensis
LENGTH 4 INCHES

This, after the Ruby-throated Hummingbird, is our smallest bird. The crown and back are dark brown with fine white streaks. Unlike the Long-billed, the Short-billed Marsh Wren lacks a white eye stripe and its bill is shorter. The throat is white as is the abdomen, the two being separated by an indistinct buffy patch across the upper breast. The typical wren tail is short and stubby.

It nests in bogs, moist meadows and sedge marshes, in areas usually dotted with alder or willow bushes, often close to cattails but not in them. The nest is built close to the ground, well concealed in a clump of grass, like a ball with the entrance at the side. Both Marsh Wrens, the Long-billed and the Short-billed, build several dummy nests for reasons unknown. This wren is not at all common, but because it prefers neighbors of its own species, we find areas of intense concentration of families, whereas equally suitable areas nearby will be neglected. It is unpredictable and may be present one year, absent the next.

Short-billed Marsh Wrens are best located by their song, for they are hard to flush, and when they do, fly only a short distance and then drop back into the grass. The song is quite unmusical — a series of dry, well spaced notes at the beginning, accelerating in frequency and dropping in pitch and ending in a trill. This species must be deliberately and patiently sought, necessitating a search of every likely marsh border.

The northeast is the extreme northern limit of the breeding range, for this species nests to southern South America. In Canada it is a summer visitor from central Saskatchewan to southern Quebec and again in southeastern New Brunswick and in the United States through most of the northeast, south to Virginia.

164

Mockingbirds and Thrashers
Family Mimidae

MIMIDAE are all long slender birds with long tails and down-curved bills. They eat insects, fruit and seeds and have an affinity for heavy thickets and shrubbery. Although many birds still nest in the wild in the tangles along streams and in second growth, others have graduated to the heavy cover provided in gardens, fence lines and hedgerows. Suitable habitat has thus greatly increased for mockingbirds and thrashers, with the growth of urban, village and farm sites.

The MIMIDAE are noted for their marvellously complicated and sometimes beautiful songs. In their names and reputations much is made of their facility to imitate the songs of other birds, but it seems likely that a part of the mimicry is a coincidence of the wide range of their voices.

The family is restricted to North and South America and there are thirty-one species in all. Of the eleven species seen in North America, three breed in the northeast.

MOCKINGBIRD
Mimus polyglottos
LENGTH 9 INCHES

The casual observer in the northeastern United States and southern Canada is unlikely to see a Mockingbird, for its range is limited to a few locations where it is resident throughout the year, and can be found in thick shrubbery with a few trees. Earl Godfrey, in his monumental study, "The Birds of Canada", reports nesting on Manitoulin Island in Lake Huron, from the north shore of Lake Erie east to Toronto, in southwestern Quebec near Montreal, at Tadoussac on the St. Lawrence River, in Nova Scotia at Debert and Halifax, and at St. John's, Newfoundland. In the United States it is common through the south and to southern Mexico, particularly in residential areas with plenty of thick shrubbery.

Mockingbirds are long, slender gray birds with an exaggeratedly long tail half the length of the bird. The upper parts are gray and the underparts are grayish white, the wings dark with two wide white bars which are seen clearly in flight. The tail is dark, the outer feathers white.

The song is splendid and is heard during all seasons. It is loud and melodious, consisting of groups of phrases which are usually repeated three times. The Brown Thrasher's song is somewhat similar, but the phrases are repeated twice. The mocker is well named, for it gives a sense of being a great mimic of other birds. It is one of the few birds which sings at night when the moon is bright. Some of its noises are grating and harsh, like the barking of a dog.

The Mockingbird is aggressive in defense of its small territory and it prefers thick tangles near streams or heavy garden cover. It sings a great deal, usually from a tree, but often from a roof or antenna, seeming to dominate other birds. It feeds on fruit, insects and seeds.

Mockingbird

Brown Thrasher

Brown Thrasher

Gray Catbird

Mockingbirds and thrashers are noted for their marvellously complicated and sometimes beautiful songs.

GRAY CATBIRD

Dumetella carolinensis
LENGTH 8 INCHES

The Catbird's name comes from its mewing call which is very much like that of a cat and, cat-like, it usually issues from a secretive tangle of shrubbery. The song, in contrast, is a series of melodious phrases, quite like that of the Mockingbird and the Brown Thrasher, but the groups of phrases are not repeated. Instead the individual melodious phrases are interspersed with discordant chatter. It is sung, like the call, from a hidden perch.

The Catbird is secretive in its habits and does most of its feeding in thickets where it also builds its nest.

Berries are the preferred food, but until the fruit is ripe, it feeds mostly on insects. Young birds are fed entirely on insects in the northern part of the breeding range which extends across most of the United States east of the Rockies with the exception of the extreme southeast. In Canada it extends from southern British Columbia, across the central prairies and western Ontario, and again east of Lake Superior through southern Ontario, Quebec, New Brunswick and Nova Scotia.

The Catbird has adapted comfortably to civilization and nests in gardens where the cover is suitably heavy and along the borders of fields and in hedges. In the wild it requires the heavy tangle along streams, or the emerging growth of burnt land. When approached, it stops singing with a squeak and starts its mewing call. It is inquisitive and responds quickly to squeaking on the back of the hand as it moves about in its protective bush.

The Catbird, like others of its family, is long and slender. It is a smaller, darker version of the Mockingbird, with a black cap and a rusty patch under the tail. The tail is long and rounded. When perching the body is parallel to the ground and the tail is held higher than the body. This gives the impression it is trying to peek out from under an obstruction.

BROWN THRASHER

Toxostoma rufum
LENGTH 10 INCHES

This large rufous colored bird is common in summer across Canada from central Alberta east to southern Quebec and in the United States from the mid-west south to Texas and throughout the east, including New England. It is unmistakable, either in flight or at rest, and is more visible than its close relative, the Catbird, because of its vivid, uncooked color, and because it often feeds on lawns like a Robin, digging into the soil with its long bill for insects.

In the air it moves awkwardly, flying in short unsteady flights from the lawn to nearby thickets, seemingly weighed down by its long broad tail which is longer than its body. It perches in an upright position with the tail hanging straight down. The upperparts are a rich brown, the underparts white heavily streaked with brown. The bill is long and down-curving.

167

The Thrasher nests in thickets but, despite its size, the nest is hard to find, for it is built in thick hedges and tangles, usually close to the ground amid thorns if possible. Away from civilization, it chooses stream sides and heavy second growth for nesting. Early in the season the Thrasher relies on insects for its diet, but changes to berries when they ripen.

The song is a delightful combination of double phrases, usually sung from a thicket or from the branch of a tree. It is extraordinarily varied and melodious, sounding like *chirrup, chirrup — I see you, I see you — pull it up, pull it up, pull it up*, and so on. The double phrases distinguish it from those of the Catbird.

Thrushes
Family Turdidae

The family TURDIDAE is a very large one — some 301 species throughout the world, and includes, in North America, the Thrushes, Bluebirds and Solitaires. There are eighteen species in North America of which seven either visit, or are permanently resident in the northeast. The Wheatear breeds in the Arctic Islands, the Yukon and extreme northern Quebec and Labrador, but winters in Europe.

All are insect eaters, concentrating on worms, grubs and caterpillars. They feed also on berries and some seeds. The young of all species, and adults of some have spotted breasts.

AMERICAN ROBIN
Turdus migratorius
LENGTH 9 INCHES

The Robin is surely the most familiar bird in North America. There is not a part of the continent which they do not visit at some time of the year with the exception of northern Alaska and the treeless eastern Arctic on both sides of northern Hudson Bay. They breed everywhere except in the extreme southern United States, and in wild areas they prefer open patches near the edge of a forest, along streams and lake shores and in other natural openings. Civilization has provided ideal habitat with shade trees for nesting and lawns and berry trees for feeding. The spraying of elms with toxic poisons affected the worms and grubs on which they feed, and killed great numbers for some years.

Pairs nest twice each season and lay about four blue eggs with each nest. The nest is usually placed on a branch of deciduous or coniferous trees from five to fifteen feet above the ground, but buildings are often used. A favorite location is against a wall where wires join a building.

A small number of Robins remain in southern Canada during the winter, but most retire southward, returning early in the spring to liven the world with their presence and their beautiful song. This consists of two and three note phrases which are loud and clear, each note on a different pitch. This song should be learned well as a comparison for the songs of other birds.

Hermit Thrush

Wood Thrush

Eastern Bluebird

American Robin

The Family Turdidae is a very large one — some 301 species — and includes, in North America, the thrushes, bluebirds, and solitaires.

The American Robin was named by early settlers in North America as a reminder of the true Robin of Europe, which also has a red breast but is much smaller and is a member of another family entirely.

The American Robin has dark upper parts, white eye ring, rufous breast and abdomen. The bill is yellow, the throat speckled white, the legs and the area under the tail are white, as is the tip of the tail. The head of the male is darker than that of the female and the breast is brighter. Young birds are similar to adults, but have pale spotted breasts. Robins tend to albinism more than other species, and pure white birds with pinkish breasts are sometimes seen.

WOOD THRUSH
Hylocichla mustelina
LENGTH 7 INCHES

The Wood Thrush is one of five species of spotted-breasted thrushes which migrate through, or summer in, the northeast. The others, described in the following pages, are the Hermit Thrush, Swainson's Thrush, Gray-cheeked Thrush and the Veery. They are either single colored or of two uniform shades of brown — rusty red and olive — but in differing combinations. It would be well to memorize the color combinations and to relate them to the song.

With the Wood Thrush the head and back are rusty brown, the wings and tail olive. The breast and belly are white and heavily spotted with dark brown, the heaviest spotting of any of this group. There is a pale eye-ring and the bill is fairly long and Robin-like. It might be confused with the Brown Thrasher, but the Thrasher's tail is much longer and it has white wing-bars.

This thrush has the most southerly range of the five species mentioned, for it is limited to Maine, southern Ontario and Quebec, and south throughout the eastern half of the United States. It winters in Mexico and Central America.

The habitat selected for nesting is in moist, mature deciduous woodland where there is heavy undergrowth. The area is usually associated with a stream or lake. In the United States this Thrush has settled in residential areas, but does not seem to have done so in Canada. It feeds close to the ground, scratching among the dead leaves for insects and grubs.

The song, which is sung close to the ground, is a beautiful flute-like series of phrases of three to five notes, with a considerable range in each phrase, and is similar to that of the Hermit Thrush. With the Wood Thrush the opening note of each phase is higher than the second and is followed by a high trill. Roger Tory Peterson has described the song as *ee-o-lay* which is apt. The alarm note is a rapid *pip, pip, pip, pip*.

HERMIT THRUSH
Hylocichla guttata
LENGTH 6 INCHES

The markings of the Hermit Thrush are the reverse of the Wood Thrush. The Hermit has a rufous or rusty brown tail and olive back and wings. The throat and breast are spotted dark brown on white, but the spots are smaller than those of the Wood Thrush. The abdomen is mostly white. This thrush, when disturbed, raises its tail slowly several times a minute.

The song which is seldom heard outside the nesting territory, is one of the most beautiful of all of our birds. It is almost bell-like and consists of phrases separated by a deliberate pause. Each phrase is similar, but the pitch varies considerably. The opening note is longer and lower in pitch than the rest.

This is very much a bird of the wilderness. It breeds in mixed and pure coniferous forest, in bogs and in areas which have been burned or logged. The Canadian range extends across the southern Yukon and Northwest Territories, British Columbia and the southern half of Ontario and Quebec throughout the Martime Provinces and south to Maryland. In the west it nests in the mountains, south to southern California, and in the east in the Appalachians. It winters in the southern half of the United States and south to Guatemala.

The Hermit Thrush is a ground nester and feeder. It scratches among the dead leaves for insects during the summer and in the autumn and winter feeds on berries.

SWAINSON'S THRUSH (formerly called the Olive-backed Thrush)
Hylocichla ustulata
LENGTH 6 INCHES

The upper parts of this thrush are uniformly olive in color, the breast is beige marked with small dark spots, and the abdomen is whitish. The face is buffy colored and there is a yellowish eye ring. It is very similar to the Gray-cheeked Thrush, but the latter lacks the eye ring and its cheeks are darker. During the nesting season there is little likelihood of confusing the two for the ranges scarcely overlap in settled areas.

The habits and habitat of the thrushes are much the same. All feed on insects during the summer and berries for the most part during the rest of the year, and all feed and nest in the lower storey of the forest. Swainson's shows a preference for spruce and fir forests in damp areas, but it is also found in mature forests. In Canada the summer range extends over most of the forested parts of the country with the exception of the central prairies. It is also absent from southern Ontario south of a line from Georgian Bay to Kingston. In the eastern United States it breeds in Maine, New Hampshire and the Appalachians. It winters in South America.

The song is less formidable than those of the Wood or Hermit Thrushes, but is still remarkably beautiful. Each phrase consists of about twelve double notes, of which the second is lower. The full phrase rises gradually in pitch, is rather gurgling and lacks a bell-like quality. There is also an abrupt *whit* as a call note.

GRAY-CHEEKED THRUSH
Hylocichla minima
LENGTH 6 INCHES

The Swainson's and Gray-cheeked Thrushes have similar drab olive upper parts and lack any of the rusty coloring of the other thrushes. The Gray-cheeked has dark spots on the white throat and breast, and the flanks are spotted with pale olive. The cheek is grayer than that of the Swainson's which is buffy, but this is not a reliable identification feature unless the bird is clearly visible in good light, which it seldom is. The Gray-cheeked lacks the buffy eye ring of the Swainson's and is the only one of our thrushes which fails to have a large-eyed look.

This is the most northerly nesting of the thrushes — from the Yukon, across the Northwest Territories, northern Quebec, Newfoundland, the northern part of Gaspé, in parts of Nova Scotia and in New York and Massachusetts. It is seen in the eastern half of North America on migration when it may be found in the woodland and roadsides. It winters in the Caribbean, southern Mexico and South America.

On the nesting ground it prefers spruce and tamarack and in the tundra uses willow and birch clumps. The song, which is not heard often on migration, is a series of notes slurring downward, the final notes somewhat higher in pitch. By contrast the Veery runs down the scale.

VEERY

Hylocichla fuscescens
LENGTH 6 INCHES

The Veery is the only spotted-breasted thrush to have uniformly rusty colored upper parts. The cheeks, flanks, and breast are pale brown with small dark spots, the throat and belly are white. The song of this bird is unique and cannot be mistaken for any other. It is quite loud and is a series of three or four rolling, descending notes which sound like *veeur, veeur, veeur*. Each note lasts about half a second and descends in pitch, each being slightly lower than the preceeding one. The song may be heard at any time of the day on the nesting ground, but is more frequent at dusk when the sky darkens with the coming of a storm or even a passing cloud. While the song is rolling, the call note is a clear whistle descending in scale and may be described *phiew*.

In common with the other thrushes, the Veery makes its living on the ground, scratching among the dead leaves for insects and feeding on wild berries and seeds. This one usually nests on the ground in second growth deciduous forest, with the heaviest concentrations close to the borders of streams and lakes.

Most thrushes respond to squeaking on the back of the hand by hopping up to a prominent perch, but it is difficult to see a Veery on the nesting ground when the cover is heavy. It is quiet in its movements, and will not show itself readily.

The summer range extends across the northern United States and southern Canada. In the west it breeds as far south as Arizona, and moves out of North America entirely to winter in South America.

EASTERN BLUEBIRD

Sialia sialis
LENGTH 6 INCHES

This is a most unthrush-like thrush both in appearance and habits. The male is bright blue above, with a vivid rusty breast and flanks and a white belly. The female is a grayish blue above with wings bluer than the head and back. Young birds are heavily spotted and resemble other thrushes more than adults.

173

While other thrushes nest on branches or on the ground, the Bluebird requires a cavity, either an old woodpecker hole, a natural cavity or a nesting box. The Bluebird is less common today because competition from the Starling and the House Sparrow, two aggressive species introduced from Europe, has restricted Bluebird nesting opportunities. Bluebird enthusiasts in North America have done much to encourage nesting by placing vast numbers of boxes in suitable areas. If the boxes have holes of less than one and a half inches in diameter, they should keep out Starlings, but will let in other competitors — the Tree Swallows and House Wrens. Bluebirds had been unknown in a certain area in the Laurentian Mountains until a man placed boxes near his country home. Within a year or two they were fully occupied.

The call note, which may be heard in flight or at rest sounds like *chur-weee* and is pleasantly musical. The song is a soft and gurgling warble, and sometimes sounds like two birds singing together.

The Eastern Bluebird is present in the northeast only in summer from southern Saskatchewan eastward to Nova Scotia and throughout the eastern United States. It prefers open country with some trees, abandoned fields, second growth and orchards. It consumes many grasshoppers, crickets and caterpillars and in winter switches to berries.

Gnatcatchers and Kinglets
Family Sylviidae

These are small drab birds with long thin bills which roam the forests with nuthatches, creepers, chickadees and titmice in search of insects and insect eggs. This is a large family comprising some 325 species living in both hemispheres, but only three appear with any certainty in the northeast. SYLVIIDAE divide unevenly into two distinct groups: the small slender gnatcatchers with long tails, and the small stubby kinglets with short tails. Both are not unlike warblers and vireos.

BLUE-GRAY GNATCATCHER
Polioptila caerulea
LENGTH 4 INCHES

This southern bird has a limited breeding range in the northeast. In Canada it is seen occasionally in southern Ontario. On migration it is sometimes seen as far east as Ottawa and in southwestern Quebec. Its normal territory is the central and southern United States where it is a common bird in summer, withdrawing in winter to the Gulf Coast and to South America.

The Gnatcatcher is usually seen from below as it moves restlessly about the tree tops, taking insects from the leaves and fluttering about as it chases them. It is best identified by its slender shape and long tail, which is white on the underside with a narrow black bar down the center. The undersides are pale bluish-gray and a large white eye ring is obvious. The

Blue-gray Gnatcatcher

Ruby-crowned Kinglet

Golden-crowned Kinglet

Water Pipit

Gnatcatchers and kinglets roam the forests with nuthatches, creepers, chickadees, and titmice in search of insects and insect eggs. The Water Pipit is seen only on migration in the northeast.

upper parts are a medium blue-gray, the flight feathers dark, and the upper part of the tail, black. There is a narrow dark line curved around the top of the bill and extending over the eye. The Blue-gray has a habit of wagging its tail (which is often cocked like a wren's) from side to side.

The song is unremarkable, but is a pleasant, thin warble, rather lisping in sound. The call note is a high pitched and rather complaining *zpee*.

The nest is usually built high in a tall tree and may be made like a saddle either across a horizontal branch or in a crotch.

GOLDEN-CROWNED KINGLET
Regulus satrapa
LENGTH 4 INCHES

Kinglets are tiny, short-tailed, puffy birds which arrive in the northeast in the spring well before the warblers. They sing on migration, and in April add to the songs of the chickadees and sparrows, bringing a welcome chatter after a silent winter.

The summer range extends from southern Alaska across Canada, excluding the central prairies and southern Ontario, and includes New England and the Appalachians. In the west, the nesting range extends south to California and Central America in mountainous areas. Some birds remain in the northeast in winter, but most move south of the Great Lakes.

Golden-crowned Kinglets are olive-green above and pale below with tiny bills, dark wings and tails. Males have an orange central crown with a yellow band on each side, while the female's crown is entirely yellow. Both sexes have a broad white stripe over the eye with a black stripe above it. They lack the distinctive eye-ring of the Ruby-crowned Kinglet.

Kinglets feed on insects and insect eggs. Early in the season they rely on eggs which they find in the needles and bark of coniferous trees. Later on they become flycatchers, flitting out from the trees to capture passing insects, characteristically flicking their wings as they move about the branches. Although they nest only high up in coniferous trees, they like to settle in an area with a mixture of deciduous trees. During migration they may be found in bushes and trees of all kinds.

The call note which is heard all year is a high, wiry *see, see, see*. The song is similar, but rises in pitch and ends in lively unmusical chatter.

176

RUBY-CROWNED KINGLET
Regulus calendula
LENGTH 4 INCHES

This is a tiny bird, olive colored above, pale gray below, with two white wing bars. The distinguishing feature is a distinct white eye-ring which gives the bird a rather wide-eyed appearance. The male has a ruby colored crown which is usually totally concealed, sometimes is partially evident but rarely is seen fully erect. When so seen in sunlight it is one of the rare treats of patient observation, for it is quite startling.

The habitat is similar to that of the Golden-crowned Kinglet, coniferous forest or mixed forest edges, muskegs with sparse tree cover and woodlots. It is an early spring arrival and is easily identified by its remarkable song which is loud and complicated for such a small bird. It starts with a series of *tee, tee, tee,* then drops in pitch to a *chew, chew, chew,* and ends with a tinkling chatter of rapid notes in groups of three. The song is somewhat similar to that of the Winter Wren, but is not as elaborate or prolonged.

The range in summer extends across Canada to northern Maine, with the exception of southern Ontario and southwestern Quebec south of the St. Lawrence River. In the west it breeds as far south as Arizona and winters in the southern half of the United States and south to Guatemala. On migration it is common in bushes and trees of all kinds, but does most of its feeding in conifers. Insects make up most of its diet but in winter it takes some seeds.

Pipits
Family Motacillidae

Pipits are long slender birds with long tails and straight thin bills which live almost entirely on the ground in open places, usually associated with water. They walk, rather than hop, and wag their tails up and down.

Pipits, and the more colorful wagtails which are common in Europe, belong to the same family. In the northeast we are only likely to see the Water Pipit, and then on migration, for it breeds across the far north and winters in the southern United States. Sprague's Pipit summers in the prairies and migrates south to the southern United States and Mexico. Two wagtails nest in North America, but migrate to Europe and Asia from the Arctic, the White Wagtail in Greenland and Alaska and the Yellow Wagtail in Alaska and the Yukon.

WATER PIPIT (also called American Pipit)
Anthus spinoletta
LENGTH 6 INCHES

The pipit is seen only on migration in eastern Canada and the northeastern United States when it passes through in large flocks, sometimes numbering thousands.

177

Pipits are best identified in flight by their slender appearance and by the white feathers on the outside of the tail. The flight is swift and erratic with the birds continually changing position, giving the appearance of being blown about by the wind. The call on migration is a sharp *tsip, ip, tsip, ip,* especially when the bird flushes.

On migration and in winter they feed on mud flats, dunes, fields with low vegetation and on wet plowed land. They nest close to or under rocks, always on the ground. They seldom perch in a tree, only occasionally to sing. The song given from the ground, or in flight, is tinkling and sibilant, but rather weak.

Pipits are slim birds with long tails which wag up and down while at rest. The top of the head and back are grayish brown, the wings somewhat darker, the tail dark with white outer feathers. The undersides are pale brown with narrow dark streaks. There is a pale line above the eye and a dark cheek patch. The tail wagging and white tail feathers are the things to look for.

The Pipit nests in the north. Its far-flung breeding range includes the Arctic Islands, the treeless eastern Northwest Territories, extreme northern Ontario, Quebec and Labrador and Newfoundland. In the west it chooses alpine locations, usually above the tree line from Alaska to Arizona. The wintering areas are in the southern United States and Central America.

Waxwings
Family Bombycillidae

This is a small family of birds of the northern hemisphere. Of the eight species, only two are resident in North America, the Bohemian Waxwing in the northwest, and the Cedar Waxwing across the center of the continent. Waxwings are prominently crested and finely masked across the

Bohemian Waxwings

Bohemian Waxwing

Cedar Waxwings

Top: Bohemian Waxwings feeding. Above: Cedar Waxwings — young, female, and male.

eyes. The wings are long and pointed with wax-like red tips on the secondary feathers. The tips look as if they had been dipped in colored wax. Both species are noted for their sleek plumage and silky appearance. The bills are short and wide, hooking downward at the tip.

Waxwings eat fruit and berries and migrate depending on the berry crop. They are late nesters, using thistledown in the nest. They are usually seen in flocks of varying sizes but, unlike the Starlings whose flocks and flight silhouettes they resemble, they are quiet almost covert birds which settle silently in a tree without one being aware that they have moved in. They feed amiably without bickering, unlike many other flocking birds.

CEDAR WAXWING
Bombycilla cedrorum
LENGTH 6 INCHES

The Cedar Waxwing is the height of elegance with its erect posture, high crest and sleek plumage peering at the world through a hard-edge upslanting black eye mask. The throat is black and there is a bright yellow tip to the tail and, although there is quite a range of colors in the rest of the feathers, they are so well blended in the sleek plumage that the overall look is of light brown. The crest and back are cinnamon brown fusing to gray on the tail. The chest is paler blending to yellow on the belly and to white under the tail. The wings are dark gray without bars. Often the waxy tips of some of the secondary feathers, which form a bright red fleck half-way down the wing, are not clearly visible. The black face mask is outlined in white. The whole gives a sleek, unruffled appearance.

Waxwings feed on berries, dried in winter and ripe in summer, and are often a menace to small berry crops such as cherries. They will take flying insects in summer, especially to feed their young. For most of the year they travel in tight flocks of up to one hundred birds, often as late as August when they become territorial for a period while nesting. They nest late — we have seen young in the nest at the end of August. When in flocks they remain close together, often alighting as one bird in the same tree before feeding. They prefer fairly open woodland, orchards and tree borders of lawns and fields.

They nest in both coniferous and deciduous trees and in bushes, building loose nests of twigs and grass haphazardly lined with down.

Cedar Waxwings range erratically across Canada to the 60th Parallel and throughout the United States from California to Georgia. Some birds remain in the northeast in winter, but most wander south through the United States as far as Panama.

The Bohemian Waxwing is larger but quite similar to the Cedar Waxwing. It has white patches on the wings and the patch under the tail is rust colored rather than white. The Bohemian is a western bird which sometimes wanders eastward in flocks during the winter. Every flock of Waxwings seen in winter is worth checking carefully to see if the birds are Bohemians.

180

Shrikes
Family Laniidae

Of the some seventy-four species of shrikes extant in the world (Europe, Africa, Asia and Malaysia), only two are present in North America.

Shrikes are predators, killing and feeding on anything from insects to rodents to small birds, but their impact on other birds is quite small, for there are so few shrikes. The title "butcher bird" is probably unjustified for they consume most of what they kill, but leave a good many carcasses rotting on thorns. They hunt from perches or close to the ground, flying with a fast wing beat, then swooping upward to another perch. They have comparatively weak claws and legs and are unable to grasp their prey for eating; to compensate, they have developed the habit of impaling the bodies on thorns and barbed wire. They sometimes leave the carcasses and when one sees them, it is good evidence that a shrike is nearby.

NORTHERN SHRIKE
Lanius excubitor
LENGTH 8 INCHES

This is the larger and paler of our two shrikes and will be seen, if at all, only in winter in southern Canada and in the northern United States. It is a northern bird and the breeding area extends across Europe and Asia and in North America from Alaska across the Northwest Territories to northern Quebec, in areas where there are trees. It wanders south in winters when the mouse and lemming populations are low, often as far as California and Virginia. It is one of our rare birds and the chances of seeing it are not very high. It feeds entirely on insects, small rodents and birds.

The Northern Shrike is a large-headed bird, about the size of a Robin, pale gray on the top of the head, neck and back and turning white on the rump. The bill is sturdy and hooked down at the tip. A black mask runs through the eye and is outlined in white. The throat is white, the breast pale gray and finely barred with white, the wings dark with white spots which are obvious when the bird flies. The tail is black, but is outlined with white. Juveniles have similar markings to mature birds, but are brown in color.

It is reported that this shrike sings late in the winter, before migrating north to its breeding ground, and that the song consists of a variety of squeaks, mews and melodious trills, warbles and whistles. The call is a harsh scream.

The hunting habits are described in the introduction to this section. This shrike will almost invariably be found in a prominent observation point at the very top of a tree or pole. From such a perch the bird drops low toward the ground, flying swiftly to pounce on its prey.

Loggerhead Shrike

Common Starling

Solitary Vireo

Red-eyed Vireo

Representative members of the shrike, starling, and vireo families. Note starlings in flight.

LOGGERHEAD SHRIKE
Lanius ludovicianus
LENGTH 7 INCHES

The Loggerhead is similar to the Northern Shrike but smaller and darker, the breast is unbarred and quite white. While not as rare as the Northern, it is still an uncommon bird. A shrike seen from late spring till late autumn in the United States or in southern Canada is almost certain to be a Loggerhead. It breeds across the central prairies, southern Ontario, Quebec, parts of the Maritimes and through the United States, and winters from the central United States south through Mexico.

In summer we see this shrike in fairly open brushy country having suitable high perches on trees or poles. They sometimes hover in one spot while hunting, but usually wait patiently on a high perch watching the ground for larger insects, frogs, mice and small birds.

Both shrikes have the weak legs and feet of perching birds. Although they are predators, they do not have the talons of hawks.

Starlings
Family Sturnidae

Starlings are not native to the western hemisphere. Two species were introduced about 1890, the Common Starling from Europe, which has spread so widely, and the Crested Myna, and Asian species located in the Vancouver area.

The Myna has maintained a small population of 2,000 to 3,000 birds in this area, but the Common Starling has flourished to pest proportions all over North America, except the far north.

COMMON STARLING
Sturnus vulgaris
LENGTH 6 INCHES

The scientific name VULGARIS describes this thoroughly unpleasant bird small numbers of which were introduced from Europe to New York City in 1890. Since then it has spread gradually throughout the continent, millions of birds now pestering every community and rural area. The starling first reached Canada at Niagara Falls in 1914 and had spread to British Columbia by 1945.

They are beneficial birds to the extent that they feed mostly on beetles, weevils, grasshoppers and other insects which they take on the ground, but when they descend in flocks on an orchard, they are harmful to the berry crops. Their principal impact is on the status of native birds for Common Starlings, like House Wrens, Martins, Tree Swallows, Bluebirds and many others, require nesting cavities. They favor old woodpecker holes, although they will use cavities in buildings and cliffs. The starling

183

is an early nester and takes the suitable locations before other birds arrive in the spring. Later nesting starlings frequently compete with those species already established, and eat their eggs while dislodging them.

This is a dark ugly bird with a long bill, yellow in summer and dark in winter, a flat head and very short tail. It is often mistaken for the equally offensive Grackle, which is also dark, but long-tailed. It is speckled dark brown in winter, but in spring takes on a dark blue sheen on the breast and green on the head. The wings and back remain brown. They have short legs and waddle about rather than walk.

When not nesting, starlings are extremely gregarious, feeding by day on lawns, fields, dumps, marshy places and shores, and flocking by night to a variety of roosts, depending on the season. They are non-migratory and congregate in trees until the leaves have fallen, then in marshes, and later around warm buildings, usually at the center of urban areas. On a winter evening, it is a remarkable sight to see great numbers converging in flocks on the city center. On their way, they stop briefly at high points.

Vireos
Family Vireonidae

This family of forty-two species, all living only in the western hemisphere, is essentially tropical. Twelve species reach North America in summer and, of these, only five appear in the northeast.

Vireos are small rather drab birds of the woodlands which live entirely in trees and bushes, taking their insect diet either on the wing or by foraging on the undersides of leaves. They can easily be confused with some of the warblers because of a similarity in coloring with the females, and with the autumn coloring of both sexes; but a close look distinguishes the vireos readily, for their bills are thicker and less pointed. In addition, they have a heavy headed appearance and, when seen in a tree, are flat from head to tail with little curve at the nape. When perching the head is usually lower than the tail, as if always poised for flight.

The movements of vireos are slower and more deliberate than those of the warblers which are in a state of constant motion.

YELLOW-THROATED VIREO
Vireo flavifrons
LENGTH 5 INCHES

The Yellow-throated Vireo may easily be confused with the Pine Warbler, for both have a yellow throat and breast, white belly, two large white wing bars on dark brown wings and an olive head and neck. The vireo, however, shows a gray rump, a much heavier bill and a yellow line from the base of the top of the bill to, and curling around, the eye. The eyestripe on the Pine Warbler goes almost to the back of the head.

The Yellow-throated Vireo is found in mature deciduous woodlands where it forages half-hidden among the upper leaves for insects. It prefers to be near water, but also uses residential areas and orchards where there is little undergrowth. The movements are slow and deliberate.

This vireo can best be located by its song which is like that of the Red-eyed Vireo, but slower and more musical. The phrases, which are slurring and rise at the end, are uttered about two seconds apart, while that of the Red-eyed is almost constant.

In Canada it nests locally in southern Manitoba and from southern Ontario east to southwestern Quebec, in the United States throughout the east. The nest, which hangs from the fork of a tree, is beautifully made, using much spider web and moss. It is usually about ten feet from the ground.

Wintering is from Mexico, across South America to Venezuela.

SOLITARY VIREO (formerly Blue-headed Vireo)
Vireo solitarius
LENGTH 5 INCHES

For many years this bird was known as the Blue-headed Vireo and a number of field guides, including early editions of Roger Tory Peterson and the Audubon Guides, use this name. To avoid such confusion throughout this book, we have also used the scientific names, in this case *Vireo solitarius*.

This common vireo occurs across Canada from British Columbia and the Mackenzie Valley to southern Newfoundland, and across the northern United States. In the west it breeds in the mountains south to Central America and in the east to Georgia.

It is the most attractive of the vireos with its blue-gray head, heavy bill, white undersides, olive back and tail, two white wing bars and yellowish-olive flanks. There is a prominent white eye-ring which extends around the base of the top of the bill. The song is not unlike that of the Red-eyed Vireo, but more musical and not as frequent. The notes are slurred and whistling, ending on a rising pitch. The call is rasping and harsh.

The nest is built in coniferous trees, like most vireos, usually from five to ten feet up in a fork near the end of a branch. I once inadvertently cut down a branch with a nest containing eggs. After I had replaced the eggs and tied the branch carefully to the one above, the mother bird returned and hatched her brood. Solitaires are quite fearless and feed close to the observer.

185

RED-EYED VIREO
Vireo olivaceus
LENGTH 5 INCHES

Probably the most abundant summer bird in North America, this species breeds over the whole of the continent to the limit of the trees, with the exception of Alaska, the Yukon, the southwestern United States and New-foundland. Wherever there are trees, the Red-eyed can be heard singing in the summer, and it has been estimated that there may be one pair for each acre of deciduous forest in their range. The song, while not unpleasant, can become tedious: it sings as it feeds, non-stop. It is rather robin-like with each phrase separated by a distinct pause, the song being repeated thirty or forty times a minute. The call note is a harsh *quee*.

As with other vireos, the line from head to tail is almost straight. The bright red iris of the eye, under a wide white eye-stripe, can be seen at a reasonable distance through binoculars. The head is gray-capped, the cap bordered in black above the white stripe, the cheek-patch buffy. The bill is heavy, unlike the needle-like bills of the warblers. The back is olive and unstreaked, the wings and tail darker, the undersides white and the flanks tinged with pale olive.

The Red-eyed Vireo feeds in the upper canopy of deciduous trees, shrubbery, alders and willow. The cup-shaped nest is usually five to ten feet from the ground, but may be higher. It is built in the fork of a branch and, like all vireo nests, hangs from its edges.

In the autumn most birds have left the northeast for South America by mid-September, but stragglers are sometimes seen until early November.

PHILADELPHIA VIREO
Vireo philadelphicus
LENGTH 5 INCHES

This vireo can best be described by the things it does not have, for it lacks the usual distinguishing features — wing-bars, eye-ring, streaks, distinctive markings. With its drab relative, the Warbling Vireo, the Philadelphia is probably our least conspicuous bird. The undersides are pale yellow in most individuals, although there is considerable variation, the upper-parts

186

are olive-green with a tinge of gray, there is a whitish streak above the eye and a narrow dark line through the eye. Even the song is not much help for it is similar to that of the Red-eyed Vireo, but the pitch is higher and the pauses between the phrases are longer.

The only apparent individuality is in the behavior, as the Philadelphia is more active than other vireos, which tend to be sluggish. It flutters a good deal when taking insects and frequently flies to capture them on the wing. It also feeds on fruit and berries in the autumn.

The nesting range of this uncommon vireo extends from Alberta to southwestern Newfoundland, but not Nova Scotia and includes a number of northern States. The nest is almost invariably built in a deciduous tree above ten feet from the ground, although it chooses a wide range of habitat including mixed forest, burnt lands, aspen stands and alder.

In the autumn it migrates south through the eastern United States to Central America.

WARBLING VIREO
Vireo gilvus
LENGTH 5 INCHES

The Warbling Vireo is drab, the dullest of all the North American birds. It is pale gray above and paler below, the wings being somewhat darker. The only distinguishing feature is an indistinct whitish line above the eye and the heavy bill. The song is quite unlike that of the other vireos, being a pleasant warble lasting about three seconds, and ending in a higher pitch than the rest, similar to that of the Purple Finch, but huskier.

The nesting range covers most of southern Canada except the Maritimes. It has been seen in New Brunswick and Nova Scotia, but is not known to breed there. Nesting occurs in all of the United States except the extreme southeast. The nest is built in the upper branches of deciduous trees, usually in open woodland. It also uses orchards and frequently urban areas.

The winter range extends from Mexico to Central America.

Wood Warblers
Family Parulidae

The family of Wood Warblers (PARULIDAE) lives exclusivly in the Western Hemisphere, and differs greatly from the rather drab warblers of Europe and Asia (MUSCICAPIDAE). Wood Warblers are nervous little birds, generally brightly colored with narrow pointed bills. They are chiefly insectivorous, but a number of species can survive for a considerable time on seeds and fruit in cold weather when insects are not available. Most insects are taken from the leaves of the trees in which they feed or from the ground, and on occasion most species will take some flying insects as well.

In almost all species the male and female differ, the male being more dramatic in its brightly colored markings. All moult after nesting and the new feathers are invariably duller and in some cases markedly different

Yellow-rumped Warbler

Tennessee Warbler

American Redstart

Yellow Warbler

Black and White Warbler

Common Yellowthroat

Yellow-breasted Chat

Ovenbird

Wood Warblers are nervous little birds of the forests, generally brightly colored. The male has more dramatic, brighter markings.

188

from the breeding plumage. Most species, especially those which feed in the leaves, are vivacious fluttering birds, those which feed on the ground or on the branches are less so.

There are 115 species of warblers present at some time of the year in North America, of which forty visit Canada in summer. Of these, twenty-seven appear regularly east of the Manitoba border, and are present in the northeastern States.

Many of the species described occur in inhabited areas only briefly on migration, sometimes only for a few days. The peak of northern migration in southern Canada is mid-May. In some particularly good viewing areas there are usually more watchers than birds on the mid-May weekend.

BLACK AND WHITE WARBLER
Mniotilta varia
LENGTH 5 INCHES

Most warblers arrive in the northeast with a rush in mid-May, but this one, because of its feeding habits, usually arrives a month earlier and stays longer in the autumn. While others rely on insects which depend on foliage, the Black and White forages in crevices in the bark of the trunks and large limbs of deciduous trees for its food. Like the nuthatches and the Brown Creeper, it moves slowly and deliberately over the bark searching every cranny for insects.

The Black and White is quite easy to identify in both spring and autumn for, unlike most warblers, its appearance does not change much with the seasons. It is the most clearly striped of all the warblers — all black and white except for the abdomen which is unmarked white. The head is heavily striped, white in the center of the crown, flanked by black, a white stripe through the eye and black cheeks. The throat is black and the back and wings are boldly striped as is the breast. The female is similar but lacks the black cheek patches, black throat and heavy breast stripes. The Blackpoll Warbler is somewhat similar but the top of the head is solidly black and the back is olive and black.

The voice is variable, but the most common song is a thin and wiry *weezee* repeated about seven times.

The breeding range extends across Canada from central British Columbia to the Maritimes and throughout the eastern United States, south to the Gulf States.

TENNESSEE WARBLER
Vermivora peregrina
LENGTH 4¼ INCHES

As with many other bird species, the name of the Tennessee Warbler has little to do with its location or origin. In this case the bird was first discovered in that state by Alexander Wilson, the great 19th century naturalist, in 1832. This species is now more common than in the past, perhaps because of the clearing of the forests, as it prefers open and second growth for nesting. Audubon saw only three of these birds in his many years of travel and careful observation in the 19th century.

The Tennessee is a plain, unstreaked warbler, plain white below and olive green on back, wings and tail. There are no wing bars. The crown is gray and there is a white stripe above the eye. The bill is long and needle-like. In the autumn both sexes and juveniles are similarly bright olive-green above, but paler below. The Tennessee is similar in spring to Red-eyed and Warbling Vireos, but the movements differ. The Tennessee is warbler-like and moves about nervously, while the vireos are less active.

The breeding area covers almost all of Canada and New England with the exception of the northern Northwest Territories, the southern prairies and northern Quebec. Migration is through the eastern States to Central and South America.

The song is loud for a warbler and is in two parts, the first a series of about six *teezips* followed by a rapid succession of *zits* getting louder towards the end. In the nesting area the song is repeated time after time. The nest is made on the ground concealed from above by dead vegetation, often in boggy areas of sphagnum.

ORANGE-CROWNED WARBLER
Vermivora celata
LENGTH 4¼ INCHES

Alexander Sprunt (Warblers of America — Chapter II) says, "the principal field mark of the Orange-crowned Warbler is that it does not have any". Indeed, even the name is confusing for the crown patch, when it can be seen at all, is not orange but a dull rust color. The head, back and tail are a uniform drab olive green, the wings somewhat darker. The breast and abdomen are lighter and have pale gray stripes which are only visible in a good light. There is a yellowish stripe above the eye. The song is a trill, rather like that of the Chipping Sparrow, but more musical. It starts slowly, builds in pitch and fades in volume towards the end.

In the east, the Orange-crown breeds in second growth and brushy deciduous woods and shrubbery in northern Ontario and central Quebec. It is far more common in the west where it breeds from Alaska south to Mexico. In most of the northeast it is seen only in migration and in the autumn is difficult to identify. It winters in the extreme southern United States, Mexico and Central America.

NASHVILLE WARBLER
Vermivora ruficapilla
LENGTH 4 INCHES

The Latin name for the Nashville, *Ruficapilla,* or red cap, describes a feature of this warbler which is less obvious than its white eye-ring, for the cap is seldom seen unless one can see the top of the head. The throat and underparts are unstreaked yellow, the head grayish, the back, wings and tail are olive gray. In its autumn coloring this warbler closely resembles several of the unstreaked members of the warbler family. When one catches a glimpse of fall warblers moving about nervously in the trees there is a great temptation to make convenient judgments of identification. This species then closely resembles the Connecticut (which has a gray throat), the Mourning (also with a gray throat), the Wilson's (no eye-ring and more yellow on the back), the Tennessee (a pale wing-bar and eye-stripe) and the Black-throated Blue (a tiny white patch on the wing). Altogether, autumn warblers are confusing unless seen in comparison in a series of good colored drawings, which does not help much when one gets a look through the binoculars for a second or two.

In the spring the song is in two parts, the first a series of *see-it, see-it, see-it,* followed by a more rapid *si, si, si, si.* It arrives with the early warblers on migration and settles in two quite different habitats for breeding. In the more primitive areas it chooses a location near bogs with a growth of coniferous and suitable ground cover. In more settled areas it has adapted to the drier environment of young forests growing up after cutting.

The eastern race breeds from Manitoba east to the Maritimes and south to Virginia. The western race, which is separated in breeding range, nests from southern British Columbia to California.

NORTHERN PARULA WARBLER
Parula americana
LENGTH 4 INCHES

The name Parula, which means little titmouse, describes the actions of this lovely little warbler. It has the habits of a creeper as it moves about in a deliberate and purposeful way in the hanging moss which is its home. During the summer the explosive song is the first thing which attracts attention. It is a buzzing trill which rises in pitch and, as Peterson says, "snaps over at the top" sounding like *seeeee-wip.*

The Parula requires hanging moss for its nest which it builds in a hollow in the mass of lichen. In Canada and the northern States it uses usnea lichen which is also called old man's beard. In the south it uses Spanish moss, which hangs from live oaks. Where moss is not available it will settle for a dense mass of hemlock or spruce, usually quite high in the tree.

The Parula is a bluish warbler with a yellow throat and breast and a white abdomen. The head and neck are blue and there is a white eye-ring. In the center of the back there is a patch of olive green in the form of a saddle which extends in a "V" over the wings. The lower back is blue, as are the wings which display two prominent white bars. Across the throat is a blackish necklace with a line of red below. The female is paler and similarly marked, but it lacks the necklace.

The breeding range in the north extends from central Manitoba east throughout the Maritimes with the exception of Newfoundland. In the

United States it breeds throughout the east near swamps, ponds and streams or other areas where hanging moss is present. It winters in Central America and the Caribbean.

YELLOW WARBLER
Dendroica petechia
LENGTH 4 INCHES

This common warbler, together with the Goldfinch, is often called a wild "canary" by the inexperienced, but the canary is a European bird and is not present in North America.

This is the most yellow of all our birds and, at first glance, appears to be entirely so. In fact, the back is somewhat olive and the wings have dark feathers with yellow bars. The male has reddish streaks on the yellow breast and abdomen. The female is more olive and duskier than the male, and only sometimes shows traces of breast streaks. There are several races, or sub-species of Yellow Warblers, all with great variation of coloring. Some, particularly the western birds, have brown or even rufous heads.

The breeding range covers almost the whole of North America with the exception of the eastern Arctic and extreme northern Quebec. In natural areas it prefers alder and willow thickets along streams and beside ponds, but it has adapted to civilization and is a common nester in gardens and orchards.

Cowbirds, which never make their own nests but lay their eggs in the nests of other small birds, regularly victimize the Yellow Warbler. In this event the Yellow Warbler often builds a floor over the unwanted egg and lays more of its own. Multi-storied nests with as many as six floors have been recorded, illustrating the persistence of this species. Other warblers are not so determined and in summer one frequently sees them feeding a Cowbird much larger than themselves.

The song varies considerably in different parts of the range, but everywhere is musical and high pitched. There are a series of *sweets* followed by a number of shorter notes in a lower pitch.

MAGNOLIA WARBLER
Dendroica magnolia
LENGTH 4¼ INCHES

The yellow throat and the broad white band across the tail are the best identification points for this warbler as both features are dominant in spring and autumn coloring. The head and neck are gray, there is a clear yellow spot at the base of the tail, the wings have a large white spot, the throat is yellow, the breast and abdomen yellow with black streaks.

This bird feeds low enough to be seen clearly. It is also quite tame as it moves about in young conifers in which it nests. It is found in wet second growth forests, in clearings, along streams and at pond edges. Forest roads provide sufficient clear area and nests are found there in small spruce and hemlock.

Nesting range extends from central British Columbia, north to the Mackenzie River and east through the northern prairies, south of James Bay, central Quebec and the Maritime Provinces. In the United States the range extends across the northern States east from Minnesota and south to Virginia in the mountains.

The song is short and distinct, consisting of three double phrases and a final one — either dropping or rising in pitch — *wissa wissa wissa witsy* —the whole somewhat suggestive of the first bar of the William Tell Overture. The song is similar to that of the Yellow Warbler, but the latter is unlikely to be heard in evergreen forest.

In the autumn the Magnolia migrates south through the United States but does not stop. Its wintering area is in Mexico, Central America and the West Indies.

CAPE MAY WARBLER
Dendroica tigrina
LENGTH 4¼ INCHES

Alexander Wilson, the great 19th century naturalist, named this warbler in 1831 from a specimen collected on the eastern seaboard at Cape May in 1811. Wilson never saw one alive and the bird was not seen again at Cape May for over a hundred years. This is truly a bird of the conifers for it requires a fairly open forest with a good number of tall trees reaching through the canopy for nesting and singing. The nest is built in the clumps at the very top of a tall tree and the bird can usually be seen only from a distance. It feeds mostly on insects caught in the air, but does descend to lower levels in search of larvae.

This is an uncommon warbler, especially in the west, for its main breeding area is east of Ontario. During periods of spruce budworm infestation, significant numbers may concentrate in the affected area. This is unfortunate, for heavy spraying of such an area can be catastrophic for the Cape May population.

This is perhaps the handsomest of warblers although not the most gaudy. The distinguishing feature of the male is a chestnut colored triangular patch on the cheek which can be seen at some distance. The top of the head is dark, the back mottled gray and yellow, the wings dark with a large white patch. There is a yellow patch on the rump similar to the Yellow-rumped and Magnolia. The throat and lower face, below the chestnut patch, are yellow and the breast and abdomen are yellow streaked with black.

The song is a series of weak, rapid notes in the same pitch.

The breeding range extends across Canada from the Mackenzie River to the Maritimes, and in the northern States from North Dakota east to New England. It migrates through the east to the West Indies.

BLACK-THROATED BLUE WARBLER
Dendroica caerulescens
LENGTH 4½ INCHES

Its name aptly describes this elegant and immaculate warbler. The top of the head, neck and back are a uniform grayish blue, the tail is dark and fanned. The face and throat are black with a black line continuing along the flank, the breast and belly are pure white. The female is rather drab dark olive on top and paler below, with a white eye-stripe. A key distinguishing feature of both sexes is a white spot on the lower part of the wing.

On migration the Black-throated Blue is common and unusually tame as it travels with other warbler species. It may then be found in any habitat and seems quite at home in gardens and parks. For breeding it requires second growth deciduous woodland with plenty of ground cover in the form of young trees. It can be found usually, but not invariably, on dry forested hillsides. The nest is built close to the ground in a small tree or bush, making it vulnerable to chipmunks and predatory birds. The fluttering of the adult birds in defence also tends to attract predators.

The song is quite distinctive and worth learning. It consists of loose, almost lazy *swee, swee, swee, swee, swee-a* with the last note rising in inflection.

The breeding range is slightly more limited than most warblers. It extends from western Ontario across central Quebec and the Maritimes, but not Newfoundland, and in the United States east from Minnesota to New England and south in the Appalachians to northern Georgia. Migration is through the eastern States to the West Indies.

YELLOW-RUMPED WARBLER
(name changed from Myrtle Warbler in 1973)
Dendroica coronata
LENGTH 5 INCHES

The Yellow-rumped was originally, and appropriately, given this name by Audubon, although it is now best known by the name of Myrtle, which it bore for more than a hundred years. It winters farther north than any other warbler, as far as Maine and Nova Scotia, where it feeds on wax myrtle and bayberry when insects are not available. It is also the most abundant species, in winter congregating in great numbers on beaches and dunes and in thickets feeding on various seeds.

It is the only bird with a yellow rump and a white throat. The crown is yellow, the face black, the back and wings bluish with two white wing bars and the belly is white. There is a large yellow patch on either side of

194

the breast. The female is similar, but brown where the male is blue. The tips of the tail feathers are white which is apparent when the bird flies. The Yellow-rumped is very active and much like a butterfly as it flies about.

In Canada the breeding range covers the whole country with the exception of southern British Columbia, the eastern Arctic and extreme northern Quebec. In the United States it is present in the northeast from Minnesota eastward. Nesting is in coniferous forests at the edge of clearings and along streams.

The song during migration northward and during the nesting season is a mixed jumble of weak notes which may either rise or fall at the end. While the song is not particularly lovely, it is a pleasant association with this busy bird.

BLACK-THROATED GREEN WARBLER
Dendroica virens
LENGTH 4¼ INCHES

In the coniferous forests of Canada east of the Rockies, in New England and in the mountains south to Georgia, this warbler is more often heard than seen. The distinctive song with its *zee, zee, zee, zee, zur, zee,* can be heard on any lazy summer day. The second to last note is lower than the rest, the whole repeated several times a minute. While it is a bird which does most of its searching for insects high in the trees, it sometimes feeds near the ground. Curiosity and a tame nature makes it respond well to squeaking by the observer, and it will come quite close when called. It is relatively common and, on migration, can be found in woodlands and shrubbery.

The Black-throated Green is a very handsome bird, the most distinctive feature of both sexes, besides the black throat, being a large triangular yellow patch on the face and neck. The top of the head is grayish green, the back greenish, usually mottled with black spots, the belly white and the wings dark with two white bars. The outer tail feathers show some white. The female is similarly marked, but paler.

Nesting usually takes place in a coniferous tree at any elevation, but an area which is interspersed with aspen and birch is preferred. A second growth forest is ideal, usually on dry ground.

Migration takes place on a broad front throughout the eastern United States and the winter is spent from northern Mexico, south through Central America and in the West Indies.

BLACKBURNIAN WARBLER
Dendroica fusca
LENGTH 4¼ INCHES

This is my favorite warbler, if not my favorite bird. My first sight of it, in the very early morning in the Laurentian Mountains, in the first rays of the sun, is unforgettable. The throat, which is brilliant orange fusing to yellow below the eye, is suggestive of molten steel. Much of the upper parts are black. This would indicate that the bird's name emerges from its distinguishing features, but not so; it was named for a Mrs. Blackburn, an English ornithologist of the 19th century, to whom a skin was sent and who described the bird.

With the exception of a tiny yellow spot on top, the head, and most of the back are black. The cheeks are black, with a yellow eye-stripe above, descending in a jagged line at the sides of the neck. The throat is orange, the breast and abdomen white, the wings and tail black, with a large white patch on the wings. There are black streaks on the flanks. The female is similar, but paler in color.

The song, which is usually heard from the top of a tall tree, is a wiry series of high pitched *zips* followed by a *zeeeee*.

The breeding range extends from central Saskatchewan, east to James Bay and through the Maritime Provinces, excluding Newfoundland, and south through New England and the Appalachians to Georgia. In winter its range extends from the Yucatan Peninsula to Peru.

Nesting is in coniferous forests, usually high in a tree and well out towards the end of a branch.

CHESTNUT-SIDED WARBLER
Dendroica pensylvanica
LENGTH 4¼ INCHES

In the early 19th century the Chestnut-sided was rare and Audubon saw only one. Its current prevalence is an example of how human interference can encourage a population explosion. Land clearance and the subsequent regrowth of bushes and saplings provide the ideal habitat for this bird and, when the emerging forest becomes too dense, it will disappear. In earlier times, fire was the only agent which created suitable conditions for nesting, today lumbering interests do the job.

This bird is noted for the remarkable narrow chestnut colored streak which curves from the side of the neck, back below the wing on an otherwise white throat, breast and belly. A black line extends from the bill to the back of the head curving downward from the eye to meet the chestnut line on the side. The top of the head is yellow, fusing to grayish yellow on the neck and back. The wings are brown, marked with two white bars, and the tail is dark with showings of white on the outer feathers. The female has similar markings but is paler, and the chestnut flank streak is somewhat jagged.

196

The voice — it can scarcely be described as a song — is an emphatic, unmistakable, and often repeated: "Pleased to see you Miss Beecher". The bird is tame and responds quickly to squeaking.

Nesting is in a shrub or small tree, quite close to the ground, from the central Canadian prairies eastward to the Maritimes and New England, but not in Newfoundland, and south of the Great Lakes to Georgia in the mountains. Wintering is in Central America.

BAY-BREASTED WARBLER

Dendroica castanea
LENGTH 5 INCHES

This is probably the most exciting of the warblers for the male, especially in breeding plumage, is extraordinarily handsome. The chestnut coloring is dominant on the top of the head, throat and along the side of the neck and flank. The coloring on the head and throat is separated by a black mask over the eyes and side of the head and there is a buffy patch on the neck. The back and rump are gray with black stripes, the wings and tail brownish with two white bars on the wings, the abdomen is white. After the moult in mid-summer the contrast is extraordinary for such a spectacularly marked bird because it is then olive on top with some dark streaks. The wing bars are pale, a trace of chestnut remains on the crown and the underparts are greenish on the throat and buffy on the belly. In spring the female is similar to the male, but the colors are paler.

On migration the Bay-breasted can be found almost anywhere, including urban areas, providing insects are available. It usually nests in coniferous trees in forest clearings, with a good second growth. It nests to about forty feet above the ground, but often feeds at lower levels. The range extends from the southern Mackenzie River to Nova Scotia and in the United States from Minnesota to Maine.

This is not a prevalent species, although it may be fairly common in suitable areas. It sings from a medium height with a very high, sibilant song which sounds like *teezy, teezy, teezy,* all much in the same pitch. It is deliberate in its movements as it searches the leaves for insects.

BLACKPOLL WARBLER

Dendroica striata
LENGTH 4½ INCHES

The Blackpoll is unique in two ways —it has the highest pitched song of any North American perching bird and it has the longest migration route of any of the warblers. The song, which lasts about three seconds, is high and wiry, several notes higher, in fact, than the highest note on a piano. The song is a series of short notes, building in pitch and volume, then falling away towards the end. The pitch is often beyond the hearing range of people over fifty-five.

The extremes of the migration range of an individual Blackpoll might be as high as 7,500 miles each way, or a minimum of 3,500 miles. The winter range extends across South America from Guyana to Colombia. In late winter it moves eastward to Venezuela, crosses the Caribbean and arrives in Florida in mid-April. Progress north is then slow, and it is among the last of the warblers to arrive in the northeast, moving through from mid-May to mid-June. It then speeds up, making a rush for the breeding grounds which extend from Alaska across Northern Canada to the Maritimes.

The male Blackpoll is mostly black on top and white underneath, with olive-gray on the wings and tail. It can be distinguished from the Black and White Warbler by its sharply defined black poll, or cap, and all-white cheeks, instead of the striped face of the Black and White. A smudged black line extends from the bill outlining the lower face and throat. The underparts (throat, breast and belly) and wing bars, are white. The female is dingier and lacks the black crown. In autumn following the moult, the adult birds and immatures are similar, all being a rather dull green streaked with black on the upper parts.

The nest is usually built in the lower branches of a spruce tree, in an area of burnt or cleared land.

PINE WARBLER
Dendroica pinus
Length 5 inches

This retiring bird is best found by its song, and then sought in the upper branches of pines where it searches for insects in the needles. It may occasionally be seen on the trunk and lower branches, especially those rich in gum, poking into crevices in the bark.

The song is a series of soft rather sweet notes, all sung in the same pitch, and similar to the Chipping Sparrow's whistled trill, but slower and more musical.

Ironically, the Pine Warbler is relatively uncommon in Canada and the northeast. It is primarily a bird of the southern United States where it remains relatively abundant, although reduced from its former numbers through elimination of much of the south's pine forests.

It is less migratory than most warbler species, although birds of the northern portion of the range must, of course, move south in autumn. It feeds entirely on insects in summer, but its ability to live on pine seeds and berries permits it to winter as far north as New Jersey. The breeding range in Canada extends in a thin line from southeastern Manitoba across to southern Ontario and extreme southwestern Quebec. It covers the whole of the eastern United States from Minnesota south to the Gulf of Mexico.

The Pine is noted for its yellow breast and throat, plain greenish olive back and head and two prominent wing-bars on otherwise dark wings. The eye has a yellowish stripe above and a black one running through it. The cheeks are olive. Females and young birds are plain olive above and whitish below. After the summer moult when both male and female can be confused with several other warbler species, their association with pine trees usually helps identification. The nest, which is invariably in pines, is built from ten feet upwards near the ends of branches and usually well-concealed from below.

PRAIRIE WARBLER
Dendroica discolor
LENGTH 4 INCHES

The Prairie Warbler is badly named, for it is really a bird of the scrub and brush. A preference for new growth probably contributes to very erratic nesting behaviour, for an area may be suitable one year but be neglected the next. Saplings and brush which grow up after cutting provide an ideal habitat. The nest is seldom more than five feet from the ground and the combination of its distinctive song, active behavior, low feeding and brilliant color, make it an easy bird to locate if it is present.

Two warblers are constant tail waggers — the Prairie and the Palm. The Prairie often flutters like a Hummingbird when feeding, and darts after flying insects. The undersides are plain yellow from throat to belly with a patch of white under the tail. The top of the head and neck are olive, and the cheeks are yellow with two black lines — one through the eye and one around the lower side of the cheek. The flanks are marked with black streaks. The back is olive and marked with reddish streaks, although these cannot always be seen. The wings have two white bars. The female is similar to the male, but less brilliantly colored, and lacks the red streaks on the back.

In Canada, the Prairie Warbler is found only in the east. It breeds sparsely in southern Ontario, as far north as Georgian Bay and east to Kingston. In the United States it occurs throughout the east, in dry brushy areas and in dunes.

When singing the Prairie throws its head back, with the bill pointed straight up. The song is an ascending series sounding like *zee, zee, zee, zeet.*

PALM WARBLER
Dendroica palmarum
LENGTH 4½ INCHES

The Palm Warbler, like the Prairie, constantly flicks its tail up and down. The top of the head is chestnut colored, the cheeks brown and there is a narrow yellow line over the eye. The back is olive brown with dark streaks and the rump is yellow-gray. The underparts of the eastern race are entirely yellow with fine brown streaks on the breast and the wings are dark with two indistinct bars. The western race has a yellow throat but the underparts are white. Ludlow Griscom, the American ornithologist, describes this warbler as "dull and relatively uninteresting" but I suspect this is because he has spent much of his life in Florida where, in winter, the Pine Warbler in its dull white plumage is a very common sight. Its winter plumage is uninteresting for the yellow changes to dull white.

The nesting range extends from the Mackenzie River to Newfoundland and the Palm is seen in southern Ontario only as a migrant. It also occurs in small numbers in Minnesota, Michigan and Maine. It winters in the southern United States and in the Caribbean.

"Palm" is a particularly inappropriate name for this bird, for even in the south, and in the islands, it is everywhere but in palms. During the winter it is common on lawns and gardens as well as in wild areas which are bare and open. Unlike most warblers, it feeds almost entirely on the ground and, apart from its insect diet, will take seeds and berries when insects are not available.

In summer it chooses either wet or dry ground around the edges of bogs and marshes. The nest is built on the ground, usually on a hummock, and often close to a small tree.

The song is a buzzing trill, rather flat in tone, and looser than that of the Chipping Sparrow.

OVENBIRD
Seiurus aurocapillus
LENGTH 5 INCHES

The Ovenbird takes its name from its unusual nest which is built on the ground in heavy leaf cover, with the entrance at the side, and roofed over like a Dutch oven. It is unusual too in that it walks, or teeters, whereas most small birds hop. It spends most of its time on the ground in the forest foraging among fallen trees or branches.

The voice is unwittingly familiar to all who have walked in the forest in spring and early summer, even though they may not have seen the bird. The strident shouting of *teacher, teacher,* repeated several times, ever louder, is sure evidence of the Ovenbird. A flight song, usually presented above the trees in the evening, is an outpouring of lovely liquid sound and an occasional *teacher.*

The ground nesting habit of this bird leaves it much exposed to predation by chipmunks, squirrels and snakes. It is also a favorite target of the Cowbird, which lays its eggs in the Ovenbird's nest for incubation. The young are generally raised by the host Ovenbird.

This is a bird of the forest. It chooses an area of dry mature woods with only a modest cover of underbrush. In suitable territory, the nesting area for each pair may be quite small.

The Ovenbird is larger, chunkier and browner than most warblers. The neck, back and tail are olive-brown and unstreaked. The distinguishing feature is the orange crown, flanked by black stripes above the eyes. Below that there is a pale eye-stripe. The cheeks are olive, the underparts white, heavily marked with black spots, more or less forming streaks.

Breeding is from northern British Columbia to Newfoundland and south from Colorado to Georgia. It winters in the southern United States, the West Indies and South America.

NORTHERN WATERTHRUSH
Seiurus noveboracensis
LENGTH 5 INCHES

Like the Ovenbird, the Waterthrush is a walker and not a hopper and is similar in appearance. Both have a "flat" appearance in that the line from the head to the tail is almost straight. Again like the Ovenbird, it teeters along, the body appearing to move up and down as if on a pivot. The top of the head is dark brown, the back and tail dark olive-brown. There is a buffy stripe over the eye, the cheek is dark and the underparts white, heavily striped with dark brown.

Despite its name, the Waterthrush is a warbler and not a thrush. It is found in the cool forests, beside ponds, marshes, bogs, lakes and streams. The nest is usually built in the roots of an upturned tree, very often over the water. In a suitable area several pairs can be found breeding in close proximity, sometimes with two pairs sharing the same upturned tree. It is somewhat shy and elusive and, in order to watch it successfully, one is advised to remain still for some time and wait for the bird to go about its business. It is reasonably active when undisturbed and walks about seeking tiny insects, worms and grubs.

It has one of the longer migration routes, and the breeding range is enormous, extending from the Arctic coast and Alaska throughout Canada to the limits of the tree line and in the northern States eastward from Idaho. The winter is spent from Mexico across northern South America and in the West Indies and Bahamas.

CONNECTICUT WARBLER
Oporornis agilis
LENGTH 5 INCHES

This warbler was first identified in Connecticut in 1812 by Alexander Wilson and, like most early nomenclature, it is inappropriate. It is uncommon in the northeast and New England and is seen, if at all, during fall migration, for most Connecticuts use the Mississippi flyway on their journey north from Brazil in the spring.

The breeding range extends in a fairly narrow band from northeastern British Columbia to Ontario north of the Great Lakes and into western Quebec, south of James Bay. The main concentration is the northern parts of Minnesota, Wisconsin, Michigan, and in the central prairies.

The preferred nesting habitat is in spruce or tamarack bogs, and the nest has been seen only rarely since it was first discovered by Ernest Thompson Seton in 1883 in a Manitoba bog. The nest is built on the ground in bogs rich in the typical northern plant community of moss, pitcher-plant and Labrador tea. It is placed deep in the moss, usually at the base of a sapling.

This is a large unstreaked warbler, similar to the Mourning Warbler. There is a slate gray hood extending fairly far down the breast, as if the bird had been held by the tail and dipped in gray dye. The Connecticut has a distinct white eye ring and the Mourning does not. The rest of the breast and belly are a rather drab yellow. The female is similar, but the hood is brown.

The song is ringing and loud, consisting of a series of two or three note phrases in the same key *peechoo, peechoo,* or *whippity, whippity,* repeated four or five times.

MOURNING WARBLER
Oporornis philadelphia
LENGTH 4½ INCHES

Alexander Wilson, who identified so many species, gave this bird both its scientific label and common name. He saw it once near Philadelphia and never again. The common term, Mourning Warbler, is more appropriate because of the sombre dark gray hood and jet black bib. The rest of the undersides are yellow, rather brighter than the Connecticut, the back and wings are plain olive-green. There is no eye-ring, except on immature birds, in which it is broken both in front of and behind the eye. The female is similarly marked but is paler and lacks the black on the upper breast.

The Mourning is a bird of slashings and thickets. Its song is a loud and cheerful *chorry, chorry, chorry, chorry,* the last two notes being lower. It is usually well hidden deep in the brush and can best be found by following the song. It responds to squeaking and can be encouraged to show itself for a few moments. The nest is built on or close to the ground. On migration it seeks the same cover it requires for nesting.

Although one does not see many individuals in the course of a day, it is a numerous species, for the breeding range extends from western Alberta to Newfoundland and from the northcentral and northeastern states, south in the mountains to Virginia. It is best found in recently cleared or burnt land which is at an early stage of re-growth or in clearings at the edge of forest roads. It may choose either dry or wet areas.

It winters in South America.

COMMON YELLOWTHROAT

Geothlypis trichas
LENGTH 4¼ INCHES

The Common Yellowthroat is probably the most familiar of all warblers to the beginner for it is abundant in marshy areas and along the edge of streams as well as in dry brush. Its range is vast for it breeds throughout Canada to the limit of the tree line, and all over the United States with the exception of the Gulf Coast and Florida. For a bird of this range it is not surprising that it exists in many forms — at least twelve sub-species have been established, varying slightly in size, color and song.

The male is unmistakable with its wrap-around black face mask which stretches from the front of the head across the eyes to the lower cheeks. A whitish line separates the upper extent of the mask from the crown which, like the neck, wings and back, are uniform olive. The underparts are unstreaked yellow. The female is quite different. The top of the head is brownish, the back olive, the underparts are yellow, tinged with buff along the flanks. There is a whitish eye-ring. The female may easily be mistaken for several other species, but with practice, and attention to habitat, identification becomes easier.

As with many other birds, the Yellowthroat is best found by its song in spring and summer. Although there is much variation, the most common is a strident *witchity, witchity, witchity,* heard from the dense cattails, brush or rank vegetation — most often near water. It ranges on the ground and lower vegetation and nests on the ground or low in bushes.

Yellowthroats are very active and appear to be shy. They are inquisitive however, and come quite close when "squeaked".

The winter range extends from the southern United States, through Mexico and Central America.

YELLOW-BREASTED CHAT

Icteria virens
LENGTH 6¼ INCHES

The Chat appears regularly at Point Pelee National Park on migration each spring, but in eastern Canada it only ventures a short distance beyond, to the northwest shore of Lake Erie for nesting purposes. It occurs on the south side of the Great Lakes as far east as Connecticut and else-where throughout the United States, with the exception of the north-central States. In western Canada it appears in southern Alberta and Saskatchewan and in a small area of southern British Columbia.

That the Chat is a warbler is often hard to accept, for its behavior suggests a Mockingbird or Catbird. It is the largest warbler and its bill is significantly heavier, even in relation to its size. It has a pure yellow throat and breast and a white belly. The upper parts are uniform olive, and there is a white line from the bill over the eye and under the chin. Between them a black line runs through the eye to the back of the cheek.

One seldom gets a good look at a Chat for it lives in the thickest branches, vines and shrubs it can find. Nests are almost impossible to find, for they are usually protected by thorns. The song is ridiculous. It lasts, in patches, for about twelve seconds and consists of an uneven series of whistles, gurgles, grunts and caws. The Chat frequently leaps up, often at night, and sings in mid-air with its feet hanging straight down.

WILSON'S WARBLER
Wilsonia pusilla
LENGTH 4½ INCHES

This bird is named for the 19th century naturalist, Alexander Wilson. It is largely yellow, more lemon on the underparts and face than the Yellow Warbler. The upper parts are yellowish olive. The male wears a black cap on the top of his head, the female sometimes has a less distinct cap. Another point of identification is the habit of constantly twitching its tail.

In the east the Wilson's is seen principally on migration, for the breeding range is north of most inhabited areas, with the exception of the Maritime Provinces, Vermont and Maine. In the west it breeds as far south as southern California and as far north as the Arctic Ocean.

Both Wilson's and the Canada Warbler are noted flycatchers. They spend much of their time on the wing, snapping insects out of the air. The bill is adapted for this, for it is wider than it is high, and clicks as it closes on its prey.

204

The favorite nesting habitat is similar to that of the Yellowthroat: wet open places with good cover of cattail, alder and willow, not exceeding five feet in height. Streams and pond edges are ideal.

The song, which lasts about three seconds, is in two parts. It consists of a series of rapid chattering notes, quite loud and forceful, sounding like *chee, chee, chee, chee, chee, chet, chet*, the second part being lower.

Migration occurs throughout the whole of the United States, with the exception of Florida. It winters from Mexico to Panama.

CANADA WARBLER

Wilsonia canadensis
LENGTH 5 INCHES

The breeding range of this warbler is certainly not limited to Canada, although it is likely that the largest numbers do nest in the north. The range extends from the central prairies of Alberta to the Maritimes, although not as far north as many other warblers. In the United States it breeds from Minnesota east to New England and south to Georgia in the Appalachians.

This is a gem-like, brilliantly marked warbler. It has a yellow chest and throat and matching spectacles. A black necklace is dotted across the throat with "pendants" hanging down the breast. The forehead is black, the head, wings, back and tail are clear dark gray, the wings unmarked. Females are similar but much paler.

Like the Wilson's, the Canada is a flycatcher. It is very active as it flutters from its perch to catch flying insects on the wing. In its breeding territory it chooses the undergrowth of a mature forest or the clearings at its edge. The nest is built on the ground, in the root system of an up-turned tree or in the moss on fallen logs.

The song is irregular and varied, consisting of a brief explosion of notes, usually preceeded by a *chip* and then a pause. While hard to describe, it is distinctive once learned.

Migration is through the eastern United States and Texas to Colombia, Venezuela and Peru.

AMERICAN REDSTART

Setophaga ruticilla
LENGTH 4½ INCHES

This delightful black, orange and white warbler is known in Latin America as "the candle of the forest" because of its extraordinary aerobatics. It can change directions within inches, literally resembling a flickering flame. Its habit of fanning the tail and wings and then fluttering off to take an insect on the wing resembles the performance of a butterfly.

In the male the head, throat, flank, back and wings are black. There is a large orange patch at the front of the wing, another farther back on the wing and two wedges of orange on the outer tail feathers for the first two thirds of their length, leaving the final third entirely black. The belly is white. The female is gray on the head, brownish on the back, entirely white on the undersides and shows the same patches as the male, but the orange is replaced by pale yellow.

The breeding range covers all of Canada to the limit of the trees and most of the States of the northwest and all of the east except the extreme south. Deciduous and mixed woodland with good ground cover are favored and the nest is almost invariably built in a deciduous tree at elevations above six feet. It is quite common in suitable territory throughout its range.

The Redstart enters the southern states from Florida to Texas and moves north on a broad front to the breeding grounds. The winter is spent from Mexico to northern South America and throughout the West Indies.

Weaver Finches
Family Ploceidae

This family of birds is native to the old world; two species, the European Tree Sparrow and the House Sparrow have been introduced into North America. The former is established in a small area around St. Louis, Missouri, while the latter has spread all over the western hemisphere in the last 125 years. As with most tampering with the natural order, this introduction has been an unfortunate mistake. It was undertaken originally as a measure to control insect pests, but the number of useful native birds displaced has probably outweighed any benefit derived from House Sparrows.

HOUSE SPARROW
Passer domesticus
LENGTH 6 INCHES

This robust nuisance is not a sparrow at all, but a member of the family of Weaver Finches which are native to Eurasia and Africa. The House Sparrow was introduced from Europe about 1850 to Brooklyn, New York,

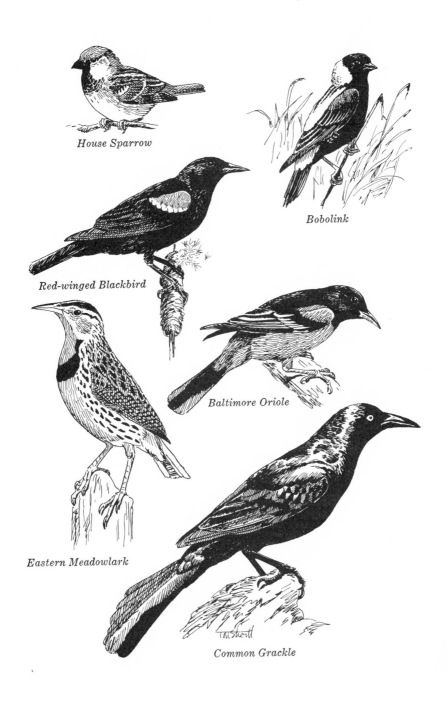

House Sparrow

Bobolink

Red-winged Blackbird

Baltimore Oriole

Eastern Meadowlark

Common Grackle

Representative members of the weaver finch and meadowlark, blackbird, and oriole families.

and later to Halifax and Quebec City. Like the starling, it is a cavity nesting bird, and has impacted severely on the populations of some of our native species, such as the Cliff Swallow and the Bluebird, by pre-empting its nesting sites. Following an explosive population growth in the first seventy-five years or so of its residence in North America, it now appears to be stable and to have filled its place in the bird society, albeit at the expense of other species. It has been suggested that the reduction of the number of horses has contributed to this stabilization.

The House Sparrow is gregarious both in cities and on the farm. Except in the nesting season large flocks gather at night in a protected location, in a building, a large tree or a thick vine. Nesting is usually in a cavity, but may be in bushes or vine, where a domed nest which is entered by the side is built. There is little migration, although some birds may move south in winter. The range extends from the Mackenzie Valley, across the central prairies to the Maritimes, southward through the whole of the United States to South America.

The male is a handsome finch with a gray crown, a chestnut colored stripe from the eye and around the nape, whitish cheeks, a black throat and breast and pale abdomen. The back is brown striped with black, as are the wings, and the rump is gray. The paler female is striped on the back, has a dingy beige breast and belly, pale eye stripe and dark cheek patches. For those who have only seen the filthy city bird, the immaculate farm bird looks like a different species entirely.

Meadowlarks, Blackbirds, and Orioles
Family Icteridae

This family of birds, numbering eighty-eight species, is limited to the western hemisphere. Of these, twelve visit, or are to some extent permanently resident in the northeast. The family diverges widely in appearance, ranging from all-black birds to brilliantly colored orioles. Some have short conical bills, others long pointed bills. The tails can vary from very long to short. They are all largely insectivorous in summer and seed-eaters in winter. The blackbirds flock after the breeding season in vast numbers, not only with their own species, but in a mix with other blackbirds and starlings. In the southern United States evening roosting flocks are counted in millions of birds. In marshes in Canada during the autumn it is not unusual to find roosts of hundreds of thousands.

BOBOLINK
Dolichonyx oryzivorus
LENGTH 6 INCHES

The Bobolink has the distinction of being the only North American bird to be lighter colored on top than on the bottom. The male, from arrival in spring until mid to late summer, is an exceptionally handsome bird. The back of the head and neck are pale yellow, the back striped black and white, the wings dark with large white shoulder patches, and the face and undersides black. The bird, with its conical bill, is more like a sparrow than a blackbird, but somewhat larger; the female and autumn males are often mistaken for sparrows. They are then brown with dark stripes on the uppersides, a buffy median stripe on the crown flanked by black stripes, and then another buffy stripe over the eye. The undersides are buffy and faintly striped. The tail feathers come to sharp points.

The Bobolink nests in the tall grasses in open meadows, in hay or alfalfa, a habitat which has increased enormously in recent years. It has also increased the dangers of nesting, for if the field is cut before mid-July the chance of the flimsy nest surviving is small. The song of this bird is a lovely bubbling chatter of metallic notes which may be given while flying slowly on fast beating wings over the nesting area, or from a perch. In summer they feed mostly on insects, and in the autumn switch largely to seeds. On the southern migration large flocks form and sometimes do considerable damage to crops.

The nesting range is a fairly narrow band across the continent from the mid-prairies of Canada to southern Quebec and the Maritimes (except Newfoundland), south to California, Ohio and New Jersey. Southern migration is through the eastern United States to South America as far as Argentina.

EASTERN MEADOWLARK
Sturnella magna
LENGTH 9 INCHES

WESTERN MEADOWLARK
Sturnella neglecta
LENGTH 9 INCHES

In spring and summer the Meadowlark's song is heard from nearly every field as one drives through the country. The high, slow *tsee-you, tee-yair* is distinctive, the last note slurring downward in pitch. The Meadowlark usually sings from a fence post or wire and sometimes from a tree. Meadowlarks seldom leave the open fields where they build a domed nest in clumps of high grass.

The distinguishing feature is a broad black crescent across the brilliant yellow breast and undersides. The bill is long, as long as the flattish head, which has a white central stripe, flanked by dark lines and a white stripe over the eye. The cheeks are pale, the back and wings brown with white stripes, the flanks white with black spots forming streaks, the tail short and wide with white outer feathers and brown in the center. In flight one is conscious of the broad wings, long bill and, particularly, the widely fanned tail with white borders. When the bird flies, low to the ground, it uses a series of fluttering wing-beats and short glides, typical also of the Ruffed Grouse.

Like most blackbirds, the Eastern Meadowlark feeds almost entirely on grasshoppers and other ground insects during the summer. In winter it relies more heavily on weed seeds.

The Canadian summer range is limited to southern Ontario and Quebec and to parts of New Brunswick and Nova Scotia along the Bay of Fundy. In the United States it is permanently resident through most of the east from Arizona eastward, but moves out of the New England and northern States in winter. It also breeds in South America.

The Western Meadowlark is identical except for its song which is deeper in pitch, rich and bubbling. It consists of six or seven notes of varying pitch with a descending jumble of short notes at the end, the whole lasting about two seconds.

The Western Meadowlark is a summer resident throughout the open grassy parts of the west and is also present as a breeding bird in parts of the east to Michigan and southern Ontario. Where the ranges overlap one may find the two species in close proximity.

RED-WINGED BLACKBIRD
Agelaius phoeniceus
LENGTH 8 INCHES

This is one of our most abundant summer birds and, perhaps, the most obvious. The male is entirely black, except for red shoulder patches, outlined on the lower side with pale yellow. During mating displays and in flight the red epaulet is apparent but when at rest, only the yellow edge may be seen. The female is striped black and brown with a black line over the eye. Young males look much like the females, but show an obscure orange patch on the wing.

The males arrive early in the spring, usually when snow remains on the fields and ice in the marshes. They are then much in evidence on the roadsides, mixed with flocks of grackles and starlings. The females arrive later and the move to fresh water marshes is made. The nest may be built suspended above the water from two or three cattails, but those which nest before the cattails have grown do so in bushes and low trees as close to the marsh as possible. Individual territories are very small, sometimes only a few feet, so that even a small marsh may have hundreds of pairs.

The song is the familiar *och - a - reeee*, rising in pitch and ending in a quavering trill. From a distance one may only hear the *reee*. The alarm note is a descending whistle and also a harsh call. When nesting is complete the birds form large flocks, ranging through the country by day feeding on insects in summer and seeds and waste grain in winter, returning to a marsh at night to roost.

The Canadian range is from coast to coast and north to Great Bear Lake in the west, James Bay in the center and southern Newfoundland in the east. A few birds remain in southern Ontario in winter, but most move into the central and southern United States and Mexico.

ORCHARD ORIOLE
Icterus spurius
LENGTH 6 INCHES

This oriole is a rarity in the northeast, and is an established summer resident south from Massachusetts and in only a few small areas of southern Ontario and in one area of southern Manitoba. These are the extreme northern limits of a breeding range which covers the eastern half of the United States and Mexico, where it is reasonably common. It winters in South America.

The markings are similar to the Baltimore Oriole, the male having a black mantle over head, breast and back, a brick red belly, rump and wing patches. The wings are black with whitish edges on the flight feathers and the tail is solid black. The female is yellow below and olive above, with two whitish wing bars. Males of the first spring are much like the females, but have a clearly defined black bib and eye-patch.

The preferred habitat is among the scattered trees of orchards, roadsides, streams and near houses. It feeds almost entirely on insects, but takes some berries.

The song is Robin-like, loud, clear and short, in various pitches, slurring downward at the end. The male sings a great deal, often while making a vertical flight from its tree to which it then returns.

As with other orioles, the Orchard builds a nest in the form of a pouch suspended in a forked branch, usually from ten to twenty feet above the ground. The nest is about six inches deep, somewhat shallower than that of the more widespread Baltimore.

BALTIMORE ORIOLE
Icterus galbula
LENGTH 7 INCHES

The piping, flute-like song of the Baltimore Oriole makes this one of my favorite birds. It is rather low in pitch, and consists of irregular two note phrases, rich in musical quality. The song differs considerably from bird to bird, and where several pairs are nesting close together, it is not difficult to identify the individual singing. This is also true of Song Sparrows.

The Baltimore and Orchard Orioles have quite similar markings, but different colors, the Orchard having a red belly, the Baltimore orange. The male Baltimore has a black head, upper breast, throat, back and wings, the wings being marked with a yellow patch on the shoulder and white patch lower down. The tail is black with orange patches on the outside for the final two-thirds of its length. The breast, belly and rump are a brilliant orange. The females and first year males are a rather drab orangy yellow below and somewhat spotted olive-yellow above, with two white bars on the wings, which are darker than the body.

The Baltimore Oriole, named for the colors of Lord Baltimore, is fairly widespread in Canada in summer, from central Alberta east across the south. It is common through the eastern United States north of Georgia, but is seen as a migrant only in the southern States, for it does not stop to nest. It winters in Mexico and northern South America.

RUSTY BLACKBIRD
Euphagus carolinus
LENGTH 8 INCHES

The male Rusty is the blackest appearing of all the blackbirds, for it lacks the iridescence of the grackle and of the Brewer's Blackbird — the Cowbird has a brown head. The female is dull slate-gray. In autumn, and during the winter, both sexes show brown feather ends over their normal mantle, which gives them the rusty appearance. Both sexes have pale, almost white, eyes. The Brewer's Blackbird is a similar western bird seen in the east fairly frequently. It now nests north of the Great Lakes and is extending its range.

The Rusty nests in the thick conifers at the edge of forest swamps from Alaska to Newfoundland and again in New England, but not in southern Ontario and Quebec where it is only seen on migration. It migrates through the center of the eastern United States to winter in the southern States. It arrives on its breeding ground early in the spring, before the ice is off the swamps and the snow from the woods. It then searches for food in large flocks, often in company with grackles, and other blackbirds. Its song sounds something like the creaking of an unoiled hinge, interspersed with other gurgling, more musical notes. The call is a harsh *guck*.

In summer the Rusty feeds almost entirely in swamps, walking about in the shallow water searching for insects. It also feeds on weed seeds and some grain and berries. It is seldom seen in fields, except occasionally on migration.

COMMON GRACKLE (Bronzed Grackle)
Quiscalus quiscula
LENGTH 11 INCHES

The Common Grackle is one of the many birds whose habitat has been expanded vastly by man, through agriculture and the growth of ornamental trees. Before huge areas were opened by farming it is likely that grackles were limited to the edges of marshes and streams for feeding. They require fairly open areas, for they feed almost entirely on the ground, searching for insects and larvae. They also take seeds and have the unfortunate habit of eating the eggs of other birds and young in the nest. In

212

the early autumn large flocks form and they sometimes do considerable damage to unharvested grain. In early spring and in the autumn, grackles feed in fields with other blackbirds.

The favored nesting tree is a dense conifer, but it uses ornamental bushes in gardens, particularly lilacs, and sometimes cavities in buildings and trees. The fact that the grackle habitat, both urban and rural, has been expanded is not always a blessing, for the Grackle is not an attractive bird.

The Common Grackle is the largest of our blackbirds in the northeast, but is much smaller than the Boat-tailed Grackle of the Gulf Coast. It looks black from a distance, but is not — the head, breast and nape are highly iridescent and show a green and blue sheen. The rest of the bird is dark bronze. The tail is longer than the other blackbirds, rounded at the end, and when the bird flies, the tail is wedge-shaped like the keel of a boat. The bill is long and pointed and the pale eyes are obvious for some distance. The song is a short squeaky thing of no beauty and there is much clucking.

It breeds widely in Canada from northeastern British Columbia to southern Newfoundland and all through the eastern United States. In winter a few birds remain in southern Canada but most move south to the United States.

BROWN-HEADED COWBIRD

Molothrus ater
LENGTH 7 INCHES

The Cowbird is noted as a parasite. It does not build its own nest, the female laying four or five fertile eggs, one day apart, in the nests of other birds. It appears to lay after the host bird has laid its first egg. The incubation period is only ten or eleven days, a little shorter than most others, and the young Cowbird grows more quickly than the chicks of the host. It throws all or most of the others from the nest, thus assuring the full attention and food supply of the foster parents. It parasites many species, usually those of the thrush, warbler, vireo, sparrow and flycatcher families. Some species react to the intrusion, the thrushes by breaking the eggs and throwing them from the nest; others, like the Yellow Warbler, by building a second storey over the offending egg and its own, and laying again. Most others tolerate the new egg and raise the single Cowbird as their own. It is a ridiculous sight to see a fledged Cowbird being fed by its much smaller foster parent.

For most of the year it mixes with flocks of other blackbirds, feeding on insects, seeds and grain. It associates with horses and cattle in the pastures, taking the insects they have stirred up. The head, neck and upper-breast are coffee colored, the body dark with an iridescent sheen of greenish blue. The bill is short and stubby, more like that of a sparrow.

The Cowbird breeds across North America, north to the southern Mackenzie Valley in the west and central Quebec and southern Newfoundland in the east. A few birds remain in Canada in winter, but most move to the southern United States and Mexico.

213

Scarlet Tanager

American Goldfinch

Rose-breasted Grosbeak

Cardinal

Rufous-sided Towhee

From May until August the male Scarlet Tanager is our most vivid bird.
The male Rose-breasted Grosbeak (shown above) is one of the loveliest of
North American birds, with an almost parrot-like bill and markings.

214

Tanagers
Family Thraupidae

Tanagers are a numerous family of 191 species particular to the western hemisphere. They are essentially tropical birds, and only three species reach the northeast. The Western Tanager, which breeds from Saskatchewan west, is by far the most northerly nester. The Summer Tanager, which is a dull red, breeds as far north as central Ohio, and is an occasional visitor to southern Ontario. The Scarlet Tanager is the one seen regularly in the northeast.

Tanagers are somewhat like finches, many of the tropical species having conical bills.

SCARLET TANAGER
Piranga olivacea
LENGTH 6 INCHES

From its arrival in May until August, when it loses its scarlet plumage, the male Scarlet Tanager is our most vivid bird. During these months the male is a brilliant scarlet, except for the wings and tail, which are black. The bill is stout and fairly long. During the fall moult the male gradually loses its scarlet coat and becomes greenish above and yellowish green below, the wings and tail remaining black. During the transition the feathers are a mottled mixture of scarlet and green. Females are much like autumn males, but the wings are dark, not black.

The summer range extends from southeastern Manitoba to southern Quebec and southern New Brunswick, south to Oklahoma and Georgia. It migrates through the southern United States to South America.

The Scarlet Tanager is described as common in its breeding range, but I have not found it so. During the height of migration when it is often seen close to the ground, one is lucky to see more than a few birds in a day, and during nesting when they become very spread out, few are seen.

Tanagers prefer the upper canopy of mature deciduous woodland for feeding and nesting. They are somewhat sluggish in behavior, as they move about the foliage feeding on leaf-eating insects. Even with its brilliance, the Scarlet Tanager may be overlooked in summer if one does not recognize its song which is much like that of a Robin, but huskier. Roger Tory Peterson describes it as "a Robin with a sore throat". In some conditions it nests in urban areas.

Sparrows, Gosbeaks, Finches, and Buntings
Family Fringillidae

The world's largest family of birds — some 566 species — divides conveniently for purposes of identification into two distinct groups, so disparate as to be almost separate families. Those in the first group, which includes the cardinals, grosbeaks and finches are quite colorful. Those in the second group are the small brown sparrows which subdivide again into those with plain breasts and those with streaked breasts. In this second general group the differences in appearance are minor and, while we attempt to pinpoint these, it is more important in the field to recognize the differing habitat requirements of these look-alikes. Some are quite specific in their needs, which vary from low bush and ground cover to swamps and trees in open country.

Sparrows are essentially seed eaters in winter and insect eaters in summer. Most raise the young birds almost exclusively on an insect diet. The common feature of all FRINGILLIDAE is the conical stubby bill which is adapted for opening and eating seeds. Their principal diet of weed seeds and harmful insects and larvae makes them valuable birds.

There are eighty-nine species of FRINGILLIDAE in North America of which twenty-six species are seen in the northeast.

CARDINAL
Richmondena cardinalis
LENGTH 8 INCHES

Despite its size and color, this all red grosbeak can vanish into green shrubbery as if it were camouflage material and, were it not for its penetrating and delightful song, it might not be there. It is, as Audubon says "a proud musician" and sings earlier in the season than most other birds. Its emphatic song, which can be heard early in the morning (about fourA.M.) in late winter, starts with a series of double whistled notes, followed by a number of *weets*, as if it were enjoying the sound of its own voice. It is not particularly shy, but prefers to remain deep in thickets and shrubbery along the tangle at the edge of fields and near streams where it feeds and nests.

The Cardinal is common east of the Mississippi, north to Connecticut but was unknown in Canada one hundred years ago. It is now widely spread throughout Ontario to about fifty miles north of Lake Erie and Lake Ontario and is constantly extending its range northward; a few birds turn up in southern Quebec but so far, only in winter. Most individuals are non-migratory, except at the northern limits of the range. It has adapted well to urban living and appears to be comfortable in gardens with sufficient cover. A fondness for sunflower seeds makes it a regular visitor at feeding stations and, in areas outside the normal breeding range, regular feeding can encourage wanderers to remain. It is not aggressive at the feeder preferring to eat alone, choosing its seeds sedately after the other birds have fed, usually late in the morning and just before dark. The female usually feeds first, the male watching from a nearby perch.

The Cardinal has a large conical pink bill and a prominent red crest. The face and throat are black, the crest and underparts the red of a cardinal's robes, the back and tail somewhat grayer and darker. Where the male Cardinal is red, the female is mostly yellowish olive with the exception of the crest which is red. The wings and tail have a reddish tinge through the olive.

ROSE-BREASTED GROSBEAK
Pheucticus ludovicianus
LENGTH 8 INCHES

The male of this species is one of the loveliest of North American birds, almost parrot-like with its conical white bill, black head and back, flashing black and white wings, white stomach and a spectacular V-shaped carmine breast patch. The female, by contrast, is rather dull, mostly brown with a striped breast, heavy pale bill and distinct pale crown and eye stripe. The song is Robin-like, but richer and more melodious, as many as twenty-five notes pouring out in rapid succession, usually quite loudly, but at times very gently.

On migration it may be found in reasonable numbers feeding in deciduous woodland, usually in small to medium-sized trees. When nesting, its choice of habitat is somewhat limited, as it favors an area where large trees and dense shrubbery grow close together, usually near water. It also nests in parks and suburban areas where conditions are favorable.

The Rose-breasted Grosbeak summers from north of the 60th parallel, in British Columbia, across the prairies, and in the northeast from Georgia to southern Quebec and Ontario. Unlike its close relatives, the Cardinal and the Evening Grosbeak, which can tolerate hard winters, the Rose-breasted withdraws entirely to Mexico and northern South America.

INDIGO BUNTING

Passerina cyanea
LENGTH 5 INCHES

All perching birds can be seen best against a dark background with the bird itself in full light. This is particularly true of the Indigo Bunting. Against the sky it appears to be black, but when seen clearly, the blue head and body are spectacular. There is also some brown on the wings and tail. The Indigo Bunting is best found by its song, which is quite loud and clear. During the breeding season and into the summer, it sings regularly from a high perch, either near the top of a tree or from an exposed branch or wire. The song may be described as *twee, twee, twee, sorry, sorry, tsu, tsu,* declining in strength and clarity toward the end.

In the United States it is widespread east of the Mississippi and in Canada it is a summer visitor breeding from southern Manitoba, east through southern Ontario and Quebec and possibly in New Brunswick. It nests close to the ground in thick bushes, but requires a few high trees or wires as singing perches within its territory. It is usually found at forest edges and openings or burned areas, and in pastures with plenty of cover.

It feeds principally on insects during the summer, but in the autumn changes to seeds.

EVENING GROSBEAK

Hesperiphona vespertina
LENGTH 8 INCHES

This bird is a recent arrival in the east, having first nested in Ontario in 1920. The expansion from the coniferous forests of the west and northwest started about sixty years ago, and nesting has since spread through the forests of Ontario, into Quebec and the Maritimes.

It is among the most colorful of North American birds, like a miniature black and yellow parrot with its large white bill, brilliant yellow forehead, back and stomach, black throat, neck and tail, and the showy white wing patches. The female is more modestly dressed and has much white in the tail. The voice, while musical, is not especially attractive. It consists of a series of short warbling whistles heard on the wing and as they congregate in trees.

Grosbeaks move about in large flocks in winter time, feeding on seeds of Manitoba maple or box elder. In summer it is more gregarious than most forest species and nests in close community and feeds in loose flocks. At feeding stations in winter it is aggressive, both with its own kind and with other species. Within each flock the pecking order appears to be clearly established and the more aggressive individuals dominate. It is not unusual to see up to a dozen birds feeding quite amicably for some minutes, then the arrival of one more is the signal for much bickering and threatening. It has been suggested that bird feeders have had much to do with the growth in numbers, reducing winter mortality.

In summer many birds are killed by automobiles along forest roads as they pick up gravel for seed grinding.

PURPLE FINCH
Carpodacus purpureus
LENGTH 6 INCHES

Purple is a poor description for the color of this finch, for it is really raspberry colored, like a sparrow dipped in raspberry juice, according to Roger Tory Peterson. The throat, breast and back are almost the same color of red, the head somewhat brighter and with the brightest spot at the base of the tail. The belly is whitish, the wings brown tinged with red. The bill is short and stubby. It is possible to mistake the male Purple Finch for the Pine Grosbeak, but the grosbeak is much larger, more the size of a Robin. The female Purple Finch is quite unlike the male, having a brown striped back, spotted breast, dark crown and cheeks, with a broad white line through the eye.

The original breeding areas in the northern woods were in forest openings, near ponds and streams where suitable nesting was found in isolated trees. This species has also adapted to the artificial environment of parks, farms and orchards where evergreens are found. During the winter they move about erratically in flocks and are seen frequently at feeding stations. During the breeding season the male is a frequent and beautiful singer. The song is almost invariably presented from a high perch and consists of a high-pitched warble — strong and liquid.

During summer the Purple Finch ranges from coast to coast from north of the 60th parallel in the west to California, and from Labrador to Virginia in the east. During the winter some individuals remain in the southern areas of their breeding range, but most migrate south into the United States and northern Mexico.

PINE GROSBEAK
Pinicola enucleator
LENGTH 8 INCHES

This is the largest of the grosbeaks. In winter the male is a pinkish red which becomes noticeably brighter in summer. The head, cheeks, neck, back and rump are red, the rump being the brightest, the front and belly are mottled gray and red, the wings dark with two narrow white bars. The form and color is somewhat similar to the Purple Finch and to the Red and White-winged Crossbill, but the Pine Grosbeak is much larger. The female is a rather attractive combination of gray and olive, the head, back and rump being olive, the sides gray and the front a plain olive-gray. The wings are dark with white wing bars and the longish tail is dark.

Pine Grosbeaks breed in conifers near natural openings in the forest, along streams and near pond edges. In the developed areas of their range, they nest near fields and orchards.

It is not unique to North America for it nests in coniferous forests from Scandinavia to Siberia and in Japan. In North America it breeds from Alaska south in the mountains to California, and across northern Canada south to New England, where the habitat is suitable. In winter some birds wander in flocks throughout the northern half of the United States, but most remain in the north providing food remains abundant.

They appear to be slow and deliberate in their movements. The flight is noted for its undulation or roller-coaster movement, accompanied by a trilling whistle. The song is lovely, consisting of a series of warbles, whistles and trills.

COMMON REDPOLL

Acanthis flammea
LENGTH 5 INCHES

This delightful pink and brown finch is one of the joys of winter in some parts of the northeast where it is seen in tight flocks one year and then may be absent from the area for several. They are unusually tame little birds and, when feeding, can be approached within a foot or two and then move only to the next tree or bush. During winter they migrate south of their Arctic and sub-Arctic summer range, which extends across Eurasia and North America, to the northern half of the United States and southern Canada, where they feed principally on the seeds of birch and alder. They hang in improbable positions to open the seeds from their sheaths and, when the seeds have been spilled, they fly down to the snow to pick up those which have fallen.

On their breeding grounds in the north, Redpolls feed on insects and buds. They nest either on the ground or in the low forks of willow and birch trees.

The Redpoll is recognized by its bright red cap which seems to sit on the front of its head. The area around the bill and a small patch on the throat are black. The breast of the male is washed with pink, as is the rump. The neck, back and abdomen are streaked brown, the tail dark and the wings are brown with two white wing bars. Its near relative, the Hoary Redpoll (*Acanthis hornemanni*), shares the breeding range of the Common but rarely comes south of the central prairies and northern Quebec and Ontario. When it does, it may appear singly, or in small numbers, with flocks of Common Redpolls and, although paler, the Hoary can only be identified with certainty by its unstreaked whitish rump.

PINE SISKIN

Spinus pinus
LENGTH 5 INCHES

We tend to associate the siskins principally with winter, for they then travel about in large noisy flocks, and are much in evidence in some areas. They are distinguished from other finches by the slim head and pointed bill, most finches having stubby conical bills. The Pine Siskin gives the appearance of being uniformly streaked above and below, the upper side being grayish brown with dark streaks, the underside much lighter. The wings are dark with two white or yellow bars and there is a yellow patch at the base of the tail. Siskins frequently associate with Goldfinches in winter and, when they flock together, can be mistaken for females of the latter. A close look at the flock quickly separates the striped Pine Siskin from the unstriped Goldfinch. They are most often seen in conifers, and in urban areas are often attracted to parks with tall spruce and pines.

The siskins are irregular in their winter travels and in their presence in an area, for they move about in large flocks mixed with Goldfinches, Redpolls and Crossbills, and, in summer, non-breeding birds maintain their flocks. Even breeding birds tend to nest in close association with overlapping territories. The voice is a rather plaintive yet harsh *shreeet*, which rises in pitch toward the end. The call of the Redpoll is somewhat similar but less harsh.

Nesting is in conifers at varying heights, from Alaska to Central America in the west and across southern Canada and New England in the east.

AMERICAN GOLDFINCH
Spinus tristis
LENGTH 5 INCHES

The Goldfinch gives the appearance of being constantly cheerful as it flies about in fairly large flocks, chattering good naturedly. The undulating flight is quite distinctive as it bounces along, the whole flock suddenly dropping into a tree, where they all seem to sing at the same time with a series of trills and twitters. The song is interrupted periodically with a querulous note, *swee*.

In summer the male is distinctly lemon yellow with a black forehead, wings and tail, the wings and the base of the tail heavily patched with white. Females and winter birds of both sexes are olive-brown with pale bills, although the males retain their black wings and yellow shoulder patches. Females are similar to some of the autumn vireos and warblers, but the bills are different — those of the warblers are long and thin, those of the Goldfinch, stubby and short.

The Goldfinch nests later in the season than almost any other bird and simultaneously with the Cedar Waxwing, in August. A preference for ripe thistle-down as a nesting material and as a source of food is thought to be the reason. The nest is usually placed in a low bush or up to about twenty feet in a tree, beautifully made and well concealed. The thistle-down lining remains clean and soft while the young are in the nest. A location is chosen in relatively open ground. Goldfinch are normally found around weedy fields, pastures, orchards and open woodland.

Nesting is in southern Canada from coast to coast and as far south as Colorado in the United States, most birds moving somewhat southward in winter, some to the Gulf Coast and Mexico.

RED CROSSBILL
Loxia curvirostra
LENGTH 6 INCHES

This heavy headed finch, about the size of a House Sparrow, uses its remarkable crossed bill to force the seeds from the cones of coniferous trees. It is rather like a parrot in that it is often seen hanging upside down working on a cone. The male is a lovely brick red, brightest on the rump and head, the back and breast are somewhat mottled with brown. The wings and tail are dark. The female is olive-gray, somewhat mottled and becoming yellowish on the rump.

The Red Crossbill and its close relative, the White-Winged Crossbill (distinguished by large white patches on the wings), are highly unusual in their distribution. Most small birds are limited by oceans and only a few occur on both sides of the Atlantic and the Pacific. The Crossbill breeds in Canada in coniferous forests from the Yukon, in a narrowing band southeastward to Newfoundland and New England and, in the western United States, as far south as Mexico. It also occurs throughout most of Europe, the Mediterranean, North Africa, parts of Asia and Japan.

In all their ranges, the two crossbills are highly nomadic, traveling about in flocks, and breeding irregularly both as to season and location. They depend upon seeds in the cones of conifers. Their presence in an area is no indication that they breed there and they are seen infrequently. A breeding population in a suitable area one year may be followed by several years without a sighting of any kind.

RUFOUS-SIDED TOWHEE
Pipilo erythrophthalmus
LENGTH 8 INCHES

There are four species of towhees in North America, but only the Rufous-sided occurs in the east. It takes its name from its call note which is a distinct *to-whee*. This is one species which can scarcely be mistaken for any other. The head, back and tail of the male are black with patches of white in the wings and outer tail feathers. The sides and under tail coverts are an attractive chestnut color, and the belly is white, the eye red. The female is similarly marked but the black areas are replaced by chocolate brown.

222

Towhees are usually heard before they are seen. In addition to the call note, the song is distinctive and quite loud — two notes followed by a trill — *drink your teeeeee*, heard from a dense bush. It should be sought in the heavy tangle growing up in abandoned fields or in the brush along field edges. In areas which are reverting to forest, it will continue to breed in openings where heavy cover remains. The nest is built either on the ground or close to it where the bird finds its living scratching in the dead leaves, uncovering insects and feeding on seeds.

In Canada this towhee breeds in a narrow band from southern British Columbia and across the prairies to Manitoba. It occurs again in southeastern Ontario and into southern Quebec. In the United States it breeds extensively, but not in the central plains, and it winters throughout the southern United States and Mexico.

SAVANNAH SPARROW
Passerculus sandwichensis
LENGTH 5 INCHES

This little sparrow fits easily into the large group of undistinguished brown birds which we see in the fields and which lack distinguishing features or any dramatic coloring. Its only feature of any real note is a short yellow line running from the base of the bill, above the eye toward the back of the face. The breast is streaked, dark on white, the crown dark, the back and wings streaked brown, the forked tail is short and dark with the two outer feathers being lighter than the others. It is quite similar to the Song Sparrow, which lacks the yellow face stripe and has a roundish tip on the tail.

The Savannah has an enormous breeding range, virtually the whole of Canada except the Arctic Islands and the northern third of the United States in the east and south to Baja California in the west.

This is a bird of the grasses. It nests and feeds along stream sides, in meadows, hayfields, dunes and marshes. It is not easy to flush as it will sit tight until closely approached. It then flies a short distance and seems to stop flying, dropping abruptly to the ground. It can best be observed in short grass or when it rises to fences or shrubs to sing. The song is a lisping series of similar notes followed by a buzzing trill and a final note dropping in pitch.

Vesper Sparrow

Sharp-tailed Sparrow

Song Sparrow

Chipping Sparrow

Savannah Sparrow

Tree Sparrow

White-throated Sparrow

Common Snow Bunting

Slate-colored Junco

A variety of sparrows in their natural habitat.

The Savannah Sparrow, though often overlooked, is the most common sparrow in many agricultural and grazing areas. It has distinct economic value, for it consumes large quantities of weed seeds and insects.

GRASSHOPPER SPARROW
Ammodramus savannarum
LENGTH 5 INCHES

Like the Savannah Sparrow, the Grasshopper is indistinguishable from the mass of small brown birds to the casual observer. It is noted however for its rather humped-back stance, as if the head and back were connected without a neck, and for its light blue bill and very short tail. The top of the head is black with a gray stripe in the middle. The back is striped dark and white as are the wings, and the breast is buff, shading to white on the abdomen.

Again like the Savannah Sparrow, this is a bird of the grassland, but it prefers drier areas — the prairies, abandoned farmland, pastures and dry hay fields. It lives almost constantly on the ground, feeding on seeds and insects. When disturbed it flies a short distance dropping quickly into the grass like a grasshopper. The flight is rather weak and twisting. The song is more like the buzz of an insect, preceded by two or three short buzzes.

The range in Canada is limited to the extreme southern portions of the three prairie provinces, locally in central British Columbia, and generally through southern Ontario and southwestern Quebec. In the United States it breeds throughout most of the east, and from the southwest, south into Central America and the West Indies.

SHARP-TAILED SPARROW
Ammospiza caudacuta
LENGTH 5 INCHES

The quite distinct breeding areas of this rather drab sparrow are widely separated, only the habitat being similar in each area. On the east coast it breeds in salt marshes throughout the Maritime Provinces of Canada and as far south as North Carolina, and in brackish marshes on the south shore of the St. Lawrence River east of Quebec City. In central Canada it can be found along the shore of James Bay. By contrast, it breeds in the central plains of Canada north to the southern Mackenzie River, and in the United States to South Dakota, at the edge of fresh water marshes and pot holes. Similar habitat in the intervening spaces does not attract the Sharp-tailed. In winter it moves to salt marshes on the Atlantic coast south from New York to Florida and on the Gulf coast to Texas.

On the nesting ground this sparrow occurs in loose groups, each pair establishing its own small territory. Although similar habitat may exist in the immediate area, Sharp-tails do not necessarily use it. It seldom leaves the ground and then only to leap into the air, a few feet above the tall grass, to shout its curious, rasping *t - sheeeeeeeeeee*. Finishing abruptly, it plunges back to the ground. Only occasionally does one have a clear look at this bird as it perches in the high cattails. It has a general buffy appearance on the lower parts, a gray cheek patch, brown crown with a central stripe of dark gray, striped back and wings and a short sharp tail. The abdomen is white.

VESPER SPARROW
Pooecetes gramineus
LENGTH 6 INCHES

This plain brown sparrow can easily be identified from all other plain brown sparrows by the white outer tail feathers, especially conspicuous in flight. It has a lovely musical song, two clear notes followed by twitters and trills dropping in scale, which it pours out from fences and low bushes. Otherwise this bird conforms to the general description of brown sparrows: dark crown, buff stripe above the eye, brown cheek patch and a conical bill. The breast is buff, with narrow dark stripes slanting toward the abdomen, which is almost white. The back is striped brown and black and there is a fairly distinct buff bar on the wing. The tail is dark with the exception of the outer white feathers.

The Vesper is a ground-feeding sparrow which can often be seen from cars as it flushes. It prefers dry areas, weedy fields, hedgerows, pastures and the prairies. In the forests of the north it can be found in clearings, old burns and in areas which have been cleared by cutting.

The breeding range is extensive — in Canada from central British Columbia east to Nova Scotia and as far north as Great Slave Lake and James Bay. In the United States it breeds from coast to coast in the northern half of the country. It winters throughout the southern United States.

SLATE-COLORED JUNCO
Junco hyemalis
LENGTH 6 INCHES

This junco is the most elegant of the finches. It is entirely slate-gray except for its plain white lower breast and belly and outer tail feathers which are conspicuous in flight. The bill is pink.

In summer it breeds in the northern spruce and fir forests as far north as the Arctic Ocean in the west. In the east it occurs along the edge of Hudson Bay and across northern Quebec, Labrador and throughout the Maritime Provinces. In the United States it breeds in the forests of the northeastern States and in the Appalachian Mountains south to Georgia. It winters regularly in southern Ontario and the Maritimes and is widespread in the United States.

Juncos feed mostly on seeds on the ground in winter which limits their range to areas where snow is not too deep. They come regularly to feeders and if the supply of seeds is maintained a flock will remain in the same area throughout the winter and feed in mixed flocks with other finches.

The junco makes its nest on or near the ground, usually in a spot where it is concealed — in the roots of upturned trees, in a crevice on steep ground or under a fallen tree.

The song is a musical rather wavering trill, rather like that of the Chipping Sparrow, but slower, and sometimes mistaken for that of the Pine Warbler. The alarm note is a snapping or metallic *clink*.

TREE SPARROW

Spizella arborea
LENGTH 6 INCHES

This sparrow nests in the Arctic beyond the tree line and is a common winter visitor in southern Canada and throughout the northern half of the United States. In settled areas in winter it feeds in weedy fields, picking up seeds which have fallen to the ground. When the snow covering is heavy it goes after the seed pods on weeds sticking up through the snow, jumping into the air to release seeds it cannot reach from the snow. Where seed is put out in feeders, the Tree Sparrow prefers to feed on the ground with the juncos and other sparrows, picking up seeds kicked out by other birds.

The distinguishing feature of this handsome sparrow is a plain gray breast marked with a distinct black spot, like the head of a tack, in the center. The crown and eye stripe are a definite chestnut color, gray in between. The back is brown with dark streaks, the tail is dark brown, the wings are streaked brown with two white bars and the feathers between the bars are reddish. There is a curved chestnut patch on each side of the breast at the top of the wing which shows when the bird is at rest. When perching it flicks its tail constantly. The Tree Sparrow is similar to the Chipping, but the latter has a white head stripe, less white on the wings, and lacks the central breast spot.

When feeding the call of an individual bird is a rather thin *tseet*. In a flock it becomes an attractive twitter. The song, which it begins to sing before leaving for its Arctic breeding ground, is particularly sweet, beginning with one or two clear high notes followed by a warble.

CHIPPING SPARROW

Spizella passerina
LENGTH 5 INCHES

This tidy little sparrow can be found regularly in summer on well manicured lawns and in parks, feeding on soft insects which are found most readily in short grass. Its song, which is usually heard from a branch ten feet or more above the ground, is cheerful, consisting of a rapid series of *chips* in the form of a trill, lasting about three seconds. The note, appropriately, is a single *chip*.

The Chipping is easily distinguished from other sparrows by its chestnut colored crown and wide white head band. A black line runs through the eye, below the white band, the breast and belly are plain gray, the back and wings light brown with black streaks.

The favorite habitat is open woodlands where the grass is short and sparse, although it adapts well to orchards, lawns and parks. The nest is usually between three and ten feet from the ground, built in a crotch of a branch or in vines.

The Chipping Sparrow is widespread throughout North America. It breeds from the limit of the tree line in the north to the southern United States. States.

FIELD SPARROW
Spizella pusilla
LENGTH 5 INCHES

This sparrow is similar to both the Tree Sparrow and the Chipping, but lacks the central breast spot of the Tree and the white face of the Chipping. It has a reddish crown and eye stripe and a white eye-ring. The back is brown striped with black, as are the wings, which have two white bars. The breast is buffy gray shading to a pale abdomen, with a rusty hook on each side of the breast. The bill is pink.

In summer the Field Sparrow has a clear sweet song which is rather plaintive and sad and quite often sung late at night when the moon is out. It starts with two or three slow clear notes which speed up to become a trill, fading out at the close.

It prefers an open area of grass and weeds close to bushes or shrubs, usually in rough pasture, abandoned farms, burnt land or near cuttings. In summer the diet is largely insect, but for the rest of the year it feeds on the seeds of weeds and grasses.

In Canada this sparrow nests in southern Ontario, east to the Ottawa River and in extreme southwestern Quebec. In the United States it breeds throughout the east with the exception of the Gulf Coast and Florida. It winters from mid-central United States south to Florida and northern Mexico.

WHITE-CROWNED SPARROW
Zonotrichia leucophrys
LENGTH 6 INCHES

In eastern Canada and in the United States east of the Rockies, this elegant and tidy sparrow is seen only on migration during May and October, feeding in loose flocks on the ground in relatively open places, in short grass and low bushes. It breeds north from northern Alberta to just south of Hudson Bay, across northern Quebec, Labrador and northern

Newfoundland. In the west it breeds from Alaska south to New Mexico. It winters from Kentucky south to the Gulf Coast, Mexico and Cuba.

The White-crowned Sparrow is similar to the more familiar White-throated Sparrow. Both have heads striped like a referee's jacket. The white crown stripe is broad and clearly defined and flanked by black stripes which, in turn, are edged by narrow white stripes, with a second black stripe through the eye. The white throat patch of the White-crowned is smaller and less distinct than that of the White-throated. Additionally the latter has a distinct yellow patch in front of the eye which is absent in the White-crowned. The bill is pinkish, the breast pearl gray, becoming more white on the belly. The back is brown and striped as are the wings, which have two white bars. The tail is dark and long.

The song, which can be heard on migration, is rather plaintive, consisting of two clear notes at the beginning followed by a series of rapid notes, descending in scale and volume.

The White-crowned Sparrow is much more a bird of the open, grassy patches than the White-throated, which prefers underbrush in wooded areas.

WHITE-THROATED SPARROW
Zonotrichia albicollis
LENGTH 6 INCHES

This bird's song is the familiar "I love Canada, Canada, Canada," or "Old Tom Peabody, Peabody, Peabody", which pours forth from the top branches of bushes or small trees in spring and early summer. The White-throated Sparrow sings with its head thrown back so that its white throat is revealed, and with its whole body involved. It begins with two clear notes, the first higher than the second, and followed by a series of three or four quavering notes. As summer wears on, however, the song becomes weaker and more ragged, and by August is usually reduced to a plaintive performance of the first two notes.

It is similar to the White-crowned Sparrow with the same sharply marked white and black head, but the small yellow patches in front of the eyes enable the observer to distinguish it from the White-crowned. The white throat resembles a tiny bib, the breast is pale gray and the belly whitish. The back and tail are brown and the wings have two distinct white stripes.

The White-throated Sparrow breeds in clearings, forest edges, burnt areas and young forest from the Great Slave Lake area east across northern Canada and south into the northern United States, south in the Appalachians to Virginia. It nests on the ground beneath thick growth and, when disturbed, dashes about on the ground and through the bush making a distinctive "chink" note. It is particularly valiant and noisy in defense of its eggs and young.

FOX SPARROW
Passerella iliaca
LENGTH 7 INCHES

Named for its fox-red coloring, this is perhaps the most striking looking of the sparrows, and is noticeably larger than other species in the family. Its wings and tail are long and have the brightest coloring, the crown and back being liberally mixed with gray. A triangular face patch, which is outlined in white to the eye, widens toward the back of the head. The breast and abdomen are white, but are so heavily dotted with large reddish brown spots as to look striped. There is a fairly well defined central spot on the breast, somewhat like that of the Song Sparrow.

In the west, the Fox Sparrow nests from the Arctic Ocean to as far south as the mountains of California. In the east, however, it only breeds close to the tree line in the sub-Arctic. As a result, it is present in southeastern Canada and the northeastern United States only on migration. It passes through these areas quite quickly early in May and in October and can be found in the underbrush searching for animal life. The Fox Sparrow is difficult to see clearly for it tends to skulk and hide when approached. One should look for signs of great activity as it throws leaves about and, in spring, listen for its song which is loud and rich, rising at the beginning and falling toward the close.

LINCOLN'S SPARROW
Melospiza lincolnii
LENGTH 5 INCHES

In most of the east, Lincoln's Sparrow is present only during migration. Although it is reasonably common it is usually difficult to find because of its skulking habits, its nondescript markings and the fact that it does not sing when migrating. Furthermore it is hard to flush, and when it does, will disappear again as soon as possible.

Its best identification feature is a buffy breast streaked with black, and a whitish abdomen. The upper parts are olive-brown and streaked with black. The head is dark brown with a gray streak through the middle.

The breeding range of Lincoln's Sparrow extends from Alaska, across the Northwest Territories, the northern part of the Prairie Provinces, Ontario and Quebec except the extreme southern parts, and into the Maritimes. In the eastern United States it is present in the northern parts of New England, New York, Michigan and Minnesota. In winter it moves to the southwestern United States and Central America.

This sparrow nests on the ground at the edge of wet meadows, ponds and bogs where alder and willow trees are present. It sings from perches with a curious series of buzzing, liquid notes, as if it were in a hurry to finish. If disturbed during the song it will stop and hide. Because it is silent on migration and has a retiring nature, even careful observers may fail to spot one.

230

SWAMP SPARROW

Melospiza georgiana
LENGTH 5 INCHES

The Swamp Sparrow is a nondescript dark brown sparrow easily confused, even by experienced observers, with the Lincoln's Sparrow with whom it is often found. Identification is problematical unless lighting is good and the bird is in clear view and reasonably still.

Unlike Lincoln's Sparrow, the Swamp Sparrow is resident through most of the east. Its breeding range extends from the Mackenzie River in the northwest, across Canada (except in Quebec north of James Bay) and the northern United States.

It breeds in fresh water marshes, and builds its nest on a hummock of cattails or at the base of willows or alders. Sluggish streams and pond edges are also favored provided the vegetation is suitable. During the breeding season it seldom leaves the ground except to sing from a low bush.

On migration it prefers to stop in areas similar to its nesting ground, but when these are not available, it feeds in fields and shrubbery. It seeks swampy areas in winter throughout the United States, south of the Great Lakes.

The Swamp Sparrow has a chestnut colored crown, white eye stripe and throat, brown back streaked with black and chestnut wings with one indistinct wing bar. The throat and abdomen are whitish, the breast gray and slightly streaked, but not to the extent of the Lincoln's Sparrow.

SONG SPARROW

Melospiza melodia
LENGTH 5½ INCHES

The Song Sparrow is an early arrival in northern areas, heralded by its cheerful song which consists of three or four clear notes, followed by a trill and ending in a series of short notes. Later in summer only the introductory notes may be heard, almost as if it could not be bothered to finish.

This sparrow is most easily identified by the heavy streaks on its breast, which appear to converge in a dark central spot near the throat, and by its habit of pumping its tail when in flight. The crown is brown with a gray central stripe, the back and tail brown, the cheeks beige with a strong eye stripe.

It is distributed widely across North America, breeding from the Arctic to the Gulf Coast and wintering from southern Canada to Mexico. It is found in low bushes, hedgerows and shrubbery, usually along the edge of streams and ponds but not in deep forests.

There may be two nests. When this bird nests early it usually does so on the ground. The second nesting, either following the loss of the first brood, or to raise a second, is above the ground in thick shrub or conifers, sometimes as high as four feet.

The Song Sparrow is one of our most valuable small birds because it feeds largely on the seeds of weeds and, to a lesser extent, on insects.

COMMON SNOW BUNTING
Plectrophenax nivalis
LENGTH 6 INCHES

This sparrow spends the winter in southern Canada and the northern United States, seldom traveling south of areas where snow is present. It is the whitest of all the song birds and during the summer in its breeding range in the high Arctic, it is entirely white except for small black patches on the back and wings. During the winter, and until it leaves for the north, only the undersides are white. The crown is an attractive rust color and the back and wings mottled gray and rust.

Snow Buntings move about the open country in flocks which are sometimes quite large, and feed on the seeds of grasses and weeds sticking up through the snow. Suitable fields are often near roads and these birds can be seen from automobiles as they wheel erratically over the snow or grass. Even at close range, a flock seems to vanish suddenly, and then reappear just as quickly, depending on whether the gray or the white side is seen against the sky. When they are in flight a constant twittering sound can be heard. As soon as the first wave lands, feeding starts, the birds running about seeking seeds, often fluttering into the air for seeds which are too high to reach from the snow. The birds in the rear fly over the flock and alight ahead.

Snow Buntings breed in all polar regions, and are present in Europe and Asia during winter. In North America they nest in Alaska, the Northwest Territories and throughout the Arctic Islands. Their nests are built in cracks in the rocks and under stones, indeed anywhere that they can be concealed. On their breeding grounds the song is quite loud and warbling.

Bibliography

BENT, Arthur Cleveland and others. *Life Histories of North American Cardinals, Grosbeaks, Buntings, Towhees, Finches, Sparrows and Allies.* Volumes I, II and III. Washington D.C. United States National Museum, 1968.

BLAKE, Emmet Reid. *Birds of Mexico.* Chicago, The University of Chicago Press, 1953.

BODSWORTH, Fred. *Last of the Curlews.* Toronto, McClelland and Stewart Limited, 1954.

BOND, James. *Birds of the West Indies.* London, Collins, 1960.

BRAMWELL, Martin and others. *The Mitchell Beazley World Atlas of Birds.* London, Mitchell Beazley Publishers Limited, 1974.

FISHER, James and PETERSON, Roger Tory. *The World of Birds.* Garden City New York, Doubleday & Company, Inc., 1964.

FROHAWK, F. W. *British Birds.* New York, Abelard-Schuman Limited, 1958.

GODFREY, W. Earl. *The Birds of Canada.* Ottawa, National Museums of Canada, 1966.

GRISCOM, Ludlow and SPRUNT, Alexander. *The Warblers of America.* New York, The Devin-Adair Company, 1957.

KORTRIGHT, Francis H. *The Ducks, Geese and Swans of North America.* Harrisburg, Pa. The Stackpole Company and Wildlife Management Institute, 1942.

LINDUSKA, Joseph P. and others. *Waterfowl Tomorrow.* Washington D.C. United States Department of the Interior, 1964.

PETERSON, Roger Tory and FISHER, James. *Wild America.* Boston, Houghton Mifflin Company, 1955.

PETERSON, Roger Tory. *A Field Guide to the Birds.* Boston, Houghton Mifflin Company, 1934.

PETERSON, Roger Tory and others. *The Bird Watcher's Anthology.* New York, Bonanza Books, 1957.

PETERSON, Roger Tory and others. *A Field Guide to the Birds of Britain and Europe.* Boston, Houghton Mifflin Company, 1954.

POUGH, Richard H. *The Birds of Eastern and Central North America.* Garden City New York, Doubleday and Company, Inc., 1946.

ROBBINS, Chandler S. and others. *Birds of North America.* New York, Golden Press, 1966.

TAVERNER, P.A. Ottawa, *Birds of Eastern Canada, Department of Mines,* 1922. Ottawa, *Birds of Western Canada, Department of Mines,* 1926.

TUCK, Leslie M. *The Murres.* Ottawa, Canadian Wildlife Service, 1960.

Index to Illustrations

Index

237

238